2op

CLASSROOM MU

This book is dedicated to my oldest friend,

Mrs Hilda Smith

Other TIMESPAN titles include

TELLTALE - an anthology of history stories for every study unit each with a pack of colour pictures and other drawings to pass round the class.

1 — Invaders and Settlers (Romans, Anglo Saxons & Vikings)
2 — Medieval Realms (1066-1500)
3 — Life in Tudor & Stuart Times (1500-1700)
4 — Victorian Britain
5 — Life in Britain since 1930

CLASSROOM SERIES - helps the teacher to identify, classify, organise, describe and use a range of objects in the classroom and also serves as a resource1 facility when taking children out on educational visits.

Classroom Museum — a teacher's guide to artefacts with 100 examples illustrated and described. isbn 1 85450 001 5

Classroom Gallery — a colourful selection of narrative and descriptive pictures from every age, dating from cave paintings to moonwalking.

Classroom Archives — an expansion on the theme of documents for younger children, with about 100 examples.

CLASSROOM MUSEUM

John West

Elm Publications

First published June, 1990 by ELM Publications,
12 Blackstone Road, Huntingdon, Cambs. PE18 6EF (Tel: 0480 414553,
Fax: 0480 433577) who hold the copyright on behalf of the author John
West.

British Library Cataloguing in Publication Data
West, John,
    Classroom museum. — (Timespan, ISSN 0958-7640; 1).
    1.   Great Britain. Schools. Curriculum subjects: History
    I.   Title II. Series
    907.1041

    ISBN 1-85450-001-5

Printed by St Edmundsbury Press, Bury St Edmunds, Suffolk

CONTENTS

Page

ABOUT THE AUTHOR

John West taught history to primary and secondary schoolchildren before training teachers, advising in Liverpool and recently conducting a range of INSET courses.

He has researched widely in history at doctorate level on how children learn about the past, and he continues to collect and enjoy Victoriana.

His publications include:

History 7-13: a set of guidelines for teachers.

Village records, Town records.

and several books for schoolchildren.

FOREWORD

The National Curriculum for History requires that all children from 5-16 must learn History by frequent reference to primary sources, including ancient artefacts. New skills are required of Primary School children, to enable them to acquire and evaluate historical information from original sources. This requirement demands a great deal of specialised background knowledge to be readily available both to teachers and children.

CLASSROOM MUSEUM equips non-specialist teachers to collect and use these ancient sources with confidence. Each Chapter offers an unusual range of knowledge and constant reference to the wide range of museum-based resources and specialised books which are available to a well-informed teacher. Examples have been chosen to illustrate each of the Study Units for British History, European and World History and Thematic History specified by the New Curriculum. Teachers might also choose to use the book as the basis for their own School Designed Theme on A Classroom Museum.

These guidelines are firmly based upon the author's intensive research into the development of children's sense of Time. They offer models for organizing and communicating the results of the children's acquisition of very complex types of information and provides information on the best sources for follow-up work on these lines. **CLASSROOM MUSEUM** is not only a handy *vade mecum* or useful reference book, but also a mode of study which ensures the achievement of the New History Curriculum's essential attainment targets.

INTRODUCTION : AIMS AND OBJECTIVES

The **Final Report (April 1990)** of the History Working Group for the National Curriculum makes constant reference to the uses of ancient artefacts as historical evidence. In Key Stage 1 most specifically, Infant teachers are required to: "ensure that pupils have experience of handling a wide range of historical objects, so as to gather information about the past by studying and speculating upon the origins and use of artefacts, comparing them in terms of age and sophistication and asking who made and used them." **(Final Report 5.2: p.34)**. The list of "historical questions" **(ibid.6.8: p.31)** which infants are expected to ask about unusual artefacts will test the resources of most experienced Infant teachers. (See page xii.)

Key Stage 2's Study Units (2-13) "are constructed of generally familiar materials and build on the teaching approaches established in Key Stage 1." **(ibid: 5.3: p.21)** There are in fact, frequent references to the use of museums in programmes of study for Key Stage 2. These are sometimes vague, offering little if any indication of the source materials available there; as in 'Maritime museums and art galleries' (HSU 8), or simply 'museums' (HSU 4, 13). Reference to groups of objects is equally vague – glassware (HSU 2); photographs; domestic gadgets (HSU 4); articles from the Blitz (HSU 5); newspapers (HSU 5, 11, 15); Egyptian and Greek Museum objects; pottery; coinage (HSU 6); medals and coins (HSU 7); tickets (HSU 12); Roman remains; toys; domestic artefacts; children's books (HSU 13). A few more museum objects are specifically mentioned: cameras, pop discs (HSU 5); Egyptian mummies (HSU 6) papyrus, samplers (HSU 11); children's books and Mrs Beeton (HUS 13).

Every one of these groups or separate items, and many more besides, are catalogued and illustrated in *CLASSROOM MUSEUM*, with exact details of their locations in museums and loan services, the possibilities of replicas, useful reference books and essential information. The **Final Report** is frank, if brief, on the problems which this new demand will create in terms of non-specialist History teachers' knowledge and resources. It refers to "the stock of teachers' expertise, books, artefacts, films etc. (which) has been relatively fixed – and it certainly cannot be changed overnight." **(ibid, 4.38: p.18)**. *CLASSROOM MUSEUM* can effect a great deal of immediate change in this unpromising situation.

In its chapter on **Bringing History to Life** (pp.177-9) the Working Group deals at greater length with **Museums and historic sites** (10.16; p.178) There is critical reference to teachers' 'conventional wisdom' (a phrase which, like 'with respect' is always a polite term of derision!) of using museum visits and similar outings only as end-of-year treats. "It is important that field trips, and museum and site visits, form an integral part of the school curriculum for history." (10.2, p.177) This is a naive, though desirable assumption in view of teachers' increasing apprehension about reduction in available funds and time for outings of any sort, not least in view of the massive timetable demands for the New Curriculum. This is the rationale of *CLASSROOM MUSEUM*.

If schools can no longer afford Museums visits, we must make every effort to bring museums into the school. As the financial strictures of 1988's Education Reform Act begin to bite, many teachers and museum curators express doubts about the future of the traditional museum visit. The prohibition of charges for some educational outings creates problems of choice in an overcrowded New Curriculum; already, by April 1989, some Museums had received cancellations; they share teachers' doubts about future bookings. Some collections, like the Imperial War Museum, have seen their very subject matter disappear from the schools' curriculum, fortunately to be hastily reinstated by the planners. Such educational gerrymandering creates confusion and uncertainty in schools.

There is no doubt about schools' widespread goodwill towards the Museum visit as an opportunity for children's educational enrichment; many Heads will no doubt accept the new costs into their budget, raising even more profitable School Funds by means of Jumble Sales and Sponsored Breathing events to subsidise increasing costs. There are so many opportunities in museums, for role-play, hands-on experience and imaginative reconstruction which can never be transported into school. The juggernauts in Birmingham Science Museum or the fragile costumes of the V & A will never lend themselves to any school loans service. Nor can the sheer excitement of the museums, its atmosphere and wealth of choice, be boxed and transported.

Museums loans services, wherever these exist will now become indispensable to schools. For regular daily use these precious boxes, supplemented with other items, begged, borrowed and bought by enterprising teachers, must now form the basis of our own ongoing DIY classroom museum. Schools cannot be expected to dispense entirely with museums' services - any Museum's Education Officer, advisory teacher or Loans Keeper (See **Appendix B**) becomes an essential aide in our determined effort to bring the museum into school.

There is no more evocative or useful aid to the teaching of Primary School History than a growing classroom collection of ancient artefacts. Children's enthusiasm, once aroused, will be productive of a remarkable collection of bygones, culled from home and the local environment. In my own experience, these relics have ranged from small items like coins, medals, fragments of Roman glass, fossils and small prehistoric tools, to larger objects, like ploughshares or a soldier's red coat; even a Victorian cast-iron grate. Once their help has been enlisted, parents, or more likely, grand-parents and great-grandparents, will willingly loan substantial family treasures. The classroom museum soon becomes a valuable community enterprise.

A collection of turn-of-the-century family photographs or picture postcards alone, with a timeline of pre-decimal pennies, can form an important central reference core to a well-organized classroom display. These expand the museum into an archives collection, to which family documents will be added. My own treasures include the Attendance Certificate of an Infant scholar of Liverpool in 1895, and the well-authenticated typescript account of how an Australian schoolboy's great-grandfather witnessed the shooting down of the Red Baron, von Richtofen, on the Western Front in 1918.

To these borrowed items, the teacher adds his own collection, begged, found, and bought from local junk shops, Museum shops and antique fairs. Many unconsidered objects, of relatively little price, have much more lesson-value. My own purchases include a Victorian goffering-iron, a silver penny of Edward I's reign, an Elizabethan shilling, the leather-bound first edition of John Wesley's sermons, a yellowing number of Winston Churchill's British Gazette from the General Strike, and the realistic replica of a Roman oil-lamp. Carefully chosen, these items have more built-in teaching value, in terms of capitation allowance or school fund, than many a modern textbook.

Most experienced teachers will know precisely how to use these treasures as the focal points of History lessons, or as jumping-off ground for a term's project. What most of us lack are the more specialised skills of the professional museum curator. Lately, several local Museums services provide invaluable help from colleagues employed as Education Officers or advisory teachers. These, whenever they are invited to support a class-teacher's efforts in setting out and classifying a growing collection, add a new dimension to the idea of a classroom museum.

Of course, the more formal activities of research and identification are by no means the only classroom activity which these evocative relics will promote. Children love to handle them, to pretend to use them and adopt the roles of their original owners. In prompting these activities we may well decide, didactically, to *tell* the class what the object is, before inviting them to explore its possibilities. Here is ample stimulus for informal, creative activity. But children love a mystery too, and the challenge "What is it?" is another approach to some items. The making of record cards is, perhaps, more to be advocated as a more formal teacher's discipline, shared occasionally by literate, older children. Certainly all our pupils will be helped to keep adequate written records of all their conclusions. **(AT 4)**

What we must make every effort to avoid, is the abandonment of a dusty heap of half-forgotten artefacts, once used long ago, then allowed to become an elephants' graveyard, matched only by the stock room store of the last three class-teachers' perennial choices of up-to-date History books. Any item worth collecting will provide many more lessons in classification, discussion, teaching points, research and reference work.

This book then, sets out to offer suggestions based upon experience of collecting museum-type artefacts, documents and pictures and using them in their many different ways. We shall briefly survey the possibilities presented by the real world of museums, then apply the best practice to our own more modest collection. First we examine ways and means of starting and maintaining a classroom museum and a standardised method of recording our finds is recommended for teachers' consideration.

Next we look very closely at 100 items of the type which we might confidently expect to have amassed, catalogued and cross-indexed as suggested, over the course of a year's work. This wide range of record cards, chronologically ordered, becomes in effect a valuable reference book and locations list, offering in-depth information, with supplementary library and museum resources which support our own collection and make it more meaningful to children. The final chapters structure those activities from which many Primary and Middle school children children have already gained enjoyment, experiences and knowledge of the past.

Finally, in **Puzzles and Problems** a key question is posed for every one of our 100 museum objects, leading on to widening fields of learning. These problems have been carefully selected to stimulate the thinking of children of all ages and abilities; some are simple and straightforward, others demand a high degree of thought and real empathy with people of the past. Teachers, of course will select and interpret these at their own discretion. Most of the bygones which form the central core of this guide-book are found all about us in the present day. To take them in our hands as evidence of people past and gone is the very purpose of our classroom museum which, like a garden can become a lovesome thing to child and teacher.

CLASSROOM MUSEUM is aimed directly at **Attainment Target 3** of the New History Curriculum: **Acquiring and evaluating historical information**. During KS 1, at Levels 1-3 children are now required to acquire information from more than one type of historical source. At KS 2's Levels 2-5, they are to compare the value of different sources, select particular types of sources, and examine a variety of sources of evidence in terms of their contribution to an historical enquiry. For both more and less able children, the non-verbal evidence of artefacts poses essential problems.

In Chapter Five, **Children at Work**, we shall demonstrate means by which this Target can be best achieved, also in relation to the outcomes of investigation which will match **Attainment Target 4: Organising and communicating the results of historical study**. As a starting-point, to indicate the relevance of *CLASSROOM MUSEUM* to these new curricular requirements, we list the following questions posed by the Working Group at Key Stage 1:

Asking historical questions

6.8 Teachers should encourage pupils to enquire about the past by means of:

   i) asking questions; What was this object for? Who used it? Is it real, or a copy?

   ii) speculating: suggesting sensible possible answers to questions;

   iii) connecting and comparing new information with existing knowledge, or fitting a new piece of evidence into what is known already;

   iv) investigating; asking why things were as they were; seeking and testing new explanation.

   v) using historical evidence to inform the imagination: What was life like? What was that person like?

The author is gratified to see that so much of his own, and his wife's research work in schools, previously commended by the DES, *(History in the Primary and Secondary Years : An HMI View* (HMSO 1985 p.4) appears to have found some favour with the Working Group. He would emphasise however, that this brief list is only vague gesture at the possibilities of a classroom museum and certainly no basis for a complete programme of study. Those possibilities are more extensively pursued in Chapters Five and Six. First however, in accordance with the published programmes of study for every History Study Unit, Chapters One to Four offer **essential information** to teachers at Key Stages 1-3, who may be unfamiliar with this field of children's work.

CHAPTER ONE : MUSEUMS TODAY

In recent years, Museums have become attractive places. Gone is the old-fashioned image of fusty fragments in dusty cases. Nowadays, riding in a tram-car around the streets, shops and workshops of the Black Country Museum near Dudley or scrambling a Fokke-Wulf triplane simulator amongst the Fleet Air Arm's collection of 50 historic aircraft which range from Bleriot's string-and-fabric kite to Concorde, is as enjoyable for a child as any less educational outing.

We can rub brasses at Droitwich Heritage Centre and in the Tolhouse, Great Yarmouth. Bressingham Live Steam Museum in Norfolk offers footplate rides on their standard gauge locomotives, but if you prefer comfort, both Colne Valley and Severn Valley Railways provide a Pullman car Wine and Dine service. In fact, the post-war trend towards Folk Museums, from Den Gamle By in Denmark to Mystic Seaport, Connecticut, has become normal museum practice. A new trend too, is the enthusiasm for hands-on experience of all the stimuli on offer.

Many museums now incorporate elements of the living past, following the earlier example - still the most nostalgic re-creation of all - of the streets of walk-in shops at the Castle Museum York. Period streets are widespread nowadays, at Stockton-on-Tees, Kendal, Ellesmere Port, Flambard's Victorian Village at Helston and the Museum of Shops at Battle (E.Sussex). A more extensive site, 26 acres in all, houses the fast-growing open-air Museum near Dudley (West Midlands). Here we find a typical Black Country community of shops, nailers' cottages, chapel, baker's shop, pub, chain-making forges and canal-builders' workshops, all demonstrated by a team of friendly guides, who live their parts.

MUSEUMS TODAY

At the Jorvik Viking Centre in York, time-travel excites all the senses of sight, sound and smell, and Museum Experience becomes the name of the game, skilfully linking Jorvik's noisy, smelly alleys with the site as seen under excavation, archaeologists' workshops and museum showcases, including treasures you are invited to touch.

The possibilities are endless: Cobbaton Combat Vehicles Museum at Chittlehampton (N.Devon) takes us back to the Blitz with Home Front and Mum's War sections. At Chatterley Whitfield colliery (Stoke-on-Trent) visitors are issued with miners' lamps and helmets for a visit to the underground coal face. The same experience is matched, and guided by experienced ex-miners, at Big Pit, Blenavon (Gwent), at Caphouse & Overton (W.Yorks) and down the Poldark Mine at Helston (Cornwall).

More and more museums too, in the Scandinavian, Dearborn (Michigan) or Cregneash Village (Isle of Man) tradition, have specialised in rescuing, removing and restoring vernacular buildings. Of these, the most active are: Avoncroft Museum, near Bromsgrove which, starting with a medieval merchant's town house, now includes a windmill, granary, forge, toll-house and dovecot, all spanning 700 years of social history; the Welsh Folk Museum at St.Fagan's near Cardiff, said to be one of the three best folk museums in the British Isles and certainly a founder of the genre; more than a score of buildings illustrate the traditional architecture of the Weald and Downland at Singleton, near Chichester, and the North of England Open Air Museum at Beamish (Co.Durham) covers an astounding 200 acres. There we find a complete railway layout, tram-rides, market place and a 1920s street, with colliery and pitmen's cottages, a working farm and regular craft demonstrations.

Vigorous developments in archaeological techniques have given this generation a wider range of discovery than ever before - vernacular architecture, industrial archaeology, medieval deserted village sites, aerospace museums and planetaria - all have opened up new fields of study and created new museums of their own. The metal detector too, has brought new possibilities of treasure trove to the amateur searcher which though deplored by professional archaeologists, cannot be completely ignored.

Of these new sciences, perhaps the most startling to the laymen has been the dramatic development of marine archaeology and the discovery of whole ships' sunken carcases. Thus, aboard a vintage ferry-boat on West India Dock we are not surprised to discover the London Underwater Museum; nor, at Hastings, the National Shipwreck Heritage Centre.

The idea of ship-restoration is an even older tradition than the discovery of the Sutton Hoo burial in 1939. Generations of grandparents, parents and children too, have thrilled to the tarry smell of HMS *Victory* and the *Cutty Sark* clipper ship. Colourful media coverage of the raising of Henry VIII's ill-fated *Mary Rose,* following hard on the restoration of the *Vasa,* and lately, the discovery of more and more wrecked Armada galleons, have all made children well aware of exciting underwater possibilities.

New technology chimes well with children's voracious appetite for collecting, as they discover what a lively range of artefacts can justify a vivid display or audio-visual presentation. The Robert Opie Collection of Packaging and Advertising at Gloucester has put ephemera on the museums map. Puppets are especially featured at Abbots Bromley (Staffs), pencils at Keswick, dinosaurs at Dorchester. Museums of Childhood and collections of toys are, nowadays delightfully commonplace; it is perhaps, more unexpected to discover a Museum of Sweets at Halesowen (W.Midlands). And there are no prizes for guessing where to find the Museum of Tennis! But why do we sometimes call prison The Clink? (See page 12.)

In the illustrated catalogue of our own small collection (Chapter

Three) each specimen is attributed to one or more British museums which could be expected to hold a similar object. Most of those references record helpful advice from curators, either by letter, telephone or personal visit. The following list classifies other subject collections which can be used to inform and illustrate a classroom topic, or merit an out-of-school expedition. Reference to *Museums & Galleries in GB and Ireland* (British Leisure Publications 1988) gives even more extensive subject-lists on these and other topics, including many more local museums which house only a worthwhile gallery or showcase. The list below however, adds a few subjects (eg Canals, Childhood, Education etc), not specifically listed in the Guide. Telephone numbers (as for 1990) are listed for easy contact; it is well worthwhile to use the telephone to make an initial check of costs of entry, as these vary excessively from place to place. Full postal addresses and charges will also be found in the *Museums Yearbook* and other museum guides (Appendix A).

Advertising and Shopping

Black Country Museum, Dudley, W.Midlands (street of shops)	021 557 9643
Museum of Shops and Social History, Battle, E.Sussex	0426 4269
Old Mill Museum, Bourton-on-the Water, Glos	0451 21255
Robert Opie Collection of Advertising and Packaging, Gloucester	0452 302309
Rochdale Pioneers' Co-operative Museum, Rochdale	061 308 3374
York Castle Museum (street of shops)	0904 653611

Aeroplanes

Air and Space Gallery, Manchester	061 833 2244
Aerospace Museum, Cosford Airfield, Shropshire	090 722 4872
Aldershot Military Museum, Hants	0252 314598
Battle of Britain Museum, Hendon, London NW9	081 205 2266
Bomber Command Museum, Hendon, London NW9	081 205 2266
Duxford Airfield, (Imperial War Museum) Cambridge	0223 833963

Fleet Air Arm Museum and Concorde, Yeovilton, Som.   0935 840565
Museum of Army Flying, Middle Wallop, Hants.   0264 62121
Museum of Flight, N.Berwick, East Lothian   062088 308
Newark Air Museum, Notts.   0636 707170
North East Aircraft Museum, Sunderland, Tyne & Wear   0385 891702
Royal Air Force Museum, Hendon, London NW9   081 205 2266
Shuttleworth Collection of Aircraft, Old Warden Aerodrome,
   Biggleswade, Beds.   076 727288
Tangmere Military Aviation Museum, Chichester, W.Sx   0234 775223
Torbay Aircraft Museum, Paignton, Devon   0803 553540

Arms and Armour

Aldershot Military Museum, Hants.   0252 314598
Alnwick Castle Museum, Northumberland   0665 602 456
Coalhouse Fort, East Tilbury, Essex   03752 4203
D-Day Museum, Portsmouth, Hants.   0705 827261
Gainsborough Old Hall, Lincs.   0427 2669
Gloucester Folk Museum, Glos.   0452 26467
Grange Cavern Military Museum, Holway, Clwyd   0352 713455
Lichfield Heritage Exhibition, Staffs.   054 32 5661
National Army Museum, London SW3   071 730 0717
Newcastle-upon-Tyne, The Keep Museum, Tyne & Wear   0632 327938
Nottingham Castle Museum, Notts.   0602 411881
Regimental Museums (most ancient county towns and depots)
   see **Services Museums** in 'Museums & Art Galleries (1989)' pp.164-8
Royal Armouries, Tower of London, EC3   071 480 6358
Tank Museum, Bovington Camp, Nr. Wareham, Dorset   0929 462721
Warwick Castle, Warwicks.   0926 495421
The West Gate, Canterbury, Kent   0227 52747
The Wish Martello Tower No.73, Eastbourne, E.Sussex   0323 410440
York Castle Museum,York (Military Collection)   0904 653611

Battlefields

Battle (Hastings) Historical Society Museum, Sussex   04246 3792

Bosworth Battlefield, Market Bosworth, Leics.	0455 290429
Naseby Battle and Farm Museum, Northants.	0604 74021
Tewkesbury, John Moore Museum (Model) Glos.	0684 297174

Cameras and Photography:

British Photographic Museum, Totnes, Devon	0803 863664
Fox Talbot Museum of Photography, Lacock, Wilts	024 973 459
Impressions Gallery of Photography, York	0904 54724
Museum of the Moving Image, South Bank, London SE1	071 401 2636
National Museum of Photo, Film and TV, Bradford	0274 727488
Photographic Heritage Centre, Salford, Gtr. Manchester	
RPS National Centre, Bath, Avon	0225 62841
See also **Cinema and Films**	

Canals and Boats

Boat Museum, Ellesmere Port, Cheshire	051 355 5017
Canal Museum, Nottingham	0602 598835
Devizes Wharf Canal Centre, Wilts.	0380 71279
Junction Cottage, Pontymoel, Pontypool, Gwent	04955 52036
Leeds Museum Canal Trail	0532 637861
National Waterways Museum, Gloucester	0452 25524
Waterways Museum, Stoke Bruern, Northants.	0604 862229
Wigan Pier, Wigan, Gtr.Manchester	0942 44991

Childhood

Bethnal Green Museum of Childhood, London E2	081 980 2415
Dewsbury Museum, W.Yorks.	0924 468171
Museum of Childhood, Beaumaris, Anglesey, Gwynedd	0248 810448
Museum of Childhood, Edinburgh	031 225 2424
Museum of Childhood, Sudbury Hall, Derby	028 378 305
Museum of Childhood & Gillow Museum, Lancaster	0524 2808
(See also **Toys**)	

Cinema and Films

Barnes Museum of Cinematography, St.Ives, Cornwall	073679 7251
Buckingham Movie Museum	0280 816758
Chipping Campden Folk Museum, Glos.	0386 840289
Laurel and Hardy Museum, Ulverston, Cumbria	0229 52292
National Film Archive, Dean St., London W1	071 437 4355
National Museum of Photography, Film and TV, Bradford	0274 727488

Costume

Bexhill Manor Costume Museum, E.Sussex	0424 215361
Castle Howard Costume Galleries, Yorks	065384 333
Devonshire Collection of Period Costume (Bogan House Antiques), Totnes, Devon	0803 862075
Gallery of English Costume, Manchester	061 224 5712
Museum of Costume, Bath	0225 61111
Museum of Costume, Glasgow	071 632 1350
Museum of Costume and Textiles, Nottingham	0602 411881
Pitville Pump Room Gallery of Fashion, Cheltenham	0242 512740
Shambellie House Museum of Costume, Dumfries	038 785 375
Springhill Costume Museum, Moneymore, Londonderry	064874 8210
Victoria & Albert Museum, London SW7	071 589 6371
Wygston's House Museum of Costume, Leicester	0533 554100

Dinosaurs

The Dinosaur Museum, Icen Way, Dorchester, Dorset	0305 69880

Education

Armley Mills Museum, W.Yorks	0532 637861
Grammar School Museum, Heptonstall, W.Yorks	0422 54823
Museum of the History of Education, Leeds	0532 431751
St.Anne's Chapel and Old Grammar School, Barnstaple	036782 635
Tom Brown's School Museum, Uffington, Oxon.	036782 635
Royal Education Corps Museum, Beaconsfield, Bucks.	049 46 6121

Egyptian Pharaohs, Mummies etc.

Pitt-Rivers Museum, Oxford	0865 512541
Tutankhamun Exhibition, High West St., Dorchester, Dorset	0305 69571
The Manchester Museum, Manchester	061 275 2634

Famous People

Jane Austen's House, Chawton, Hants.	0420 83262
Bonnie Prince Charlie, W.Highland Museum, Fort William	0397 2169
Bronte Parsonage, Haworth, W.Yorks.	0535 42322
James Brindley Museum, Leek, Staffs.	0538 381446
John Buchan Centre, Broughton, Peebles, Borders	0899 21050
Robert Burns Centre, Dumfries	0387 64808
Robert Clive's House, Shrewsbury, Shropshire	0743 54811
Captain Cook's Schoolroom, Great Ayton, W.Yorks	0642 722327
Captain Cook's Birthplace, Middlesbrough, Cleveland	0642 311211
Cromwell Museum, Huntingdon	0480 52861
Grace Darling Museum, Bamburgh, Northumberland	06684 310
Charles Dickens's House, Doughty St. London WC1	071 405 2127
Charles Dickens Birthplace Museum, Portsmouth, Hants.	0705 827261
Elgar's Birthplace,Broadheath, H-Worcs.	090 566 224
Faraday's Laboratory & Museum, 21 Albemarle St. W1	071 409 2992
Hogarth's House, Great West Road, London W4	081 994 6757
Dr.Johnson's House, Gough Square, London EC4	071 353 3745
Keats's House, Hampstead, Camden, London	071 435 2062
Rudyard Kipling's House, Bateman's, Burwash, E.Sussex	0435 882302
David Livingstone Centre, Blantyre, Lanark	0698 823140
Lloyd George Museum, Criccieth, Gwynedd	0766 522171
Mary Queen of Scots House, Jedburgh, Borders	08356 3331
Milton's Cottage, Chalfont St.Giles, Bucks.	024 07 2313
Lord Nelson Collection, Portsmouth RN Museum	0705 822351
Lord Nelson Memorabilia, Monmouth Museum	0600 3519
Florence Nightingale Museum, St.Thomas's Hospital, London SE1	071 928 9292
The Captain Oates Memorial Museum, Selborne, Hants	042050 275

Robert Owen Memorial Museum, Newtown, Powys	0686 26220
Ruskin Museum, Coniston, Cumbria	0966 41387
Scott Polar Research Institute, Cambridge	0223 66499
Shakespeare Globe Museum, Bankside SE1	071 402 6075
The Shakespeare Birthplace, Stratford-on-Avon	0789 204016
Wellington Museum, Apsley House, London W1	071 499 5676
John Wesley House & Museum, City Road, SE1	071 253 2262
Sir Winston Churchill Museum, Chartwell, Kent	0732 866368

Farming

Acton Scott Working Farm, Church Stretton, Shropshire	06946 306
Alscott Farm Agricultural Museum, Shebbear, Devon	0409 28206
Barleylands Farm Museum, Billericay, Essex	0409 28 206
Beamish Open-Air Museum, Stanley, Co.Durham	0207 231811
Beck Isle Museum of Rural Life, Pickering, N.Yorks	0751 73653
Coate Agricultural Museum, Swindon, Wilts.	0793 526161
Cogges Farm Museum, Witney, Oxon.	0993 72602
Cotswold Countryside Collection, Northleach, Glos.	0285 5611
Elvaston Working Estate and Museum, Derbs.	0332 73799
Grove Rural Life Museum, Ramsey, Isle of Man	0624 5522
Hampshire Farm Museum, Botley, Hants	04892 87055
Hunday Tractor & Farm Museum, Stocksfield, Nmbld.	0661 842553
Institute of Agricultural History and Museum of	
English Rural Life, Reading, Berks.	0734 875123
Museum of Kent Rural Life, Maidstone, Kent	0622 63936
National Dairy Museum, Riseley, Berks.	073583 444
Newnham Grange Leisure Farm, Middlesbrough, Cleveland	0642 36762
Old Kiln Agricultural Museum, Farnham, Surrey	025 125 2300
Rural Life Museum,Stoke Bruerne, Northants.	0604 862229
Ryburn Farm Museum,Ripponden, W.Yorks.	0422 54823
Scottish Agricultural Museum, Newbridge, Lothian	031 333 2674
Somerset Rural Life Museum, Glastonbury, Somerset	0458 32903
Staffordshire County Museum, Shugborough, Staffs.	0889 881388
Warwickshire Museum of Rural Life, Warwick.	0962 493431
Wilmington Priory Agricultural Museum, Polegate, E.Sussex	0323 870537
Yorkshire Museum of Farming, Murton, N.Yorks.	0904 489966

Fire Engines

Fire Defence Collection, Potterne, Wilts.	0380 3601
London Fire Brigade Museum, London SE1	071 587 4273
The Yorkshire Fire Museum, Batley, W.Yorks.	0942 475228

Maritime Museums

Aberdeen Maritime Museum, Grampian	0224 585788
Armada Experience, Barbican, Plymouth	0752 662225
Bembridge Maritime Museum, Isle of Wight	0983 872223
Buckie Maritime Museum, Moray, Grampian	0524 32121
Buckler's Hard, Hants.	0590 63 203
Caernarfon: *Seiont II* Maritime Museum, Victoria Dock.	0248 600835
Castletown Nautical Museum, Isle of Man	0624 5522
Chatham Historic Dockyard Trust, Kent	0634 8125551
Cowes Maritime Museum, Isle of Wight	0983 293341
Exeter Maritime Museum	0392 58075
Fort Grey Maritime Museum, Guernsey	0481 65036
Hartlepool Maritime Museum, Cleveland	0429 72814
Lancaster Maritime Museum	0524 64637
Lowestoft and E.Suffolk Maritime Museum	0502 61963
Maryport Maritime Museum, Cumbria	090 081 3738
Merseyside Maritime Museum, Pier Head, Liverpool	051 236 1492
Maritime Museum for E.Anglia, Great Yarmouth	0493 842267
Museum of Smuggling History, Ventnor, I o W.	0983 853677
National Maritime Museum, Greenwich, London SE10	081 858 4422
Poole Maritime Museum	0202 683138
Royal Naval Museum, Portsmouth	0705 822351
Royal Navy Submarine Museum, Gosport, Hants	0705 822351
Scottish Maritime Museum, Irvine, Ayrshire	0294 73084
Wool House Maritime Museum, Southampton	0703 223941

(See also **Ships and Boats**)

Medicine

Florence Nightingale Museum, St.Thomas's Hospital, London	01 620 0374

Museum of Royal College of Surgeons, Edinburgh	031 556 6302
Chipping Campden Folk Museum, Glos	0386 840289
Wellcome Museum of Medicine, Science Museum SW7	071 387 4477

Mills

Avoncroft Museum of Buildings, Bromsgrove, H-Worcs.	0527 31363
Bromham Water-mill, Beds.	023 02 4330
Crabble Water-mill, Dover, Kent	0304 201066
Ifield Mill, W.Sussex	0293 36018
Sarehole Water-mill, Hall Green, Birmingham	021 777 6612
Skidby Windmill and Mills Museum, Humberside	0482 882255
Stevington Windmill, Beds.	0234 63232
Thornton Windmill, Thornton Cleveleys, Lancs.	039 17 9287

Monks and Monasteries

Beaulieu Abbey and Display of Monastic Life, Hants.	0590 612345
Bede Monastery Museum, Jarrow, Tyne & Wear	091 4892106
Birkenhead Priory, Merseyside	051 652 4177
Cathedral Treasury, Durham	091 3844854
Cistercian Museum, Hailes Abbey, Glos.	0242 802398
Fountains Abbey & Studley Royal, Ripon, N.Yorks.	076 586 333
Norton Priory Museum, Runcorn, Cheshire	092 85 69895

Motor-cars

The Motor Museum, Old Mill, Bourton-on-the Water, Glos.	0451 21255
Beaulieu, The National Motor Museum, Hants.	0590 612345
C.M.Booth Historic Vehicles Collection, Rolvenden, Kent	0580 241234
Donington Collection of Single-seater Racing-cars, Castle Donington, Leics.	0332 810048
Doune Motor Museum, Perthshire	0786 841 203
Heritage Motor Museum, Brentford, Middlesex	560 1378
ICS History of the Jaguar Museum, Maldon, Essex	0261 53311
Lakeland Motor Museum, Cark-in-Cartmel, Cumbria	044 853509

Lark Lane Motor Museum, Liverpool	051 727 7557
Myreton Museum, Aberlady, E.Lothian	08757 288
Sorn Castle Motor Collection, Mauchline, Strathclyde	0290 51555
Sparkford Motor Museum, Nr.Yeovil, Somerset	0963 40804
Stanford Hall Motor-cycle & Car Collection, Lutterworth, Leics.	0788 860250
Stratford-on-Avon Motor Museum, Warwks.	0789 69413

(See also **Transport**)

Musical Instruments

Bate Collection of Historic Instruments, Oxford	0865 276139
British Piano Museum, Brentford, Middlesex	081 560 8108
Edinburgh University Collection of Musical Instruments	031 441 3133
Harpsichords & Clavichords, Russell Collection, Edinburgh	031 667 1011
Mechanical Music Museum, Cotton, Suffolk	0449 781354
Museum of Mechanical Music, Chichester, W.Sussex	0243 784683
Royal College of Music Museum of Instruments, Kensington	071 589 3643

Police and Punishment

Bath Police Museum, Avon	0225 61111
Beaumaris Gaol, Anglesey, Gwynedd	0248 810 921
Beaumaris Court House, Anglesey, Gwynedd	0248 723262
The Clink, Clink Street, Southwark, London SE1	071 403 6515
Cotswold Countryside Collection, Northleach, Glos.	0285 5611
Greater Manchester Police Museum, Manchester	061 855 3290
Jedburgh Castle Jail, Roxburghshire	0835 63925
London Dungeon, London SE1	071 403 0606
Metropolitan Police History Museum, New Scotland Yard	071 274 9593
Police Bygones Museum, Tetbury, Glos.	0666 53552
Police Museum, Crewe, Cheshire	0270 211098
Police Museum, Hindlip Hall, H-Worcs.	0905 723000
Prison and Police Museum, Ripon, N.Yorks.	0765 3706

Post Office, Telecom and Radio

Bath Postal Museum, Avon	0225 60333
British Telecom Museum, Oxford	0865 246601
National Postal Museum, London EC1	071 432 3851
National Wireless Museum, Arreton, Isle of Wight	0983 67665
Telecom Technology Showcase, Queen Victoria Street EC4	071 248 7444

Railways

Birmingham Railway Museum	021 707 4696
Big Four Railway Museum, Bournemouth, Dorset	0202 22278
Bluebell Railway, Uckfield, E.Sussex	082 572 2370
Bressingham Live Steam Museum, Diss, Norfolk	0379 88386
Colne Valley Railway, Golcar, Huddersfield	0484 659762
Corris Railway Museum, Powys	065 473 343
Cromford & High Peak Railway, Derbs.	062 982 3204
Darlington Railway Centre and Museum, Durham	0325 460532
Didcot Railway Centre, Oxon	0235 817200
Festiniog Railway Museum, Porthmadog, Gwynedd	0766 2340
Great Central railway, Loughborough, Leics.	0509 230726
Great Western Railway Museum, Swindon, Wilts.	0793 26161
Isle of Wight Steam Railway, Havenstreet	0983 882204
Keighley & Worth Railway, Oxenhope, W.Yorks.	0535 45214
Keswick Railway Museum, Cumbria	07687 74644
Midland Railway Centre,Ripley, Derbs.	0773 44920
Narrow-gauge Railway Museum, Tywyn, Gwynedd	0654 710472
National Railway Museum, York	0904 21261
North Woolwich Old Station Museum, London E16	071 474 7244
Railway Village Museum, Swindon, Wilts.	0793 26161
Railway Museum, Ravenglass, Cumbria	06577 226
Railworld, Peterborough, Cambs.	0733 44240
Severn Valley Railway, Bridgnorth, Shropshire	07462 4361
Strathspey Railway, Inverness, Highland	047983 692
Winchcombe Railway Museum, Glos.	0242 602257
Yorkshire Dales Railway Museum, Embsay Station, N.Yorks.	0756 4727

Roman Britain

Aldborough Roman Town and Museum, N.Yorks.	0423 323768
Arbeia Roman Fort, South Shields, Tyne & Wear	0632 561269
The Roman Baths, Bath, Avon	0225 61111
Bignor Roman Villa Museum, W.Sussex	079 87 259
Binchester Roman Fort, Bishop Auckland, Co.Durham	0833 37139
Brading Roman Villa, Isle of Wight	0983 614623
Caerleon Legionary Museum, Gwent	0633 421462
Calleva Museum, Silchester, Hants.	0734 700 362
Castleford (*Lagentium*) Museum, W.Yorks.	0977 559552
Chedworth Roman Villa Museum, Nr.Cheltenham, Glos.	024289 256
Chesters Hadrian's Wall, Chollerford, Nmblnd.	043 471 2349
Colchester Roman Theatre, Essex	0206 712481
Corbridge Roman Site Museum, Northumberland	043 471 2349
Corinium Museum, Cirencester, Glos.	0285 5611
Fishbourne Roman Palace, Nr.Chichester, W.Sussex	0243 785859
Grosvenor Museum, Chester, Cheshire	0244 21616
Housesteads Roman Fort, Hexham, Northumberland	04984 363
Lancaster, Roman Bath House, Lancs.	0524 64637
Letocetum Roman Site, Wall, Staffs.	0543 480768
Lullingstone Roman Villa, Eynsford, Kent	0322 863467
Lunt Roman Fort, Coventry, W.Midlands	0203 303567
Museum of Antiquities, Newcastle-upon-Tyne	0632 328511
Ribchester Museum of Roman Antiquities, Lancs.	025 484 261
Rockbourne Roman Villa Museum,Fordingbridge, Hants.	072 53541
Roman Painted House, Dover, Kent	0304 2032790
Roman Army Museum,Greenhead,Haltwhistle,Nmbd.	069 72485
Segontium Roman Fort Museum, Caernarfon, Gwynedd	0286 5625
Verulamium Museum, St.Albans, Herts.	0727 54659
Viroconium Museum, Wroxeter, Shropshire	074 375 330
Welwyn Roman Bath House, Herts.	0438 820307

Science and Industry

Abbeydale Industrial Hamlet, Sheffield, S.Yorks.	0742 557701

Arkwright's Mill, Cromford, Cornwall	062 982 4297
Bath Industrial Heritage Centre, Avon	0225 318348
Bersham Industrial Heritage Centre, Wrexham, Clwyd	0978 261529
Birmingham Museum of Science and Industry	021 236 1022
Black Country Museum, Dudley, W.Midlands	021 557 9643
Bolton Steam Museum, Lancs.	0204 22311
Brunel Atmospheric Railway, Exeter	0626 890000
Calderdale Industrial Museum, Halifax, W.Yorks.	0422 54823
Chatterley Whitfield Mining Museum, Stoke-on-Trent, Staffs.	0782 813337
Coalbrookdale Museum of Iron & Furnace, Telford, Salop.	095245 3418
Coldharbour Mill Working Wool Museum, Uffcolme, Devon	0884 40960
Cornish Engines, Redruth, Cornwall	0209 216657
Derby Industrial Museum	0332 31111
Gas Museum, Leicester	0533 549414
Greater Manchester Museum of Science & Industry	061 832 2244
Hands-on Science Centre, Victoria Rooms, Bristol	0272 634321
Ironbridge Gorge Museum, Telford, Shropshire	095245 3522
Kelham Island Industrial Museum, Sheffield, S.Yorks.	0742 722106
Kew Bridge Steam Museum, Brentford, Middlesex	081 568 4757
Kidwelly Industrial Museum, Dyfed	0554 891078
Kirkaldy Industrial Museum, Fife	0592 260732
Leeds Industrial Museum, W.Yorks.	0532 637862
Lewis Textile Museum, Blackburn, Lancs.	0254 667130
Leicester Museum of Technology	0533 616330
London Gas Museum, Bromley-by-Bow	071 987 2000
Museum of the History of Science, Oxford	0865 243997
Museum of Lancashire Textile Industry, Rossendale, Lancs.	0706 226459
Museum of Mining, Salford, Gtr.Manchester	061 736 1832
Museum of Science & Engineering, Newcastle-upon-Tyne	091 232 6789
Museum of the Woollen Industry, Drefach Felindre, Dyfed	0559 370929
National Mining Museum, Retford, Notts.	0632 860728
National Museum of Labour History, Limehouse, London E14	071 515 3229
Newcomen Engine House, Dartmouth, Devon	080 43 2923
Newtown Textile Museum, Powys	0686 26243
Nottingham Industrial Museum	0602 284602
Paradise Mill Silk Museum, Macclesfield, Cheshire	0625 618228

Peak District Mining Museum, Matlock, Derbs.	0629 3834
Quarry Bank Mill, Styal, Cheshire	0625 527 468
Ruddington Framework Knitters Museum, Notts.	06077 2795
Science Museum, Exhibition Road, London SW7	071 589 3456
Scottish Museum of Woollen Textiles, Walkerburn, Peebles	089687 281
Sheffield Industrial Museum, S.Yorks.	0742 22106
Tonge Moore Textile Museum, Bolton, Lancs.	0204 21394
Welsh Industrial & Maritime Museum, Cardiff, S.Glam.	0222 481919
Welsh Miners' Museum, Port Talbot, W.Glam.	0639 850564
Whipple Museum of Science, Cambridge	0223 358381
Yorkshire Mining Museum, Wakefield, W.Yorks.	0924 370211

Ships and Boats

Cutty Sark Clipper Ship, Greenwich, London SE10	081 858 3445
Gipsy Moth IV Greenwich, London SE10	071 730 0096
Historic Ship Collection, St.Katherine's Dock, London E1.	071 481 0043
HMS *Belfast,* Tooley Street, London SE1	071 407 6434
HMS *Victory,* Portsmouth, Hants.	0705 819604
HMS *Warrior* (1860), Hartlepool, Cleveland	0429 33051
Kathleen and Mary Schooner, St.Mary Overy Dock, SE1	071 403 3965
Mary Rose Ship Hall, Portsmouth, Hants.	0705 839766
Museum of Roman Wreck (Operation Asterix), Fort Grey, Guernsey — ready in 1990	
Shipwreck Heritage Centre, Hastings, E.Sussex	0424 437452
SS *Great Britain,* Bristol	0272 20680
Windermere Steamboat Museum, Cumbria.	09662 5565

Theatre

Bear Gardens Museum & Arts Centre, Bankside, London SE1.	071 620 0202
Georgian Theatre Royal, Richmond, W.Yorks.	0748 3021
Shakespeare Globe Museum, London SE1.	071 928 6342
Theatre Museum, Covent Garden, London WC2	071 589 6371
The Puppet Theatre Museum, Rugeley, Staffs.	0889 52351

Toys

Arundel Toy and Military Museum, W.Sussex	0903 882908
The Motor Museum, Bourton-on-the Water, Glos	
(has a fine collection of large toys)	0451 21255
Cockermouth, Ethnic Doll and Toy Museum, Cumbria	0900 85259
Finlaystone Doll Collection, Langbank, Strathclyde	047 554 235
Hartlebury Museum, Nr.Kidderminster, H-Worcs.	0299 250416
Lilliput Museum of Antique Dolls & Toys, Brading (I.of W)	0983 407231
London Toy and Model Museum, Craven Hill, London W2	071 262 7905
Museum of Dolls & Bygone Childhood,	
Newark-on-Trent, Notts	0636 821364
Museum of Dolls, Toys & Victoriana, Strathpeffer, Ross	0997 21549
Pollock's Toy Museum, Scala Street, London W1.	071 636 3452
The Precinct Toy Collection, Sandwich, Kent	0843 62150
Potters Museum of Curiosity, Arundel, W.Sussex	0566 86838
Museum of Childhood, Ribchester, Lancs.	025 484 261
Vintage Toy and Train Museum, Sidmouth, Devon	03955 5124
Warrington Museum & Art Gallery, Cheshire	0925 30550
Warwick, The Doll Museum, Oken's House	0926 495546
(See also: **Childhood**)	

Transport

Bury Transport Museum, Lancs.	061 764 7790
British Commercial Vehicles Museum, Leyland, Lancs.	0772 451011
Christchurch Tricycle Museum, Dorset	04252 3240
East Anglia Transport Museum, Lowestoft, Suffolk	0728 2485
Gloucester Transport Museum, Glos.	0452 24131
Grampian Transport Museum, Alford, Grampian	0336 2292
London Transport Museum, Covent Garden, London WC2	071 379 6344
Mark Hall Bicycle Museum, Harlow, Essex	0279 39680
Midland Motor Museum, Bridgnorth, Shropshire	0746 761761
Museum of Road Transport, Coventry, W.Midlands	0203 25555
Museum of Transport, Glasgow, Strathclyde	041 423 8000
Museum of Transport, Manchester	061 205 2122

MUSEUMS TODAY

National Motor-cycle Museum, Solihull, W.Midlands	06755 3311
National Tramway Museum, Crich, Derbs.	077385 2565
Sandtoft Transport Centre, Doncaster, S.Yorks.	0302 62095
Stanford Hall Motor-cycle Museum, Lutterworth, Leics.	0788 860250
Steamport Transport Museum, Southport, Merseyside	0704 30693
Tom Norton's Collection of Old Cycles and Tricycles, Llandrindod Wells, Powys	0597 4513

Just one picture postcard, slide or set of teaching notes from each of these Museums would make an invaluable classroom reference collection.

In 1988, Prince Charles launched the £12 million juggernaut Museum of the Moving Image (MOMI). This is, as the Daily Telegraph's critic described it: 'the epitome of everything that is fun and fancy-free about the twin arts of film and television.' Everything moves and everyone participates. You can crank the handle of a Kinetoscope, dub your own press-button film dialogue, queue for a simulated Odeon, experience flashbacks from 450 great Hollywood films in 5 minutes or join in a filmed interview.

Then, in 1989 the Museums Association celebrated its centenary, designated as Museums Year, under the patronage of the Duchess of York. A rolling programme of events included special exhibitions, new galleries, even new museums. 'Throughout 1989 the Museums Association will be working hard to get the message across that our museums are alive and kicking, lively and stimulating places that can offer a thoroughly enjoyable day out.' (Patrick Boylan, President of the Museums Association in The Times Museums Year Guide, 1989)

In recent years, Museums have become attractive places. Gone is the old-fashioned image of fusty fragments in dusty cases .... Just a minute. As we used to say in the golden, olden age of 1936 and the cinema's continuous performance "This is where we came in."

CHAPTER TWO : STARTING A COLLECTION

As most of us soon learn from experience of collecting objects for a classroom museum, success (and failure too), comes in patches. Some historical periods are far easier to document than others.

Recent family memorabilia, for example, including a wealth of Victoriana, are very easy to find. We begin with our own family collection which is rapidly augmented by loans from the catchment area. This is the stuff of which an older school's Centenary exhibition is made. Though the socially mobile residents of some newer housing estates will have resolutely jettisoned all that old stuff - reminiscent to some of unhappier generations - the school can play an important part in reawakening a sense of values.

Indeed, escalating prices of antiques, the whole nostalgia market, the popularity of fairs, car-boot sales, and TV's Antique Roadshows have already changed parental perception of the monetary value of bygones. Nor should adults forget that, to an eight-year old, World War Two is olden days and steam railways almost prehistoric. Better to build up a truly representational collection of family history over the past four generations than none at all. What are our other sources of supply?

Finds: We begin with specimens which we acquire free of charge by one means or another and which become permanent items in our collection. Original artefacts from the earlier periods of History will be more difficult to find, though the problem need not be insurmountable. Some fortunate teachers work in regions where a particular period of history or prehistory is a commonplace aspect of the environment. At Devizes pupils occasionally produced flint arrow-heads from Windmill Hill; at Bath it was fragments of Roman glass and an infrequent coin; across the deserted villages of Yorkshire the ploughs still turn up fragments of medieval pottery;in the fields behind Chaddesley Corbett (H-

Worcs) metal detectors disclosed a scattering of medieval coins; in Wrens Nest schools, the trilobite or Dudley Bug is a long-term resident! It is a great pity that schools all over England have no facilities for swops!

Fossils can become, literally, the foundation of a school's collection. They are relatively easy to find for ourselves on guided field trips; teachers will be well advised to make contacts with The Nationwide Geology Club, (Hon.National Organizer: Chris Darmon, at 13, Acacia Avenue, Chapeltown, Sheffield S30 4PQ) for guidance. Children should also be encouraged to visit their local museum to ask for help in making their collections. There are now more than 50 *Thumbs-Up!* museums, identified by their peculiar dinosaur logo. These museums guarantee a qualified Geology Keeper who will be pleased to advise us. By the same token, the author is indebted to Colin Reid, Keeper of Geology at Dudley Museum, for some of the helpful advice which this book offers on fossils. See too, below, the additional possibilities of fossil-specimens, not only as finds but also as inexpensive purchases and very cheap replicas.

Given a limited budget, we must be dependent to a large extent upon **loans**. Parents and friends have always been generous to my own museum collection. Ensure adequate publicity of your needs, offer information and carefully presented exhibitions in return and the classroom museum becomes a community enterprise. Best of all, take some pains to involve the lenders in classroom use of their artefacts. Tape-recordings of the family memories attached to each item form the family's own descriptive notes and labels, and become the permanent record of a growing collection.

An outstanding exhibition in a Lancashire Infant school amassed the almost entire furniture of a Victorian parlour, including grandfather clock, iron grate and fireplace, corner cupboard, rag rugs and oil lamps. There was a whole picture gallery of family photographs, discarded 19th century paintings and a lovely collection of Victorian christening robes, patchwork, white-work and samplers. The classroom laundry was equipped with dollies, washboards, tubs and mangles, all capable of sploshy use. The farmyard was well represented too, by smocks and farming implements of all sorts and sizes. Most exotic of all was the generous long-term loan, by the town's theatre, of an original collection of 17th - 18th century dresses, themselves a treasured bequest to the theatre.

It goes without saying that we shall always handle and store such loans with maximum possible care and security, returning them promptly and undamaged after use. We certainly need advice from experts on the proper storage, packaging and display of fragile items, and any restoration should only be attempted with the utmost caution. This advice is offered with feeling, the author having once been horrified to watch an apparently parian bust of Lord Kitchener - fortunately his own property - inexorably dissolving after washing in too strong a detergent solution. A fate almost as terrible as HMS *Hampshire*'s! More often my more encouraging experience has been that schools have raised the community's own standard of care for some previously disregarded old-fashioned treasures, and the permanent loan becomes a regular feature of any collection.

Purchases: As a last resort we may have to rely upon purchasing power. Let us assume that it may be feasible to spend no more than £30 per academic year on museum material other than textbooks. At no more than £1 to £8 a purchase, coin collectors' shops, second-hand bookshops, antique fairs and junk-shops will provide one or two useful - sometimes surprising - additions to our collection.

One of my own most useful buys for £1 was a bag of 80 predecimal coins, ranging from Victorian bun-pennies to Elizabethan farthings and representing every reign from 1880 to 1971. Coin dealers count out pre-decimal pennies by weight not number, and are often quite prepared to give some away with a more exotic purchase. My own dealer recently threw in two barely recognizable George II specimens (00093).

A distinct advantage to the teacher is the expert's low opinion and cheap rating of any specimen not in mint condition. This applies to items other than coinage; museum curators rarely appreciate how much use a teacher can make of a broken, incomplete or even fragmentary piece of evidence. Often their response has been: "Oh well, if I had known that you could use that you could have had plenty of examples." My two earlier Georgian coins will certainly have their classroom uses, though obviously we would want the pupils to see better examples in due course. The line between children's response being "Its all old rubbish!" and "Mystery object! Brilliant! Almost impossible to decipher - Great!"is very narrow indeed, taxing the experience of the teacher and his knowledge of a class's probable reaction.

The many uses of those humble copper coins are self-evident, as dated time-line markers and problem posers. Given a long broken series of pennies, halfpennies and farthings from six reigns since Victoria, we can ask the class to work out the valid statements they can make about their chronology. For example:

What has the order of succession been during the past four generations?

Can you be sure from this time-line how many kings and queens there have been from 1900 to 1988? (The abdication of Edward VIII in 1936 will be an almost impossible trap to avoid.)

How closely can you work out the regnal dates of each monarch, given only these coins?

How closely do these different reigns correspond with the past four generations of your own family?

Is there any way of suggesting the relationship of each monarch, one to another?

Why do the heads face in different directions?

Where is the date on a pre-decimal coin, head or tail? Is this the same for our present decimal coinage? - For every coin?

What are the differences in size and shape between pre-decimal and decimal coins?

What do the abbreviated inscriptions mean? - DG; DEI GRA: REX/REG: FD: IND.IMP: BRIT.OMN.REX ? When do these seem to appear or disappear?

How many are left on a 1990 coin?

How many of these pennies were there to a pound? How many little ones make a big one?

What do the different images on the reverse represent? When do they change?

Which are the standard reference books and catalogues which teach us more about this subject?

This was certainly a very good £1's worth! Where else can we look for bargains?

There is in Glastonbury High Street, a veritable Aladdin's cave, called *Monarch Antiques*. Its owner, John Badman, unfortunately produces no catalogue of his ancient stock, but he describes the following useful items, all reasonably priced:

Paleolithic and Neolithic flint tools, scrapers, blades etc. through to hand-axes, from 50p to £30, but mainly below £3.

Ancient Egyptian amulets etc. from 1200 - 100 BC (£5-12).

Ancient Greek bronze coins in reasonable condition, all identifiable @ £3-4 each).

Roman and Romano-British bronze coins from 1st-4th centuries AD, from £2 to £10 each.

Roman bronze brooches, rings, bracelets etc. (£5-35).

Romano-British potsherds 10p to £1, depending on style and size.

Other Roman items such as beads, loom weights, small artefacts etc., from £2 to £15.

Small medieval objects of bronze, bone etc from £2 to £15.

Medieval and Tudor-Stuart silver coins from £3.

Civil War musket balls @ 50p each.

Early documents from the 16th century onwards for £6-15.

" - and all sorts of ephemera and bits of tangible history from all over the world."

This shop is such a joy to explore that it seems a shame to conduct our business by post! The specimens shown on Cards 00081 and 00085 are both from Monarch and cost a total of £8.00.

Returning to fossils as a staple item of our collection, we should certainly consider a basic range of inexpensive purchases. Nineteenth century Directories of provincial towns all featured Fossil Dealers. Though no longer in the Yellow Pages, they still survive as useful sources of supply. Although a perfect Dudley Bug could cost us more than £100, less exotic specimens come more cheaply; for £5 we can certainly make a start. Museum curators sometimes look askance at the whole prospect of fossil-purchase, but we cannot afford to be contentious!.Here are four useful addresses:-

Simon Cohen, 22 Sydenham Road, Cotham, Bristol BS6 5SJ

Gregory, Botley & Lloyd, 8-12 Rickett Street, London SW6 1RV

Kernow Fossils, New Road, St.Stythans, Truro, Cornwall

Pete Lawrence, Down-to-Earth Co. 164 Elmbridge Road, Gloucester GL2 0PH (for quality fossils)

Or why not consider extending your collection with a few reliable replicas?

Replicas*:* Asked to explain what they mean by a fake, children will soon reach the conclusion that the counterfeiter has a deliberate intention to deceive, probably in order to profit by his deception. There are however many more honest efforts which modern technology has raised beyond the level of clumsy forgery. The most difficult reproduction for even the antiques expert to detect is the copy made with loving care for a useful purpose. What in fact *do* we mean by a fake? How many *kinds* of copy are we familiar with?

For a start, let us consider: Action replay, bogus, carbon-copy, cast, copy, counterfeit, double, duplicate, fake, fax, forgery, identical (object), imitation, impersonation, impostor, likeness, look-alike, mock- (Tudor), model, pastiche, pattern, photocopy, photograph, plastic pressing, pseudo- (medieval), remake, remould, repeat performance, replica, reprint, reproduction, sham, simulacrum, simulation, stereotype, tape-recording, tracing, transcript, twin, uniform (pattern). etc.

Even as a mere vocabulary exercise, this discussion has remarkable possibilities, especially if a class of nine-year-olds are invited to offer their own suggestions. (Having made my own list long ago, I have repeatedly updated it with children's suggestions which never occurred to me - *clone* is the latest example). Is a facsimile a fake for instance? Is a copy always a forgery? And is a replica, honestly acknowledged and made for educational purposes a worthless counterfeit? Which replicas can we accept as useful, honest specimens which teach us something of their originals?

These questions become more vexed when we consider the many processes which make exact copies nowadays. Discuss, for example, the relative authenticity of:

Photographic prints made from original 19th century glass negatives.

Any object which can be cast and re-moulded from an original - fossils, coins, wax seals, fibre-glass insurance plates, a Roman thimble, medals etc.

Pages of books or newspapers reprinted from original founts of type, rather than by photography.

The Jorvik coin, struck from dies which are themselves replicas of Viking originals.

Needlework patterns or samplers which can be stitched almost exactly as the original - such as a Bayeux Tapestry kit, with canvas print, wool and tapestry needle (Rowan Tapestries @ £24.95)

Reproductions of the First Edition of the Ordnance Survey's One Inch sheets (40 x 30 ins), orginally printed 1805-73, with detailed notes on preparation and historical background (£2.95 from Past Times, Guildford House, Hayle, Cornwall TR27 6PT).

William Morris wallpaper designs, of which the original blocks are still available for printing attractive wrapping-paper.

Fibre-glass insurance-plates from Designs in Shrewsbury or, in the same town, a child's schoolroom slate from the craft-fair in St.Julians Church.

Corinium (Cirencester) Museum's beautiful wheel-made copies of 2nd - 4th century pots, priced from £4.50 to £7.50, including a rouletted pot, small storage jars and flagons.

Any sound-recording of a famous person's speech, or courtly songs of the 15th century in French accompanied by lute and medieval harp. Any gramophone record of course, however old (say Tennyson's own reading of The Charge of the Light Brigade, made c1890) is not the original voice.

Well no, a photograph of a £10 note is *not* as good as its original in every sense - but what could we use it for? Especially if it costs 50p?

For replicas fit to fool the experts, we turn yet again to fossils. Present-day scientific casting techniques, using high-grade silicone rubber moulds, acid baths and deceptive modern plastic has given us state-of-the-art reproduction of fossils. These are too authentic to be overlooked by schools. The most outstanding examples are produced by:

Stuart A. Baldwin: Educational Palaeontological Reproductions, Fossil Hall, Boars Tye Road, Silver End, Witham, Essex CM8 3QA.

A well-qualified palaeontologist, Stuart Baldwin offers more than 2,000 products priced from 20p for a single specimen to £800 for a complete evolutionary set. He has supplied over 100,000 replicas for Open University courses and his stock includes, not

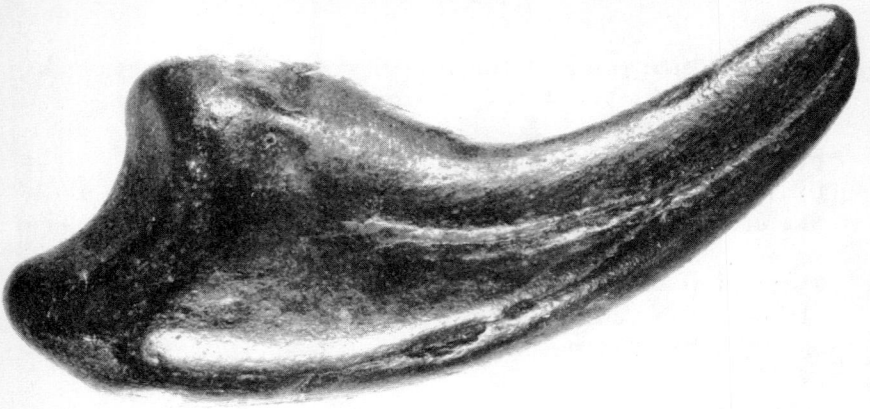

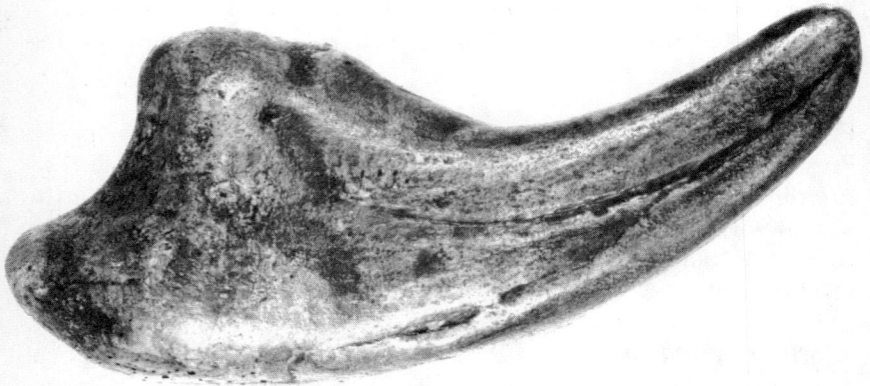

Fig 1: Can you tell the difference? One is the claw of an early Cretaceous carvivorous dinosaur, *Megalosaurus*, of about 120 million years ago, from the Sedgwick Museum Cambridge. The other is a replica by Stuart Baldwin.

only fossils and minerals, but also reproductions of palaeolithic flint implements and other artefacts. His illustrated catalogues and notes are first-rate teaching materials.

We understand that some museum Keepers of Geology may begrudge the widespread sale of original fossils for the classroom. It is as likely that conservationists too will look askance at the continual removal of natural fossils from their environment and would consider the classroom breakage of a replica far less deplorable than damaging the real thing. Children must of course be given opportunities to handle both originals and casts, asking, as in our paired illustrations of a dinosaur's claw: "How can I tell the difference?". It will be reassuring to them to know that Stuart Baldwin, has had the satisfaction of watching an international fossil-expert handle this specimen for 10 minutes under the impression that it was an original. **(Fig 1.)**

Museum Shops have become a familiar temptation all over England. Their stocks, though sometimes suspiciously similar, are also variable in types of goods, though usually of high standard and indeed some high prices. Like National Trust shops, they carry a great deal of attractive kitsch as well as a few items of unusual interest to the teacher. Much attractive costume jewellery is modelled on authentic ethnic patterns, Celtic and Scandinavian, but many of the place-mats, glassware, games and toys, though colourful and very good fun as presents are not really classroom material at capitation prices. Oddly enough, some of our best educational examples were taken from the shops' lowest price ranges. See for example, Jorvik's useful replica coins at only 50p and 85p (00020). The same shop sells realistic cooking pots, antler combs and well-turned wooden bowls, which can be matched with illustrations of their originals in the colourful guide to the excavation. Unfortunately, these beautifully authentic objects are priced in the £20-30 range, well beyond our classroom budget.

Carrying a similar range of stock for mail-order is the *Past Times* commercial catalogue: "350 fine and unusual gifts for all those who share an interest in our island heritage ... a selection of beautiful and interesting things from every age of our history .... generally ... authentic replicas or based on actual period designs. Descriptions are carefully researched too." This catalogue is particularly useful in being chronologically arranged, from Celtic prehistory to World War Two.

As with similar ventures, there is a peculiar tendency to turn most things into costume jewellery, key-rings, wrapping paper or tea-towels (all very acceptable in their own right.) Careful browsing through this very attractive catalogue however, turns up many museum-worthy items at reasonable prices. In the following cases the standard of relative authenticity is remarkably high:

A reproduction pottery Roman lamp, similar to our example 003 (£4.95)

A twelve-Caesar coin set from Julius Caesar (101-44BC) to Domitian (AD 51-96). Actual-size coin faces in cast resin, with notes on each Emperor (£9.95). These single-faced plastic replica coins, available at many Roman museums like Cirencester's are less convincing than the single sided-metal coins from Hereford Museum, from the English reigns of Charles II and William and Mary, and these too are surpassed by Westair's recent issue of double-sided Roman coins in metal. (See below)

Medieval Books of Hours of the 13th - 16th centuries, from the British Library, beautifully printed as a paperback (£5.95). A colourful collection of prints from medieval manuscripts can be built up from a lovely range of 24 Christmas cards (£3.95), a Medieval Lovers' Book of Days (£6.95), stained glass Christmas cards (from Canterbury and Ely) £3.50, and colour-plates of birds from medieval manuscripts from AD700 to the Renaissance (£10.95).

Music of the Middle Ages (13th-14th centuries) on tape, played on authentic instruments of the time (£3.95), also Motets and carols (£6.50).

Morden's playing cards, published in 1676, each card bearing a small map of an English or Welsh county - the first English maps to show roads (£4.95).

Armada playing cards published some years after the event and recording the main events of the battle (£4.95).

Glorious Revolution playing cards, published shortly after 1688 (£4.95).

The School of Manners, an attractive little book of Rules for Children's Behaviour, published in 1701 and reproduced as a clever pastiche of original print, added illustrations and a colourful cover. The book was compiled by an expert, a member of staff of the Victoria and Albert Museum, where the original text is kept (£3.95).

Cries of London playing cards, first printed c1754 (£4.95).

12 Hogarth prints, published in 1747 (£9.50).

8 authentic Victorian theatre programmes (£4.95).

Victorian magazine covers as Christmas cards (£2.95).

An irresistible pack of 20 sheets of Victorian scraps, indistingui-shable from originals - 200, all different. For younger children, these can make very realistic small scale nursery screens, pasted on card or plywood folders and eked out with period wrapping papers. Varnish with Ronseal for a convincing pseudo-antique effect (£2.95).

Victorian Toy Theatre, based on originals sold in the 19th century by Pollock's Toy Museum, with sets, characters and scripts for three plays (Cinderella, Aladdin and Bluebeard). This theatre, from my own experience, works very well (£7.50).

Two antique paper dolls, with 30 cut-out costumes of the 1890s (£3.99).

Cocoa and Corsets - 80 advertising posters from the turn of the century, produced by the Public Record Office (£9.95).

Years of Wrath 1932-45. 325 pages of David Low's famous pre-war and wartime cartoons in the Evening Standard (£5.95).

Winston Churchill: tapes of selected speeches 1939-45 (£8.95).

The Home Front: a collection of wartime advertisements from Good Housekeeping magazine (£10.95).

Not included in the colourful catalogue, but probably the serious teacher's best buys are two facsimile reproductions of historic manuscripts, on yellowed, parchment-like paper. One is a letter of Richard III in 1485, appealing to the loyal Commissioners in his own City of York, for reinforcements against rebels and traitors. The other, Nelson's last letter written on HMS *Victory* and dated October 19th, 1805, just as signals were made for the French fleet coming out of port. He hoped to live to finish the letter after the battle, but didn't. (Published by MagnaScript, 7, Bruce Street, Stirling, Scotland @ £1.50 each).

A delightful reproduction of a bronze thimble found on the Roman site of Verulamium and kept at St.Albans museum. The best buy of all, at only 85p.

The Roman thimble is is a useful Westair reproduction. Like their other replicas this is made of a nickel-tin-lead alloy, not the more usual bonded resin; the dimpled pounce-marks are carefully reproduced. Westair's reproductions are fully approved by Museums which contribute originals - the Grosvenor Museum, Chester, The Museum of London, Verulamium Museum and the Royal Armoury of the Tower of London. Their current catalogue includes the usual range of souvenir items - anointing spoons in sterling silver and period swords in miniature, as paper-knives. More educationally - and more cheaply - they offer:

More thimbles - medieval and Tudor, (£1.20 and £1.95).

A piece of eight from the Spanish Armada galleon *Girona*, wrecked off the western coast of Ireland 75p.

The Shropshire ironmaster John Wilkinson's ½d token @ 50p.

British historical coins from the Hiberno-Norse period to Queen Anne (metal, single-sided) 75p per wallet of 2.

Scottish historical coins of Robert I, Mary Queen of Scots and James VI 85p. All 16 coins in one wallet @ £5.

A high-quality reproduction of Magna Carta, with translation: £2.95.

Reproduction antique maps of 16th-18th centuries, including John Blaeu's (1638) and Norden's Britannia (c1580): £1.95.

Roman double-sided metal coins in simulated gold, silver and bronze on four themes: (1) Roman conquest; (2) Romans in Britain; (3) Rebellion in Britain and (4) Military campaigns.

All these representations have adequate historical notes and biographical details. Westair's showroom at Kings Heath, Birmingham - which shows many more fascinating replicas beyond our classroom budget, such as full-size replica suits of armour at about £85! - is well worth a visit.

STARTING A COLLECTION

This wide range of possibilities brings us to the point of reviewing our own hypothetical one-year collection, as illustrated in the previous chapter. Here, we have assumed that it will not be unreasonable for any class teacher making a start at organizing a museum to expect to collect, document and use 100 different objects in the course of one school year, if he/she has the resources of a school-museums loan service. If not, then at least 50 is a not over-ambitious target.

A century in fact, is a fairly modest beginning. It does not assume any massive all-out effort, as if for a community exhibition or centenary year. These would be far more productive. Of our own 100 items, 64% were temporary loans, including 48% from Museums' Loans Services. 36% were the school's own acquisitions by gift or purchase. Thus our model collection so far relies rather too heavily on generous museums' services but gratefully benefits from gifts (28%) and friendly loans (16%). On the other hand the reliance on purchases of authentic original objects has been kept reasonably realistically low (8%) and the reliance on replicas is equally modest (8%). The expenditure on permanent accessions (mainly a potentially profitable investment in coins), was £31.80, the total cost of our collection so far.

CHAPTER THREE : A HUNDRED A YEAR!

The following set of record cards catalogues a fairly typical collection, made by the author over a period of about a year. (A previous collection, well-known to many a Teachers' Course and collected over a far longer period was almost entirely given away in a rash fit of post-retirement generosity. Many of those items are, happily, now in regular classroom use by teachers in many parts of England and Australia.) This renewed collection also sets a realistic target - one hundred objects a year, allowing 50 as Museum loans, should form the feasible basis of a permanent collection based on gifts, semi-permanent loans and purchases, including replicas.

As the following set of record cards shows, the new collection was culled from all the sources described in Chapter Two. Like most teachers' efforts it relies heavily upon the generosity of Museums Loans services. The author is particularly indebted to Mrs. Jan Anderson of the Birmingham Schools Liaison service, to Tony Knight and Peter Good of Derbyshire LEA, and Mrs. Alison Lloyd, Education Assistant at Hartlebury Museum for their help and advice and, in Mrs. Lloyd's case the welcome excitement of developing this work with teachers and children. All these colleagues have generously co-operated in lending objects for photographing, recording and use with children. Teachers and children are fortunate in this sort of co-operation. In return, it is heartening to know that, as a result of so many lively teachers' courses, at least two county museums services circulate *John West Boxes,* with structure cards and suggestions for teachers.

Like any teacher too, the author has used several reliable replicas, seven in all. Four of these were purchases, two were loans or gifts and one was a Museum specimen. All are acceptable, hard-wearing facsimiles, each with a particularly useful function or point to

make in the classroom.   Other purchases were made in modera-
tion, with some consideration of their relatively high cost.   The
total budget for all purchases, was £31.80, (£14.80 for replicas
and £17.00 for originals, including an extravagant £8 for a
medieval coin (Card 00002).   As the previous chapter showed,
there were many, many more possibilities for another year's
budget, not included here.

Lacking a loans service, we would have to reduce our target,
perhaps collecting up to 75 items a year of our own.   I have
deliberately refrained from the more munificent possibilites of
raising money by jumble sales and suchlike private enterprise; nor
have we considered the vast number of loans and gifts that a
special local Exhibition would undoubtedly attract.

The entire collection of 100 sample items endeavours to cover as
wide a range of time as possible, ranging from fossils to the present
day.   These have been recorded on the standard pattern described
in the next chapter.   The catalogue of this hypothetical collection,
gives full documentation of each artefact, with data on reliable
sources of information in reference books and museums.   It is
intended that any teacher consulting this guide book will often
find a match with of objects collected, found or brought into
school, only to prompt the sometimes inconvenient question:
"What on earth is it?"

An interesting source of ephemeral gifts is tapped by asking a class
to become aware of the interesting problem of the NOW item,
which should be kept on prominent display in the foreground of
our collection, or at the very end of our timeline shelf.   What
article - as well as this morning's daily paper - signifies the most
up-to-date event, personality, invention or idea?   Royal weddings
and their offspring regularly produce useful memorial tins, cards,
plates, mugs etc. as dating evidence.   What else would you use,
month by month? This exercise certainly draws attention to the
remorseless passage of time and the meaning of the word
ephemera.

A HUNDRED A YEAR!

The following three pages list the full set of our first year's collection of 100 objects in order of accession. This wide range of objects, old and new, appears as we would encounter them in everyday life today - that is, in random order. In the card-catalogue which follows (pages 42-241) the contents list is re-arranged in chronological sequence. These are the accession numbers:

MUSEUM CARDS : LIST OF CONTENTS

A HUNDRED A YEAR!

A HUNDRED A YEAR!

The following pages of illustrations, facsimiles of the front and back faces of the author's own catalogue cards, have been re-arranged in chronological, not accession sequence. Thematic re-grouping, as for example in sets of coins, tools, kings and queens, cameras, photography etc., is dealt with under **Retrieval** in the next chapter.

An extra **Main Features** card, listing pairs of opposite features can be used as an elementary exercise, or test of classification skills. The boxes are left blank for children to complete by blocking or punching out the correct choices for each object, or used as a cue-card for Twenty Questions games. Suggested pairs of alternatives are:

Main features

[ ]	Natural	[ ]	Man-made
[ ]	Immobile	[ ]	Portable
[ ]	Inexpensive	[ ]	Precious
[ ]	Simple	[ ]	Ornate
[ ]	Functional	[ ]	Ornamental
[ ]	Industrial	[ ]	Domestic
[ ]	Outdoor	[ ]	Indoor
[ ]	Mechanical	[ ]	Non-mechanical
[ ]	Factory-made	[ ]	Hand-made
[ ]	Authentic	[ ]	Fake
[ ]	Facsimile	[ ]	Replica
[ ]	Dated	[ ]	Undated

Locations: Museums: M1 = Birmingham City Museum
                                 M2 = Derbyshire Loans Service
                                 M3 = Hartlebury Museum, Hereford-Worcs.

               School: H1 = History Room display
                                 H2 = History Room, locked showcase
                                 H3 = History stockroom locked cupboard
                                 S1 = School safe

Here then, are our first year's hundred items, re-arranged in chronological order:-

Our catalogue cards have been dissected, fronts separated from backs, and presented in facing pages for more convenient reading. The specimen blank card offered for duplication in Appendix C restores the more correct format.

TRILOBITE *(Calymene sp.)*

Date: 440-395,000,000 years
(at 24,000 m. max.)

Period: Palaeozoic era
Silurian period

From: Derbyshire Museums
Schools Loans Service
Box 433 No:5
(labelled from Dudley)

Measurements: Length: 40mm

Weight: 23gm

Materials: Fossilized calcium
carbonate and chitin.

Location: M2

Photo: Linda Burridge

00056

Description: A well-preserved fossilised trilobite, shiny-black on front; oval back is hard stone. Three longitudinal divisions with numerous narrowing ridges and divided laterally into head, body and tail-shield sections.

Condition: Good, slight breakage on left side of head.

Possible identity: Children say 'Beetle'.

Reference Books: L.B. Halstead: Hunting the Past (1982): Stuart A. Baldwin: Fossil Anthropod Replicas (List 6: April 1989) has full references.

Museums: Dudley Museum, West Midlands.

Data: More than 2,000 species of trilobite were a chief life-form during the Cambrian, Ordovician and Silurian periods. Marine invertebrates, now extinct, they vary in size from a few mm. to 50cm, capable of rolling into a defensive ball. Some were blind, others had lateral eyes, some with 400-5,000 facets. Typical of a warm climate which created marine deposits of coral, calcareous algae, crinoids and brachiopods, whose skeletons form ancient limestones. X-rays reveal unsuspected detail of their internal organs. Trace fossils record their feeding-, resting- and mating-trails and furrows during 350 million years from Peru, to Australia and from North Wales to Germany. Nicknamed the Dudley Bug, trilobites are numerous there, in the Wrens Nest caverns. Most fossils lend themselves well to modern processes of casting, moulding or pressing in plaster and plastics. The most reliable source of replicas is Stuart A. Baldwin of Witham, Essex. (See text). 25 catalogues of 2,000 specimens are available, plus useful teaching notes, with book lists and references to specialised articles.

FOSSILIZED SEED-FERN

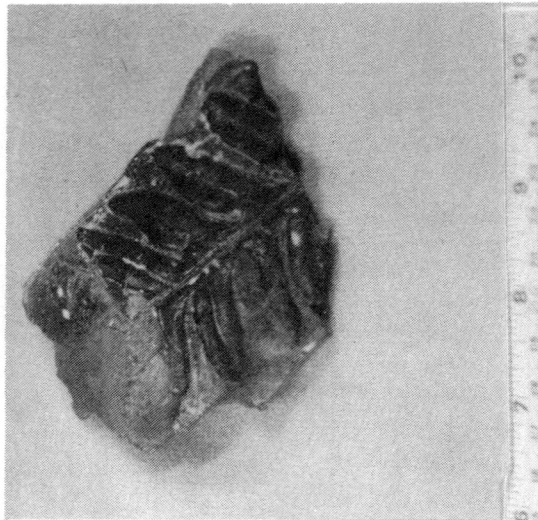

Date: 345 - 280,000,000 years (at 27,500m. max.)

Period: Palaeozoic era
Carboniferous period

From: Derbyshire Museums
Schools Loans Service
Box 463 (12)
(Yorkshire Coal measures)

Measurements: Length: 80mm
Width: 53mm

Weight: 100gm

Materials: Shale

Location: M2

Photo: Linda Burridge

Description: A small slab of black coal-like shale. Impressed on one side, part of a fern's frond with four pairs of leaves. Reverse is blank.

Condition: Poor.

Distinguishing Marks: Museum mark in white.

Possible identity: Some children believe that anything shiny is plastic - few see coal in centrally heated homes.

Reference Books: W.G. Chaloner & P. Macdonald: Plants invade the Land (1980) Barry Thomas: Evolution of Plants & Flowers (1981).

Museums: Cliffe Castle Museum, Keighley (Yorks).

Data: This specimen survives as an example of the very rich flora of the coal measures. 430m years ago the Northern Hemisphere was covered by vast swamps, where dense humid forests grew prolific of ferns and mosses. As the plants and trees decayed and were compressed, coal was formed. By the Devonian period (between Silurian and Carboniferous) within the space of 100 million years, plant life spread from the waterlogged edges of freshwater rivers and lakes to cover vast expanses of land, followed by the emergence of the first true amphibian animals. Seeds, pollen and insects are also preserved in the coal. Branches and leaves can be clearly seen in this sample.

AMMONITE (*Cephalopod sp.*)

Date: 195-136,000,000 years old
(at 16,000m. max)

Period: Mesozoic era
Jurassic period

From: Derbyshire Museums
Schools Loans Service
Box 433 No:20
(labelled Lyme Regis)

Measurements: Diameter: 45mm

Weight: 35gm

Materials: Internal mould of
a dissolved shell.

Location: M2

Photo: Linda Burridge

00057———————————————————————

Description: Flat coil of five diminishing whorls, all laterally ribbed. Grey-black colour, with tiny white (shell?) fragments embedded. Complete on both sides.

Condition: Very good.

Distinguishing Marks: None.

Possible identity: Snail?

Reference Books: David Attenborough: Life on Earth (1981).

Museums: The Lyme Regis Museum; Peterborough Museum & Art Gallery.

Data: Jurassic features were a warm, humid climate and shallow-water marine conditions. Ammonites - a now extinct marine cephalopod or mollusc (shellfish of the octopus and cuttle-fish family) were abundant and reptiles spread to land and sky. There were also dinosaurs, toothed birds and small, primitive mammals. Bivalves had a large muscular single foot, with head and back protected by shell; some original forms died out 500 million years ago, others evolved later. Their shells were partitioned as gas-chambers to float, but also weighted to keep the head forward. During the Mesozoic era, the sole surviving ammonoid evolved into the ammonite which are said to litter the beaches of Lyme Regis.

CRETACEOUS LOBSTER (*Hoploparia sp.*)

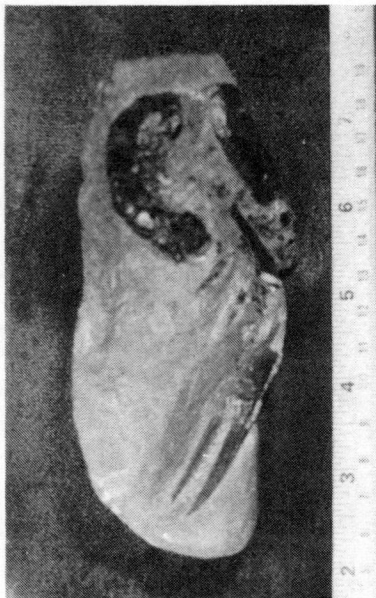

Photo: Linda Burridge

Date: 136-65,000,000 years old (at 15,500m. max)

Period: Mesozoic era
Cretaceous period

From: Derbyshire Museums
Schools Loans Service
Box 433 No:30
(labelled Blackdown)

Measurements: Length: 140mm

Weight: 288gm

Materials: sandy stone and fossilised shell

Location: M2

00060

Description: Irregular slab of greenish-white stone, with black shiny portions embedded, showing obvious claws.

Condition: Fragmentary.

Distinguishing Marks: Museum mark (30).

Possible identity: Beak? Claw?

Reference Books: A.E.Rixon: Fossil Animal Remains (1976).

Museums: Royal Albert Memorial Museum, Exeter.

Data: The Cretaceous period, last of the Mesozoic era, saw the formation of chalk deposits the first flowering plants and many modern trees (walnut, sycamore, oak etc.) This was the age of maximum extent of seas - deposits are mainly marine - with the extinction of many large reptiles and dinosaurs - even the last of the ammonites. Crustaceans like lobsters and crabs became the main scavengers of the sea-bed. They constructed elaborate living galleries within the sediment, as refuges and food-beds. These too, form trace-fossils. The Blackdown Hills (Devon), on Upper Greensand are said to be an enormously important Cretaceous deposit.

OLIGOCENE SEA-URCHIN

Date: 38-26,000,000 years old
(at 9,500m. max)

Period: Kainozoic (or Cainozoic) Era (Tertiary)
Oligocene period

From: Derbyshire Museums
Schools Loans Service
Box 433 No.36
(labelled Isle of Wight)

Measurements: 30mm

Weight: 39gm

Materials: Stone and shell

Location: M2

Photo: Linda Burridge

Description: A pretty, toy-like fossil, beautifully shaped and coloured pale ivory-cream/pink. A flattened sphere, uniformly pimpled with small crusted knobs or pores in five radial bands or ambulacra. These pores were used as a vascular system for locomotion and respiration. At top and bottom there are concave circular depressions. These conceal the mouth (bottom) and anus (top).

Condition: Good

Distinguishing Marks: Museum marks only.

Possible identity: Children might say 'pod'?

Reference Books: David Lambert: Cambridge Field Guide to Prehistoric Life (1985); J.T. Lawrence: Fossils (Granada 1982); Rudolf Prokop: Hamlyn Guide to Fossils (1981)

Museums: Museum of Isle of Wight Geology, Sandown, I o W.

Data: During this period the weather was warm; in Britain marine and estuarine marls and freshwater limestones were deposited, especially on Isle of Wight and adjacent mainland. A tropical element continued in British flora, during the period of the rise of modern mammals, prior to the appearance of man-apes in India and Africa. Sea-urchins live in salt water, crawling or burrowing on the sea-bed or attaching themselves to rocks. Their prolific period began in the Meso-zoic - Kainozoic eras, and they still survive.

RHINOCEROS TOOTH

Date: c7-2,000,000 years old
(at 5,500m. max)

Period: Kainozoic era (Tertiary)
Pleistocene epoch

From: Derbyshire Museums
Schools Loans Service
Box 433 No:40
(labelled Medway)

Measurements: Length: 65mm

Weight: 148gm

Materials: natural, mammal-tooth
protein and calcium

Location: M2

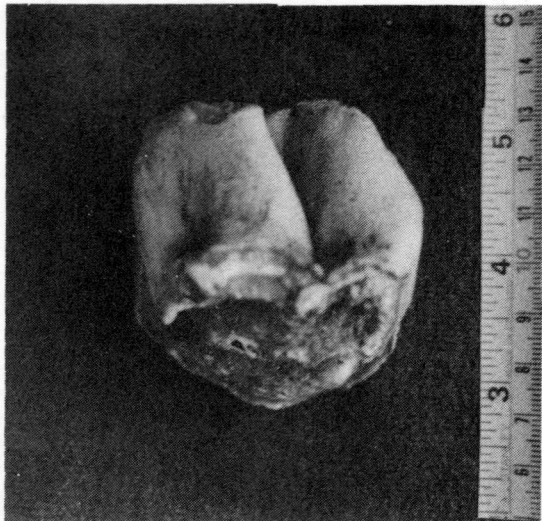

Photo: Linda Burridge

00058

Description: Wedge-shaped portion of a very large tooth, the crown broken away; two well-defined hollow roots. Yellow in colour, the unbroken surface smooth.

Condition: Fair

Distinguishing Marks: Museum mark: Rhinoceros - Medway Gravels.

Possible identity: Tooth

Reference Books: L.B. Halstead: The Evolution of Mammals (1978) A.J.Stuart: Pleistocene Vertebrates in the British Isles (1982)

Museums: Maidstone Museum & Art Gallery

Data: Pleistocene was a temperate, Mediterranean climate, with abundant flora, and mammals the dominant form of life. The British Isles began to take their present outline, mountain tracts were raised and erosion began. The Atlantic Ocean was well established, after the Americas and Greenland drifted westward. The North Sea extended over much of SE England, forming the shelly sand crags of East Anglia. Luxuriant sub-tropical vegetation covered central and southern England, with magnolias, acacia, eucalyptus and palm trees. Crocodiles and hippopotami lived on the river deltas; as grasses evolved and spread, larger herbivorous animals included the horse, tapir and rhinoceros, only the horse surviving in numbers. This tooth, like many other Pleistocene fossils, was collected from the Medway gravels around Snodland, Aylesford and Leybourne. This epoch was followed by the Ice Age.

ELEPHANT'S TOOTH

Date: 1,500,000 years ago
(at 6,000 feet max)

Period: Kainozoic era (Quaternary)
Pleistocene-Recent epoch

From: Derbyshire Museums
Schools Loans Service
Box 433 No:45
(labelled Cromer)

Measurements: Length: 130mm
Width: 80mm

Weight: 1560gm

Materials: Natural, mammalian

Location: M2

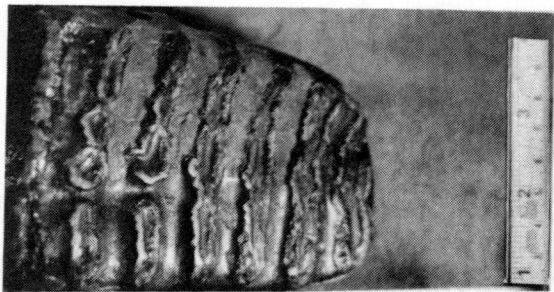

Photo: Linda Burridge

00059

Description: A brown mass of bone-like material, flat on one side, with regular corrugations; rounded on the other side and tapering to a blunt point. The top more clean-cut; highly polished, as if varnished.

Condition: Good

Distinguishing Marks: Alternating enamel-cement-dentine.

Possible identity: Probably mammoth?

Reference Books: L.P. Halstead: Hunting the Past (1982)

Museums: The Cromer Museum, Norfolk Museums Service

Data: The Pleistocene Ice Age was a glacial period in NW Europe, with Arctic plants and fauna and extensive glaciation of the northern hemisphere. Ice-sheets and glaciers spread over Britain, as far south as the Thames valley and Bristol Channel. Arctic mammals grazed the sparse vegetation, including the Southern elephant, hippopotamus, cave lion, cave bear, woolly rhinoceros, Irish deer and musk ox. The later epoch sees the evolutionary development of modern Man; the first human remains in Britain date from an interglacial of 250,000 years ago; tools have been found in older deposits.

BEAR'S TOOTH

Date: c1,500,000- 500,000

Period: Kainozoic era (Quarternary) Pleistocene period

From: Derbyshire Museums School Loans Service Box 463 (44) (Marked from Yealmpton Cave)

Measurements: Length: 70mm

Weight: 70gm

Materials: Natural tooth protein and calcium salts

Location: M2

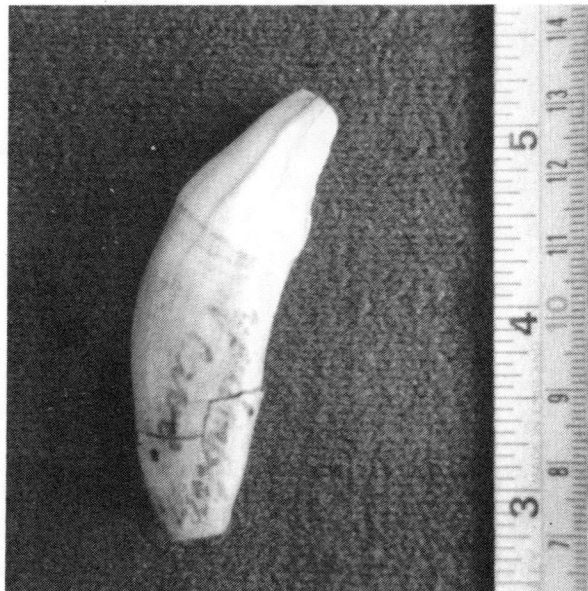

Photo: Linda Burridge

00062

Description: A well-formed, curved root and crown (incisor?), yellow-ivory colour, with smooth surface and sharply pointed end.

Condition: Good, but cracked

Distinguishing Marks: Museum mark only (Yealmpton cave) as in photograph

Possible identity: Obvious - but what animal?

Reference Books: D. Lambert: World before Man (1986) G. Welfare: Dinosaurs and Prehistoric Animals (1978)

Museums: Devon's main geological collection, including material from Yealmpton Cave, is in Plymouth City Museum.

Data: Yealmpton Cave is 11km East of Plymouth. Similar cave-finds, including bones of horses, deer, bear, mammoth, woolly rhinoceros and elephant continue into the later (500,000 years ago) age of Paleolithic Man. These are found in association with flint hunting-tools, though much of early man's diet was taken by gathering, more than by hunting. This earlier bear is more contemporary with Man's ancestor Australophecines, earlier than Uppright Man and Homo Sapiens. At the time of the greatest extent of the ice-sheet, Devon and all southwest and southern England, south of the Avon and Thames were unglaciated but climate was severe, permitting only scant vegetation, grasses, sedges and shrubs on frozen ground.

No: 00004

PALEOLITHIC HAND-AXE

Date: 30,000 years old?

Period: Prehistoric

From: Retired Museum curator, Dudley (Loan) Provenance uncertain.

Measurements: 100mm long; 70mm wide

Weight: 156gm

Materials: Flint

Location: S1

SIHC: 4.1

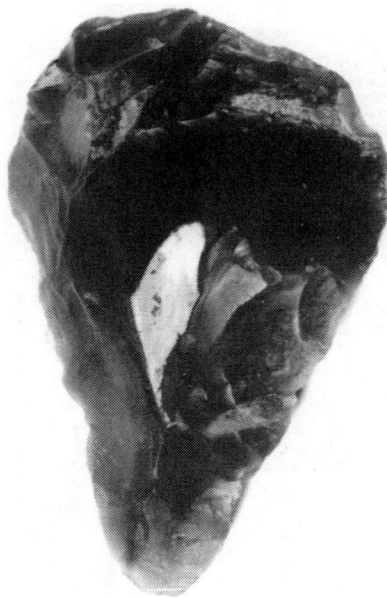

Photo: Frank Power

00004

Description: Shiny ovoid-shaped flint, rounded at one end, pointed the other. Chipped, or flaked all over, mainly towards outer edges.

Condition: Almost indestructible.

Distinguishing Marks: Some chalk-like, yellowed deposit centrally. Flaking is main feature. Fits hand neatly.

Possible identity: Tool or weapon

Reference Books: Kenneth Oakley: Man the Toolmaker (British Museum 1972); British Museum: Flint Implements (1968); W. Bray and D.H. Trump: Penguin Dictionary of Archaeology (1982); Michael Wood: Atlas of Archaeology (1985).

Museums: Devizes Museum (Wilts); Furness Museum, Barrow (Cumbria)

Data: The uncertain provenance of this object makes its authenticity doubtful. Otherwise, in size, shape etc., it matches reliable museum types. Museum experts, though dubious, make no definite judgment. Stone hand-axes were first found at St. Acheul in the Somme valley, giving the type-name Acheulian, but similar types have also been found in Palestine (of chert), in Kenya, Madras (quartzite and shale) and Suffolk (flint). (The African culture is oldest and most continuous.) These have been described as Boy Scout knives of the ancient world, mysterious, in that they are always of similar shape, unnessarily beautiful and of uncertain use. Paleolithic tools are chipped from the flint core; New Stone (Neolithic) age artefacts use smaller flakes, more finely ground or polished. Stone tools continue in use into the Bronze Age (See 053 and 054) and razor-sharp flint flakes were used by surgeons in the 19th century. (Flint remains more sterile than metal.)

STONE HAMMER

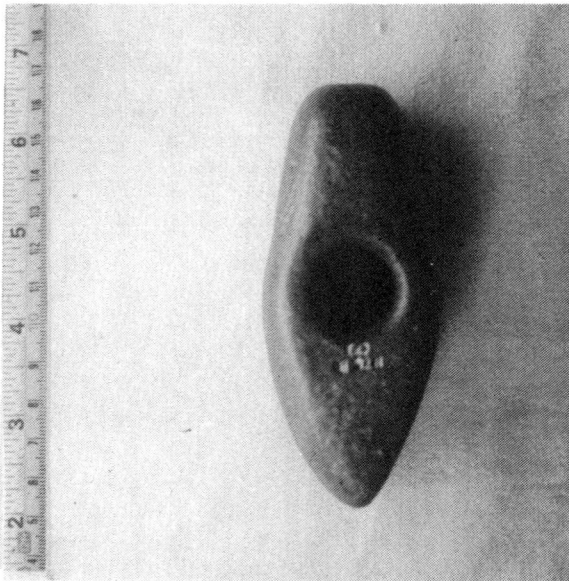

Date: 2000-1500 BC

Period: Early Bronze Age

From: Derbyshire Museums
Schools Loans Service
Box 1174B (7)
(said to be from Denmark)

Measurements: Length: 100mm

Weight: 320gm

Materials: Hard stone

Location: M2

Exit Date:

SIHC: 4.1

Photo: Linda Burridge

00053—

Description: A beautifully smooth, well-rounded hammer-head with one end slightly more pointed, the hole almost central. Edges bevelled, surface polished.

Condition: Excellent

Distinguishing Marks: none, unmarked,- even by use.

Possible identity: Obvious, though debatable whether this is a tool or a weapon, then functional or ceremonial? Or possibly unused factory stock?

Reference Books: C.B. Burgess: The Age of Stonehenge (1980); F.E.S. Roe: Battle-axe series in Britain (1966) and Typology of stone implements with shaft-holes (1979); British Museum: Later Prehistoric Antiquities (1953)

Museums: Alexander Keiller Museum, Avebury, Wilts.

Data: Stone continued long in use after the development of metals. Smooth, perforated mace-heads were used in Neolithic times and continue, as shaft-hole axes in the Beaker and Wessex phases. Axe-hammers are larger (15cm) than battleaxes. They were used as trading objects, as demonstrated by petrological (scientific study of rocks' composition) examination which identifies the regional origin of the stone used. Note that the Museum classifies this axe as originating in Denmark. The British Museum handbook (above) illustrates (Fig 4: pp.13-15) several flint and stone weapons and tools of the Beaker Culture and Early Bronze Age, including polished stone battle axes, flint arrow-heads, knives, dagger, scrapers and a mace-head.

FLINT ARROW-HEAD

Date: 2300-1200 BC

Period: Earlier Bronze Age

From: Derbyshire Museums
Schools Loans Service
Box 1174B (2)

Measurements: Length: 32mm

Weight: 4gm

Materials: Flint

Location: M2

Exit Date:

SIHC: 4.1

Photo: Linda Burridge

00054

Description: A well-flaked flint, with blunted point, two unequal barbs and an almost rectangular tang (shaft-fitting).

Condition: Fair, slightly broken

Distinguishing Marks: unmistakable hand-working of the flint. Shape too, is characteristic.

Possible identity: Obvious, but used for war or hunting?

Reference Books: Lesley & Roy Adkins: Thesaurus of British Archaeology (1980) p.67

Museums: Keiller Museum, Avebury (Wiltshire)

Data: Flint mines continued in use from Neolithic times into the Earlier Bronze Age, when leaf-shaped flint knives and daggers were made. Another type of flint arrow-head, with squared-off barbs came from Brittany. Other stone tools of the Earlier Bronze Age include whetstones, archers' arm-braces, querns and axe-heads (see 0053). Stone moulds were used for metal casting. Bone and antler were made into pins, tweezers, buttons, belt-fasteners, combs, and even daggers. Other ornamental objects were made of amber and jet. One might have thought this to be a Neolithic flint but for the Museum's description. Stone age arrow-heads (as from Windmill Hill (Wilts) are usually smaller,leaf-shaped flakes, not as fully shaped as this one. Compare also 00055.

BRONZE ARROW-HEAD

Date:	c.2300BC-1200 BC
Period:	Early Bronze Age
From:	Derbyshire Museums Schools Loans Service Box 1174B
Measurements:	42 mm long
Weight:	16gm
Materials:	Bronze
Location:	M1
Exit Date:	
SIHC:	1.8

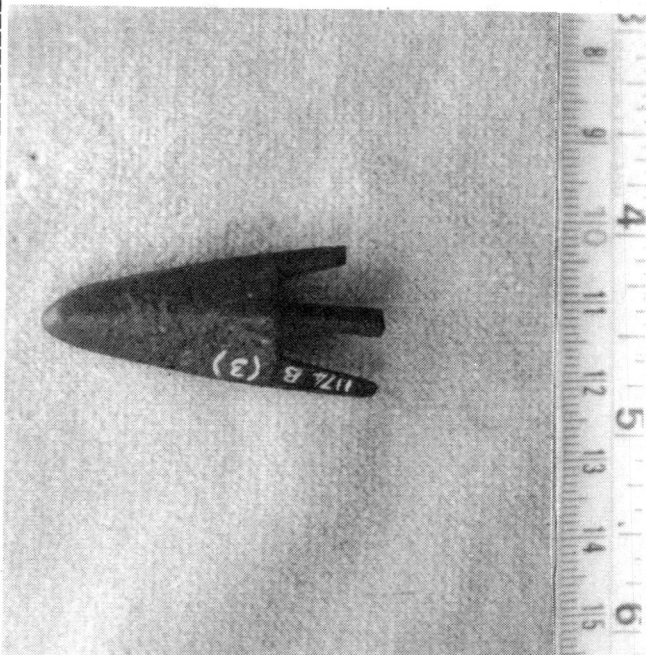

Photo: Linda Burridge

Description: A wedge-shaped arrowhead, greenish in colour, with well-defined round tang and two flat barbs.

Distinguishing Marks: Museum marks only.

Condition: Excellent, except for slight breakage of one barb.

Possible identity: War- or hunting-arrow?

Reference Books: P. Ashbee: The Bronze Age Round Barrow in Britain (1960)

Museums: Aylesbury, Devizes, Lewes and Brighton.

Data: During the Bronze Age there was an increasing tendency to single burial, usually covered by a round barrow, or mound of 12-140ft diameter, 4-10ft high, grouped in cemeteries. (There are 57 in a 3-mile area near Broad Down in Devon.) Barrows contain cremation urns, later skeletons, with grave-goods. Tools and weapons are made of both flint and bronze, ornaments of gold. Some artefacts are imports, faience beads from Egypt (Stockbridge Down: Hants and Normanton: Wilts), flint axes from Scandinavia (Julliberrie's Grave: Kent), gold and axes from Ireland (Lansdown : Avon, Willerby: Yorks.), bucket-shaped urns of migrant farmers from N. France (Sunningdale:Surrey), pins from Germany (Firle Beacon: Sussex), beads from Crete (Manton: Wilts). Bronze barbed and tanged arrowheads like this specimen are typical of the Pennard (W. Glam) phase; squared-off barbs indicate a Breton type.

EGYPTIAN AMETHYST BEADS

Date: c1900 BC

Period: Ancient Egypt
Middle Kingdom

From: Birmingham Museums
Schools Loan Service
Box 4/III Egyptian III
Item No: AL 36

Measurements: Length: 80mm (Double string)

Weight: 16gm

Materials: Said to be amethyst

Location: M1

Exit Date:

SIHC: 3.4

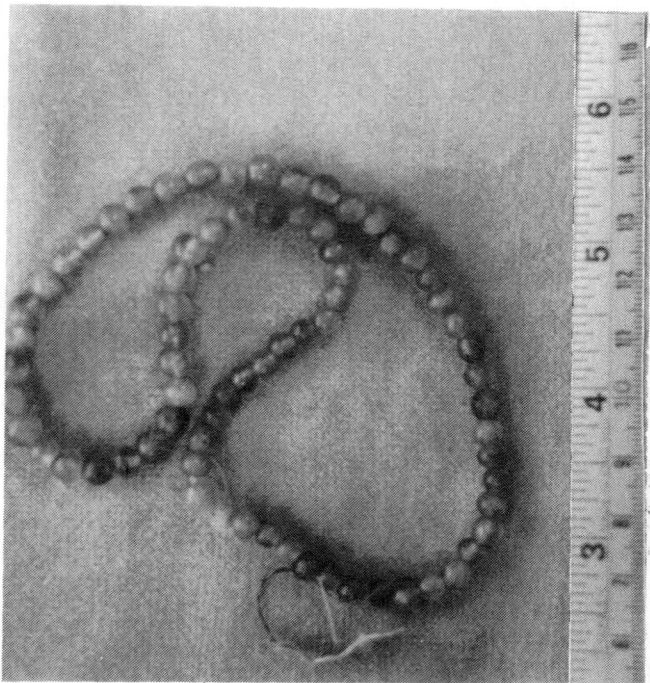

Photo: Linda Burridge

00021————————————————————————

Description: A pretty string of 72 small, spherical beads, of semi-transparent blue, each approx: 5mm in diameter, tightly strung on fine gut.

Condition: Good

Distinguishing Marks: Paper ticket AL36

Possible identity: Child's necklace?

Reference Books: Georges Posener: A Dictionary of Egyptian Civilization (1962) has useful alphabetical entries (illustrated)

Museums: Manchester City Museum

Data: It is difficult to date or authenticate this sort of item - how many lost, where found, obviously re-strung etc. The most reliable clue to the authenticity of these beads is their biconical boring. The Egyptians could not bore straight through small beads, so bored from side to side, making two narrowing, conical holes to the centre. These beads are characteristic of the Middle Kingdom. The Egyptians found their semi-precious stones in Sinai and the Eastern Desert; other necklaces, signet rings, bracelets and ear-rings used gold, carnelians, turquoise, faience, vitreous enamels, enamelled glazes, lapis lazuli, felspar, obsidian and glass imitations. Egyptian jewellery was largely allegorical, including scarabs (sacred beetles), the tau cross (Greek letter tau or T), the utchat (sacred eye), uraeus (hooded snake) and human-headed hawk.

— 67 —

EGYPTIAN MIRROR

Photo: Linda Burridge

Date: c1570 BC

Period: Ancient Egypt
Middle Kingdom

From: Birmingham Museums
School Loans Service
Box A4 III Egyptian

Measurements: Length: 170mm (Tang 55mm)
Diameter: 110mm

Weight: 295gm

Materials: Green-brown metal Copper or bronze

Location: M2

Exit Date:

SIHC: 3.1

00017————————————

Description: A perfectly circular metal disc, very smooth metal - one side has a flaky green, crusted deposit. Long, sharp tang.

Condition: Poor, badly cracked

Distinguishing Marks: Museum mark (defaced)

Possible identity: Bat? Skillet?

Reference Books: Georges Posener: A Dictionary of Egyptian Civilization (1962)

Museums: Edinburgh Museum

Data: Silvered glass was not used in mirrors before the 14th c.AD, though some strange early Coptic types stuck broken glass fragments into slabs of plaster. The lost handle might have been made of wood, ivory or papyrus-wood; it would have been carved, possibly depicting Hathor, mother of Horus and goddess of creation, love, joy and beauty. Bronze mirrors first appear during the Old Kingdom (c2,500 BC) but this example is dated to the New Kingdom (1570-1080 BC) by its round, rather than a more flattened, oval shape. The back would have been enamelled. The Romans also used metal discs, which could be very highly polished to give a clear reflection. Glass was first used in Venice c1300 to cover silver plate, then mercury. Small mirrors were first made in England in 1673 and modern silvering was invented by Liebig at Geissen in Germany in 1830.

BRONZE AXE HEAD

Date: c1300 BC

Period: Earlier Bronze Age

From: Derbyshire Museums
Schools Loans Service
Box 1174B (5)

Measurements: Length: 107mm

Weight: 187gm

Materials: Bronze

Location: M1

Exit Date:

SIHC: 4.1

Photo: Linda Burridge

Description: A fairly sharp-bladed small axe-head of blackish green colour.

Condition: Very good

Distinguishing Marks: This implement is identified as a high-flange palstave by the size of the flange and stop-ridge which are more developed than an axe would be.

Possible identity: obvious

Reference Books: C.B. Burgess: The Bronze Age in C. Renfrew's: British Prehistory; a new outline (1974) M.J. Rowlands: Production & Distribution of Middle Bronze Age metalwork in S. Britain (1976) M.A. Smith: Some Somerset Hoards. (1959)

Data: Labelled a palstave by the Museum; the dictionary gives Palstave = celt and celt = axe-like implement with a bevelled edge. Note possible confusion with Celt as Indo-European racial or linguistic group. Usually spiked to fit a slotted wooden handle, but see also Card 051. Bronze artefacts are found in round barrow burials and peat bogs. They reveal a culture which depended on mixed farming and hunting deer. Settlements include mini hill-forts. The Earlier Bronze Age (2300-1200 BC) began with the Beaker folk and Wessex cultures. This type of palstave is typical of the Taunton phase. Notice how, in our museum's timeline, the long duration of Egyptian culture from pre-Dynastic times continuing into the Roman Empire pre-dates the later development of Bronze Age techniques in the more primitive regions of NW Europe and Britain.

SOCKETED BRONZE CELT

Date: c1300 BC

Period: Earlier Bronze Age

From: Derbyshire Museums
Schools Loans Service
Box 1174B (6)
(labelled Reading)

Measurements: Length: 130mm

Weight: 303gm

Materials: Bronze alloy

Location: M2

Exit Date:

SIHC: 4.1

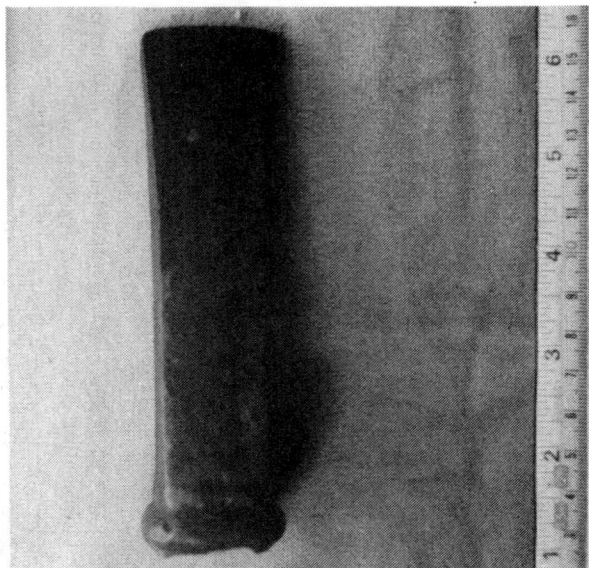

Photo: Linda Burridge

00052——————————————————————————————————————

Description: A rectangular blade with a hollow socket at one end and a ring below its raised rim. Very light green metal.

Condition: Very good

Distinguishing Marks: The shape of the socket, rim and ring identify this as a socketed axe of the Taunton-Hademarschen (W.Germany) type.

Possible identity: Evidently a tool, but exact function less certain - an adze?

Reference Books: Lesley & Roy A. Adkins: Thesaurus of British Archaeology (1982) p.57; C.B. Burgess: The Age of Stonehenge (1980)

Museums: Somerset County Museum,Taunton. Reading Museum & Art Gallery.

Data: This tool is of the same culture as OO51. Bronze, made of copper alloyed with tin, was used from c2000 BC. There is some debate on the earlier idea that each British prehistoric development was the result of a succession of invasions from abroad; more attention is now paid to the possibilities of influence by trade and itinerant workers. Other phases of bronze metalwork are found at, and named after Acton Park (Clwyd), Glentrool (Dumfries) and Penard (W.Glam). Swords were imported from Germany and developed at Chelsea and Ballintober (Ireland). Bronze Age barrow cemeteries are found in Berkshire (specimen labelled Reading) at Five Knolls and Galley Hill, grave-goods are in Luton Museum.

EGYPTIAN PAPYRUS (REPLICA)

Date: 1300-1000 BC

Period: Ancient Egypt
New Kingdom into Third
Intermediary Period

From: Gift: Miss Linda Ivell
Bought in Cairo

Measurements: 184 x 121 mm

Weight: 7gm

Materials: Papyrus, a paper, made from reeds

Location: S1

SIHC: 1.1

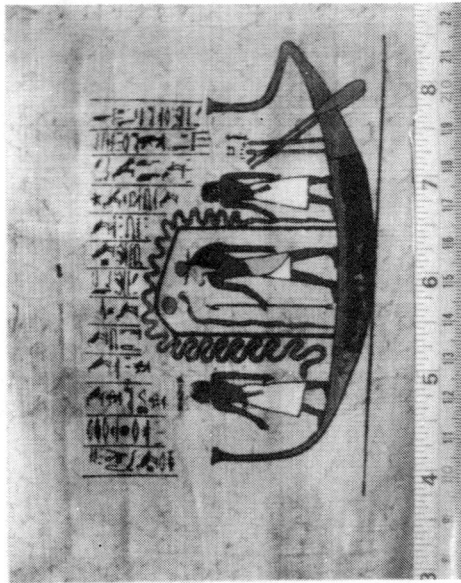

Photo: Frank Power

00019

Description: A colourful illustration with panels of hieroglyphics.

Condition: Good (replica)

Distinguishing Marks: Reverse shop's trade mark rubbed out by wear on Teachers' courses.

Possible identity: Fairly well-known to children.

Reference Books: R.O. Faulkner: Book of the Dead. T.G.H. James: Egyptian Paintings (Brit.Mus.1985)

Museum: The British Museum, Egyptian Dept. (who could not respond more helpfully.)

Data: This is a panel from a funerary book of the New Kingdom. First painted on the walls of tombs in the Valley of the Kings, these were later made into papyrus books, such as The Book of Caverns, Book of What is in the Underworld, Book of Gates etc. This picture shows the Sun God as a man with ram's head, carrying his sceptre or standard insignia, the cabin of his ship protected by a magic serpent. The sun god, having sailed the Nile of the Sky all day, by night descends into the vaults of the underworld, under the Earth, to arise from the East next morning.

BRONZE SPEAR HEAD

Date: 1200 BC

Period: Earlier Bronze Age

From: Derbyshire Museums
Schools Loans Service
Box 1174B (4)

Measurements: Length: 205mm
Width: 50mm

Weight: 202gm

Materials: Bronze alloy (copper and tin)

Location: M2

Exit Date:

SIHC: 1.8

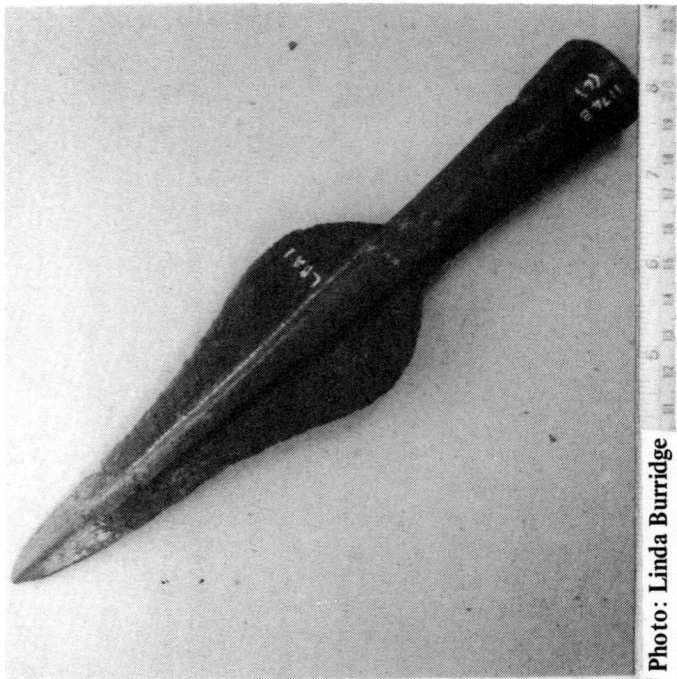

Photo: Linda Burridge

00050

Description: A medium sized spear-head, of black metal. Long leaf-shape, with socket in which is a small hole for a retaining pin.

Condition: Very good, slightly bent and worn towards tip.

Distinguishing Marks: The general shape and socket of this object identify it as a pegged, leaf-shaped spear-head of the Pennard (W.Glam) type.

Possible identity: Obvious

Reference Books: J.Evans: The Ancient Bronze Implements, Weapons and Ornaments of Great Britain and Ireland (1881). C.B. Burgess: The Bronze Age, in C. Renfrew's British Prehistory; a new Outline (1974)

Museums: The British Museum, London. Many provincial museums also have good Bronze Age collections, e.g: Brighton, Exeter, Taunton, Norwich, Lewes, Aylesbury, Dorchester and Devizes.

Data: Bronze Age metalwork is divided into several dating phases, from Beaker folk (2300BC) to Hallstatt (German) culture c700BC. Involving trade with the Continent and Ireland, industry was carried all over Britain by itinerant smiths. Bronze implements are found in round barrow cemeteries in Yorkshire, Northumberland, Peak district, Wales and Wessex, where the great temple of Stonehenge was built. Climatic deterioration changed Bronze Age economy from nomadic-pastoral to agriculture; communities have been found at Snail Down (Wilts) and Itford Hill (Sussex). The British Museum's Later Prehistoric Antiquities, (Fig.10,Plates V,VI) shows Bronze spear heads from Arreton Down, I o W; Snowshill, Glos; Bottisham Lode, Cambs; and an almost identical type from Heatherbury Burn Cave, Durham, with bronze-smith's tools, tongs and moulds.

EGYPTIAN MUMMY'S SKULL

Date: 1,000 BC - 3rd c AD

Period: Ancient Egypt

From: Birmingham Museum
School Loans Service
Box A4 III/Egyptian III
No:AL38

Measurements: Length: 140mm

Weight: 280gm

Materials: Bone

Location: M1

Exit Date:

SIHC: 3.7

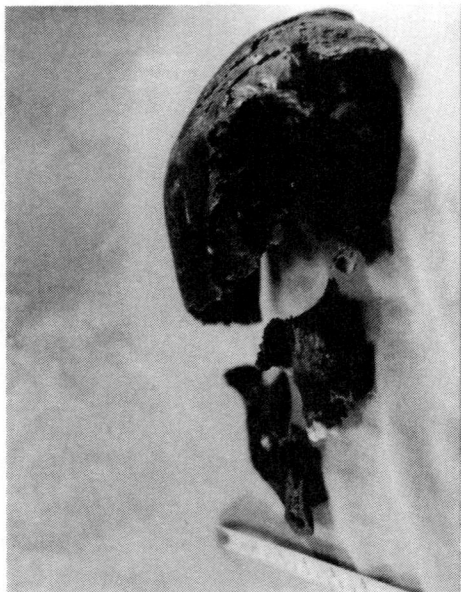

Photo: Linda Burridge

Description: A disgusting item! Smooth brown piece, (about 30%) of skull, left side to part of eye-socket. Smooth brown colour, with patches of black tar-like coating inside. Inside of bone porous or fibrous. Detached fragment of lower jaw, with 2 molars and 2 sockets. Smaller fragment with 2 molars. No traces of hair, thank goodness!

Condition: Almost fossilised. Poor.

Distinguishing Marks: Painted Museum marks.

Reference Books: See Herodotus: The Histories (Penguin Classic,1986) for a dramatic account of how to make a mummy and the building of the Pharaoh Cheops's Great Pyramid.

Museums: The British Museum, London. There are also important collections in Liverpool, Manchester, Bristol, the Ashmolean (Oxford), Petrie Museum, University College, London and Edinburgh.

Data: According to Herodotus (450BC), mummifiers were an elite profession. They offered the bereaved family a choice of wooden specimen models of various grades. To embalm the corpse the brain was extracted through the nostrils by an iron hook. The flank was opened with flint knives, contents of the abdomen removed and cavity cleansed with palm wine and spices. The body was then filled with pure bruised myrrh and other aromatics, sewn up and placed in natrum for 70 days. Then it was washed and wrapped in linen strips, smeared with gum, and placed in a wooden case shaped like a human figure. This was stored upright in its burial chamber. Embalming began c2,600 BC, the earliest surviving examples dating from the 5th Dynasty (2,300). The most productive era of mummification was from 1,000 BC, but the practice continued into the 3rd century AD. These are probably later fragments.

EGYPTIAN CAT MODEL (REPLICA)

Date: 600-200BC

Period: Ancient Egypt

From: Birmingham Museums
School Loans Service
Box A4 III Egyptian III
No: AL2

Measurements: Height: 110 mm

Weight: 163gm

Materials: Stone resin

Location: M1

Exit Date:

SIHC: 2.8

Photo: Linda Burridge

00018

Description: Small model, elegant sitting black cat on wooden plinth, with amulet on necklace.

Condition: Poor - broken ear, scratched

Distinguishing Marks: Museum mark AL2

Possible identity: Toy?

Reference Books: Juliet Clutton-Brook: The British Museum Book of Cats (1988); Cats in Art (Diary 1989: Past Times Catalogue)

Museums: The British Museum, London. Fitzwilliam Museum, Cambridge

Data: The Egyptian goddess of joy, Bast or Ubasti, was given the form of a black cat or cat-headed figure. She symbolised sunshine, and is sometimes portrayed with sun-shield and rattle. Identified by the Greeks with Artemis, in native superstition Bast became a symbol of happiness and good luck. Other Egyptian animal-headed gods were Khnomu the creator and Hershefi, as rams; Anubis, a jackal; Thoth, an ibis and Horus, a hawk. Purely human gods were Osiris, Isis, Nebhat and Horus. There were also cosmic figures - the sun-god Ra, Anher the sky, Geb the Earth and Shu, space. More abstract gods were Ptah, another creator-figure, Min the Father, Maat as Truth and Safekat, god of writing. This Museum replica is also on sale at £45 (12" high) in the Past Times catalogue. Originals date from the Old Kingdom (3-6th Dynasty, 2,700-2150BC) but this is a late example, probably copied from a 26th Dynasty Saite bronze.

No: 00030

Date: c1980 (Modern replica)

Period: Greek Dark Age, between Myceaean and Classical Ages (9th-8th century BC)

From: Gift: Mrs.A. Ivell bought in Athens

Measurements: Height: 89mm Diameter: 76mm

Weight: 9.25oz: 262gm

Materials: Pottery

Location: H1

SIHC: 2.3

Photo: Frank Power

Description: A full-bellied pot or vase with shallow neck, wide rim and single, flat handle. Terra-cotta, pale cream and black with bands of decoration, geometric designs with one band of horses and chariots.

Distinguishing Marks: Handwritten on underside: Geometric 800BC; Exact copy; Hand-made

Possible identity: Vase?

Condition: Mint

Reference Books: J.N. Coldstream: Greek Geometric Pottery (1968) and Geometric Greece (1977); Dyfri Williams: Greek Vases (British Museum 1985); Robert B. Folsom: Handbook of Greek Pottery (Guide for Amateurs) analyses shapes and patterns. Indispensable.

Museums: The British Museum, London WC1; Ashmolean Museum, Oxford; Edinburgh City Museum; Fitzwilliam Museum, Cambridge; Greek Museum, Newcastle University (by appointment); The Manchester Museum.

Data: Geometric pottery was made in many different regions of Greece, especially Athens, Attica, Crete and Euboea after the Dark Age which followed the fall of Mycenae, i.e: from c.900 to c700BC. The chief evidence for this period is archaeological, pottery is found in hundreds of cemetery and settlement sites, also in warriors' graves, wells and sanctuaries. The chequered areas, bands of hatched wolf-tooth triangles and the Greek key meander is typical of this style, with a revival of figurative art as processions and myths. Colour was not applied by pigment, but by different densities of the clay wash and a three-stage heating to oxidise (redden) and reduce (blacken) the patterns. This little vessel is a copy of a Corinthian aryballos or unguent flask.

GREEK COIN

Date: c281-261BC

Period: Ancient Greece

From: Purchased, Monarch Antiques, Glastonbury, @ £4.00

Measurements: Diameter 15mm

Weight: 0.125oz : 4gm

Materials: Bronze

Location: H2

SIHC: 1.7

ACTUAL SIZE

1 cm

mm 10

Photo: Frank Power

00085 —————

Description: A tiny, much defaced coin, needing enlargement to decipher.

Distinguishing Marks: Possible seated figure?

Condition: Poor, design almost invisible.

Possible identity: Not easily recognized.

Reference Books: Richard Plant: Greek coin types and their identification. (1979); D.R.Sear: Greek Coins and their values (1981)

Museums: Birmingham City Museum

Data: The first coins were minted c650BC in the Greek kingdom of Lydia, now modern Turkey. They were made of electrum, an alloy of gold and silver, later of either gold or silver, impressed on one side only. From 550BC coinage spread westward into the Greek city-states and their colonies in Italy and Sicily. Bronze coins were introduced c450BC, the first base metal,small-change currency for domestic use, which spread all over the Greek and Roman world. After Alexander's death (323BC), coins were minted for the great kingdoms which succeeded his Empire. After Roman conquest the last Greek mint in Egypt closed in AD296. Our coin is identified by reference to Plant's guide to 3,000 Greek coins, designed to enable the reader to begin with things which are most easily recognizable. This reveals (No 687) the figure as Apollo seated on an ompholos (a conical sacred stone, the centre of the Earth), holding a bow (behind), looking along an arrow, the Greek letters BASILEOS (monarch) but no place-name. The obverse (picture, left) has been printed upside-down and tilted left-right. The eye of faith identifies a head with braided curls,long jaw-line (bearded?), nose and eye-socket. Probably Antiochus I, king of the Seleucid Kingdom (Syria). The Greek drachm weighed 4.3gm.

ROMAN BROOCH

Date: c200-300AD

Period: Roman Britain

From: Derbyshire Museums
             Schools Loans Service
             Box 60
             (Marked South Wales)

Measurements: Length: 80mm
                Width: 50mm

Weight: 47gm

Materials: Bronze

Location: M2

Exit Date:

SIHC: 3.3

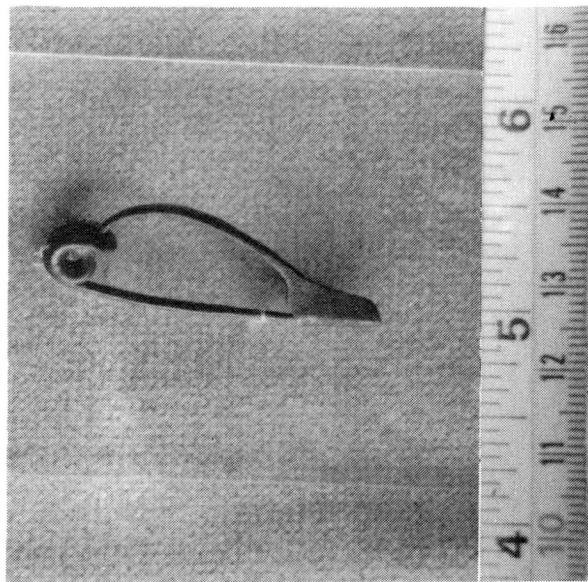

Photo: Linda Burridge

00067 —————————————————————————————

Description: Fastened to a plastic plate, a safety-pin with flattened curved bow and strong, coiled spring. Sharp pin fits into notch. The whole is shaped from one piece of wire.

Condition: Excellent - still workable.

Distinguishing Marks: None

Possible identity: Unmistakable

Reference Books: D. MacKreth: Roman Brooches (1973)

Museums: Devizes Museum (Wilts)

Data: Togas and similar flowing garments of classical times obviously needed numerous pins - similar to modern safety-pins - as everyday fasteners. (Compare the relative uses and usefulness of more modern buttons and zip-fasteners for this purpose - check durability.) Straight pins had been in use since Sumerian times (4,000 BC). The bent pin, fitting its point into a hook, was an invention of the Bronze Age, first appearing in Mycenae, Italy and Sicily. To prevent the pin from slipping, a spring was devised at the bend, by giving an extra twist. This invention has survived, though modern safety pins have the extra refinement of a completely concealed point.

BRONZE SPOON

Date: Unknown

Period: Roman Britain

From: Derbyshire Museums
Schools Loans Service
Box 60E

Measurements: Length: 120mm
Width: 60mm

Weight: 54gm

Materials: Bronze

Location: M2

Exit Date:

SIHC: 2.6

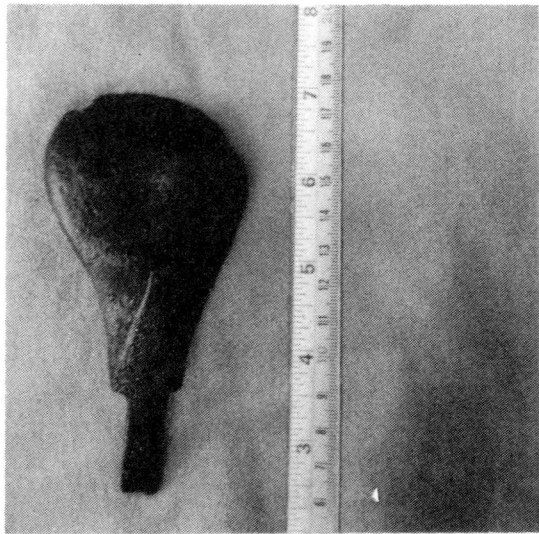

Photo: Linda Burridge

00075

Description: A broad metal spoon-bowl and tang for handle.

Condition: Fair; the metal smoothly polished and in sound condition, slightly green

Distinguishing Marks: None

Possible identity: Obvious - Domestic or ritual?

Reference Books: Lesley & Roy A. Adkins: A Thesaurus of British Archaeology (1982); British Museum: Later Prehistoric Antiquities of the British Isles (1953); and Antiquities of Roman Britain (1958). All illustrate similar spoons from Iron Age sites; Adkins (p.97) shows an almost identical shape.

Museums: The British Museum

Data: Pottery spoons have been found on New Stone Age sites and the ancient Egyptians made them of flint and ivory. Bronze spoons or scoops of similar size and shape to our example (but without handles) are found in Iron Age burials, often in patterned pairs. These may have had some ritual function. (In Roman Britain some spoons have Christian symbols) Roman spoons were made of silver, pewter, iron and bone, some with folding handles or spikes for extracting shell-fish and snails. Early pagan Saxon burials also include spoons in the grave-goods. Metal spoons of the early Middle Ages are rare, most medieval domestic types were made of bone, wood or horn. (See 092) Towards the end of the Middle Ages, cheaper metals like pewter were used.

BRONZE BROOCH

Date: Unknown

Period: Roman Britain

From: Derbyshire Museums
Schools Loans Service
Box 60E

Measurements: Length: 40mm

Weight: 12gm

Materials: Bronze wire

Location: M2

Exit Date:

SIHC: 3.3

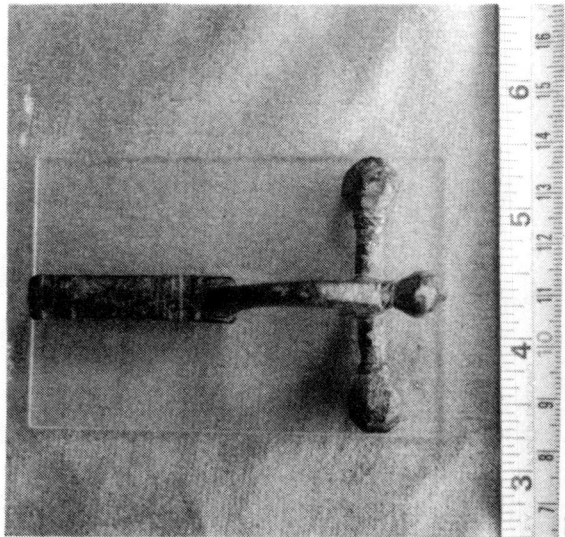

Photo: Linda Burridge

00074

Description: Light green-coloured metal brooch, hinged with surviving work-able pin. Cruciform or cross-bow shape, with high bow and long straight tail - also referred to as a P-shaped brooch.

Condition: Very good, has probably lost enamelled decoration - slight etching of metal, vestige of original pattern.

Distinguishing Marks: The characteristic crossbow shape makes easy reference to illustrated museum catalogues.

Reference Books: Best buy (10p) is Cirencester (Corinium) Museum's data sheet on Personal Ornament: Brooches and Pins.

Museums: The Roman Legionary Museum, Caerleon (Gwent) and Corinium (Glos)

Data: Flowing Roman togas and gowns needed pins and brooches as fastenings. Brooches were already in use in the pre-Roman Iron Age, more usually a simple safety-pin type (See 00074). These are found in excavations of Celtic tribal capitals, such as Bagendon, outside Corinium. The Romans introduced several new Continental patterns like the crossbow which appeared in Britain during the 3rd century as the Celtic industry declined. Roman brooch-types can be used by archaeologists as fairly reliable dating evidence. Other types include a Thistle shape, a Trumpet, Fan-tails, Studs-with-chain and various animal motifs. One type, the Aucissa, takes its name from the maker, stamped on the brooch-plate. These are usually found on sites of forts and military stations.

MINIATURE ROMAN AMPHORA

Date: c.100BC - 200 AD

Period: Roman Britain

From: Derbyshire Museums
School Loans Service
Box 60
(Marked Silchester)

Measurements: Length: 230mm
Diameter: 50mm

Weight: 225gm

Materials: Grey pottery

Location: M2

Exit Date:

SIHC: 2.6

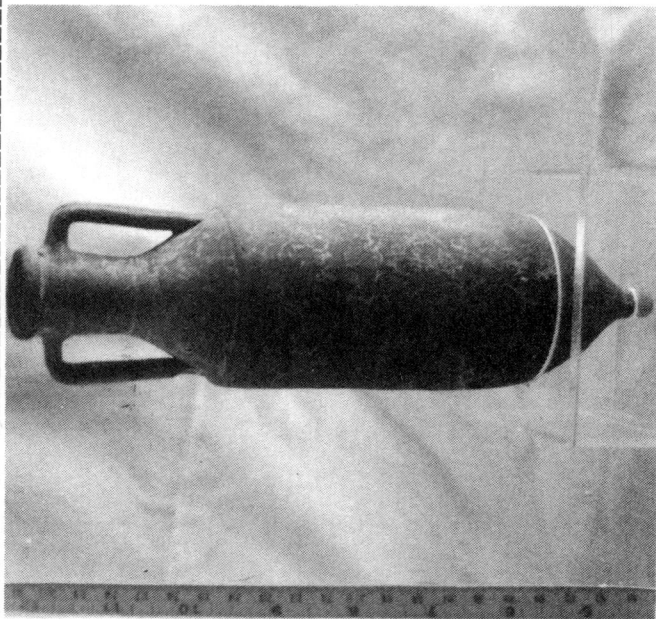

Photo: Linda Burridge

Description: Tall, narrow urn of cylindrical shape with two angled handles and a rim. Coarse, grey-black ware with gritty texture, crazed on one side with white marks (scratches?) where surface is blackened as if by fire. Other side smoother, uniformly fawn colour. Tapers to a point at lower end; neck marked with two circular divisions.

Condition: Fair; discoloration looks old, not like a modern replica.

Distinguishing Marks: None

Possible identity: Obviously a pot, but shape is unfamilar today.

Reference Books: Lesley Adkins & Roy A. Adkins: Thesaurus of British Archaeology (p.131) has an identical type.

Museums: Reading Museum; Calleva Museum, Silchester, Hants

Data: An amphora is a two-handled, narrow-necked jar for oil or wine, normally about 1m tall, widely used as cargo containers by Roman merchants. The pointed base, said to be for easy stacking, must surely have presented other problems? (Unless stuck upright in sand?) Imported to Britain from the end of the Iron Age to post-Roman times, painted labels or tituli picti sometimes gave content and origin. Like 'Samian' ware (072) Amphorae have Camulodunum form-numbers, based on finds at Colchester. Calleva was one of eleven civitas capitals, best-known of all Romano-British towns. This had been the pre-Roman Celtic capital of the Atrebates, whose territories stretched from Cunetio (Mildenhall) in the west to Pontes (Staines) in the east. Calleva stood at the central point of roads to Winchester, Chichester,London, Cirencester and Dorchester. Population was 3,000, with a 4th century Christian church and amphitheatre for 10,000.

ROMAN WINE-GLASS

Date: 2nd - 4th Century AD

Period: Roman Britain

From: Derbyshire Museums
Schools Loans Service
Box 60

Measurements: Length: 105mm
Diameter: 55mm

Weight: 140gm (plastic case)

Materials: Glass

Location: M2

Exit Date:

SIHC: 2.6

Photo: Linda Burridge

00065—

Description: An elegant conical beaker in semi-transparent blue-green glass, with patches of gold encrustations. Surface has a transluscent blue sheen, with patches of violet and yellow-green shades. Tapers to a narrow round foot.

Condition: Excellent

Distinguishing Marks: None

Possible identity: Medicine glass?

Reference Books: D.B. Harden: Ancient Glass II: Roman, in Archaeological Journal 126.pp.46-72 (1969) ; J. Price: Glass, in: D. Strong & D. Brown: Roman Crafts (1976)

Museums: Broadfield House Glass Museum, Dudley. Pilkington's Glass Museum, St. Helens

Data: Britain, glass-blowing was common in the Roman world, though very little glass has been found on earlier British sites. Most Romano-British glass was imported from the Continent - drinking vessels, window-panes, rings and brooches gaming counters, bangles and beads. Gold-band glassware, made by sandwiching thin gold foil between two skins of glass, was rare, but coloured vessels were common, superseded by colourless glassware at the end of the 1st century. Cut-glass came into use at the same time, usually in diamond patterns. Everyday glassware was usually bluish-green until the fourth century, when greenish-yellow glass became common. Some vessels were blown and moulded. Bottles were made in different shapes - rectangular, hexagonal, octagonal and cylindrical, with and without handles. By 400 AD glass was no longer commonly used in Britain, though a few pieces have been found in Anglo-Saxon graves.

ROMAN THIMBLE (REPLICA)

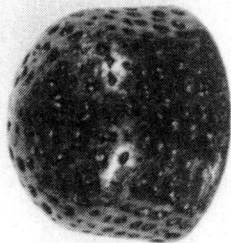

Date: c200AD

Period: Roman Britain

From: Pastimes shop, York (85p)
A *Westair* reproduction
Original in St. Albans Museum

Measurements: Length: 19mm

Weight: 23gm

Materials: Bronzed nickel

Location: H1

SIHC: 3.4

Photo: Frank Power

00022

Description: A stubby little thimble in dull-shined metal, pitted with pounce-marks as on a modern example.

Condition: Good

Distinguishing Marks: As photograph.

Reference Books: Lesley & Roy A.Adkins: Thesaurus of British Archaeology (1982); British Museum: Antiquities of Roman Britain; John Wacher: Towns of Roman Britain (1974)

Museum: Verulamium Museum, St. Albans.

Data: This attractive little replica is taken from an original in Verulamium Museum, found on the site of the Roman town. This was the Belgic site of Verlamion, capital town of the Catuvellauni. Unlike Colchester (See 00073), Verulamium was favoured as a civitas capital under pro-Roman rule. The first town was destroyed by Queen Boudicca's hordes, with evidence of fires. The new town had many metal-workers' shops and a Romano-Celtic temple. The town houses were small and timber-framed, with earth or timber floors, and plastered, patterned walls. Large numbers of coins and metal objects are found in the bed of the earlier River Ver. These are thought to be offerings to the water-spirits. Romano-British thimbles of silver and bronze are not unusual finds. They were probably cast in pottery moulds.

No: 00066

Date: Unknown

Period: Roman Britain

From: Derbyshire Museums
Schools Loans Service
Box 60

Measurements: Height: 65mm

Weight: 54gm (with base)

Materials: Bronze

Location: M2

SIHC: 2.4

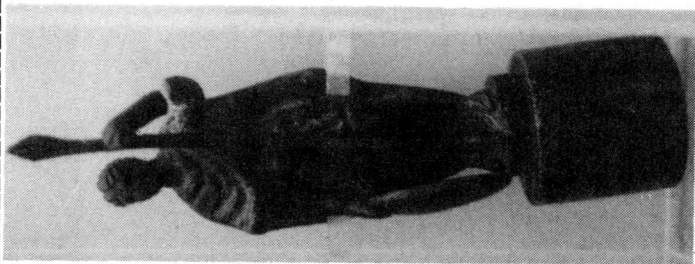

Photo: Frank Power

00066————————————

Description: A mounted and cased figurine described as a gladiator. This is a small military male, dressed in cloak and kilted tunic, barefoot, with short hair-style and laurel wreath. He carries an oval shield and a spear.

Condition: Fair - broken section of spear.

Distinguishing Marks: (none)

Possible identity: Child might say "Toy", as it is so very similar to old-fashioned lead soldier.

Reference Books: Guide to Antiquities of Roman Britain : (British Museum : 1958)

Museums: British Museum, London

Data: Similar bronze figures are illustrated in the British Museum's Guide, with 17 examples from Cheapside, Brough (Westmorland), London Bridge, Hadrian's Wall, Earith (Hunts), Barking Hall (Suffolk), Aldborough (Yorks), Colchester (Essex), Southbroom (Wilts) and Piercebridge (Durham). A figure of Mars is inscribed with the maker's name- "Celatus, the copper-smith, who contributed a pound of bronze made at a cost of 3d". These employ the classical naturalism introduced by the Romans, with official approval, though some examples reveal strongly individual native character.

SAMIAN POT

Date: c100AD

Period: Roman Britain

From: Derbyshire Museums
Schools Loans Service
Box 60E
(Marked St.Albans)

Measurements: Length: 180mm
Diameter: 110mm

Weight: 568gm

Materials: Red terra-cotta glazed pottery
ware

Location: M2

Exit Date:

SIHC: 2.2

Photo: Linda Burridge

00072

Description: A dull-red pot with wide open conical neck, embossed or decorated with an incised palmate design around body. Not as glossy or bright red as some Samian ware.

Distinguishing Marks: Museum describes as Samian.

Possible identity: Modern appearance - vase?

Condition: Holed and repaired. Brittle.

Reference Books: Guy de la Bedoyere: Samian Ware (Shire Archaeology 1988)

Museums: Corinium Museum, Cirencetser (Glos); Carlisle Museum & Art Gallery (Cumbria); Castle Museum, Norwich; Dorset County Museum; Grosvenor Museum, Chester; Lincoln City and County Museum; Verulamium Museum, St. Albans etc.

Data: Samian ware, more properly named terra cotta sigillata, was the most common, mass-produced pottery of the first two centuries AD, found in large quantities on most civil Roman sites. First made at Arezzo in Italy in the 1st century BC and in Gaul from c.15AD. Samian ware was never made in Britain, but was imported from the first years after the Conquest in 43AD. Large numbers of pots, dishes and fine table-ware were made in standard patterns or forms. Archaeologists identify and classify each specimen by shape and by reference to a series of numbers defined by Dragendorff (e.g.Dr.29, Dr30 or Dr37 - the most common types.) Most Samian pots were plain, some were decorated by pressing in clay moulds. Potters stamped their names or signs on their ware and many individual makers are well-known. This makes it easy to follow the export routes of shipments of thousands of pots per cargo, also to use the various forms as dating evidence.

ROMAN BUCKLE

Date: c.100AD

Period: Roman Britain

From: Derbyshire Museums
Schools Loans Service
Box 60 (Marked London Wall)

Measurements: Length: 43mm
Width: 25mm

Weight: 15gm

Materials: Bronze

Location: M2

Exit Date:

SIHC: 3.3

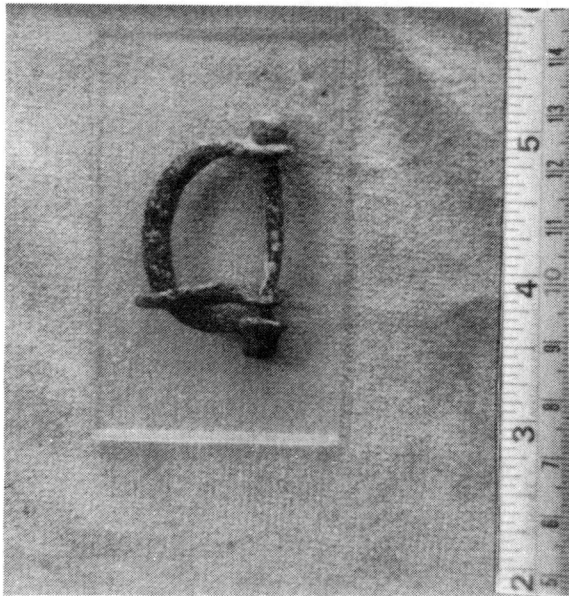

Photo: Linda Burridge

00068

Description: A workable buckle, semi-circular, with pin pivoting on bar. Very green and corroded. Mounted onto plastic plaque.

Condition: Good, still freely moving.

Distinguishing Marks: None; greenish verdigris is the sign of copper-based metals.

Possible identity: Buckle is obvious - but for belt or sandal?

Reference Books: C.J.Simpson: Belt-buckles and Strap-ends of the later Roman Empire, in No.7 of Britannia (19..)

Museums: The Museum of London, London Wall

Data: Many fittings for leather belts have been found on Roman sites, especially in the military context. They were usually made of bronze, often ornate, with enamel decoration. Belt or strap terminals were also used and buckles were sometimes attached to metal belt-plates or belt-ends. Belt stiffeners of bronze are also found. Some later belt fittings, found in SE Britain, were once thought to be patterns used by German mercenary troops who entered Britain during the late Roman period (4thc.AD) as the first Anglo-Saxon settlers or feoderati). These are now held to be late Roman. Roman sandals have been found, both civilian and military, but these were fastened by laces or thongs. Buckles for horses' harness and armour are also found with horses' leather masks, eye-guards and studded ornaments.

ROMAN PHIAL

Date: c100-200AD

Period: Roman Britain

From: Derbyshire Museums
Schools Loans Service
Box 60
(Marked Colchester)

Measurements: Length: 165mm

Weight: 148gm (with base)

Materials: Coarse pottery

Location: M2

Exit Date:

SIHC: 2.6

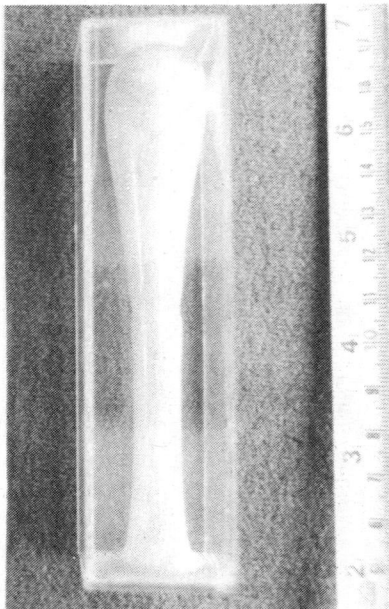

Photo: Linda Burridge

00069

Description: Tall, thin phial with bulbous central swelling and tall, narrow neck which is slightly longer and wider than its foot. A coarse, pinkish-white ware of smooth, but gritty unglazed texture.

Condition: Repair to stem, some patchy loss of surface - otherwise good.

Distinguishing Marks: None

Possible identity: Holds only a small quantity - perfume?

Reference Book: David Stephenson: The Book of Colchester (1978)

Museums: The Castle Museum, Colchester

Data: To have named Roman Colchester Colonia Claudia Victricensis, was a deliberate insult to the Celtic kingdom of Cunobelin, powerful British ruler of the Trinovantes. The name means: The colony of the Claudian victory in 43AD. The Roman town was settled with army veterans and also housed a legionary fortress. Here was the setting for the Trinovantes support of the rebellion of the Queen of the neighbouring Iceni, Boudicca in AD60. The colonia was utterly destroyed by the rebels, then elaborately rebuilt by the Romans. The suburbs were industrial, with many pottery kilns and commercial enterprises, including a man who specialised in eye-salves. Did his firm use this phial? Other finds include a group of pottery toys from a child's grave.

CAST OF CELTIC GOD (REPLICA)

Date: c150-200AD

Period: Roman Britain

From: Derbyshire Museums
Schools Loans Service
Box 60
(Marked from Corbridge)

Measurements: Length: 125mm

Weight: Unknown (cased)

Materials: Fibre-glass?

Location: M2

Exit Date:

SIHC: 1.1

Photo: Linda Burridge

00070———

Description: Cased and impossible to handle, seems heavy, like lead, but is an obvious replica (Case 60E has identical copy). A dwarfed, bearded figure in raised relief on an irregular-oval plaque, holding a rectangular shield with a raised boss and dimpled surface pattern. Figure wears a short kilted tunic, a conical, Phrygian cap and is barefoot. Holds a strange twisted flail or yoke in left hand; a chariot wheel on his left.

Condition: Excellent.

Distinguishing Marks: Costume

Possible identity: From shrine?

Reference Books: Anne Ross : Pagan Celtic Britain (1968); Miranda Green : The Gods of the Celts (1986)

Museums: Corbridge Roman Station, Northumberland has the original mould.

Data: Cast of Celtic god, Taranis, the Thunderer, whose symbols were the wheel, forked lightning, club, eagle and serpent. Specially venerated by the Druids and mentioned by Caesar in Gaul, his images are found as far afield as Brittany, the Rhineland and Jugoslavia. God of storms and the sky, Taranis was also concerned with war. Sometimes confused with Mars and Dispater, god of the dead, but was more properly identified by the Romans with Jupiter, god of the sky. Human sacrifices were offered to Taranis, people burned in tree-trunks. Taran became a legendary Welsh hero, and taran is modern Welsh for thunder. This cast was probably taken from a mould found at *Corstopitum* or *Coriosopitum* (Corchester) a fort, behind Hadrians Wall.

ROMAN LAMP (REPLICA)

Date: Modern: original c.200AD

Period: Roman

From: The Roman Museum, Bath
Purchase (£9.50)

Measurements: diam: 78mm

Weight: 3.5oz (99gm)

Materials: terra cotta pottery

Location: S1

SIHC: 2.3

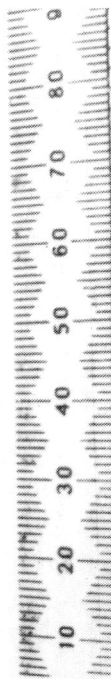

Photo: Frank Power

00003

Description: A red-clay pottery container with a spout-like aperture and 4mm circular hole off-centre; stands on a slightly raised base.

Condition: New

Distinguishing Marks: Raised pattern round rim Head on central boss, with surrounding inscription (SEPT)IMIUS SEVERUS PERTINAX (See Data).

Possible identity: Child might say "Teapot"?

Reference Books: M. Cayless and A.M. Marston: Lamps and Lighting (1983). D.M. Bailey: Pottery Lamps, in D. Strong and D. Brown: Roman Crafts (1976)

Museums: Aldborough Roman Museum, Boroughbridge, N.Yorks: Grosvenor Museum, Chester (Roman army): The Roman Palace, Fishbourne, W.Sussex

Data: Derived from a Grecian type, these lamps were used domestically and in temples, usually standing in a niche and fuelled by olive-oil. Fitted with a small wick and filled with oil, this lamp will work. Lucius Septimus Severus Pertinax was Emperor from 193-211 AD. Compare this replica with a real Roman lamp (00073) and with Victorian oil-lamp (00042). The author learned too late that an identical replica is now available from the commercial Past Times catalogue at half this one's price (£4.95)

ROMAN LAMP

Date: Unknown

Period: Roman Britain

From: Derbyshire Museums
Schools Loans Service
Box 60E

Measurements: Length: 90mm
Diameter: 60mm

Weight: 35gm

Materials: Smooth red pottery (unglazed)

Location: M2

Exit Date:

SIHC: 2.3

Photo: Linda Burridge

Description: A circular, closed dish with flat bottom, slightly concave top and projecting spout. One small (5mm) hole in top, another in nozzle which is decorated with relief volutes (curved pattern). The top around the filling hole also has a shell-like relief decoration.

Condition: Excellent, comparable with replica

Distinguishing Marks: Museum mark (60E)

Possible identity: Child might say "Vase, dipper or baby's feeding-bottle"

Reference Books: D.M. Bailey: Pottery Lamps, in: D. Strong & D. Brown: Roman Crafts (1976)

Museums: Roman Baths Museum, Bath (Avon)

Data: The oldest lamps were prehistoric, shallow stone basins, found in French Paleolithic caves. Filled with blubber and moss, these were used until the last century by Eskimos. Pottery lamps burning vegetable-oil at a wick confined by a nozzle, were invented in Mediterranean lands during the early metal ages. Lamps from c2000 BC came from the Gezer rock-tombs in Palestine. Shaped as fish, birds and animals, some with Christian designs, this is the typical lamp of the Graeco-Roman classical world. Used throughout the Byzantine and Saracen periods they were not improved in Europe, apart from finer cotton wicks to reduce smoke, until after the Renaissance. BM's Guide to Antiquities of Roman Britain (Fig.20) gives similar pot-lamps from Colchester and London. Some Roman lamps were made of bronze, with several nozzles.

ANGLO-VIKING COIN (REPLICA)

Date: 1988 (original:910-938AD)

Period: Anglo-Saxon/Viking (Dark Ages)

From: Purchase (50p): Jorvik Viking Centre. Struck by pupil, Linda Meese, on school visit.

Measurements: Diameter: 23mm

Weight: 5gm

Materials: Pewter

Location: H4 and S1 (2 copies)

SIHC: 2.7

ACTUAL SIZE

1 cm

mm 10 20

Photo: Frank Power

00020

Description: A thin pewter mule coin, i.e. stamped with differently dated dies back and front, a two-headed silver-coloured penny. Obviously new and shiny, and clearly legible. Slightly milled edge.

Condition: Excellent

Distinguishing Marks: One side: EDELSTANRETOBRIT and small central cross. Other side: Sword in centre, tiny cross at top, another at edge. Thor's hammer. Runes or letters SCIPI.TnIIo

Possible identity: Looks more like a token than a familiar coin. A fairly obvious fake.

Reference Books: Jorvik's information sheet; Details from striker, Matt Ransom. See also P. Seaby & P.F. Purvey: Coins of England p.55

Museums: Usher Gallery, Lincoln

Data: During excavation of the Coppergate site in 1981, two Viking coin-dies were found, the only ones ever discovered. Made of iron with steel tips, they have been copied and replicas used for visitors to strike souvenirs @ 50p. Peter's Pence has an interesting combination of Christian cross and Thor's hammer, struck by Viking kings of York, c910-920. Aethelstan King of Wessex (924-939) and grandson of Alfred, drove the Vikings out of Northumberland, styling himself King of All Britain and facing a league of Scots, Danes, Britons and Irish at Brunanburh in 937. His victory song is in the Anglo-Saxon Chronicle. The silver penny, introduced by Offa of Mercia c.780, was sole English coinage for 500 years. Jorvik's shop sells two other coin-replicas (85p), one of the Irish-Norse king Sihtric of Northumbria (921-27) whose successors Aethelstan overthrew, and Guthfrithsson(939-41). The coiner's name is stamped on the back, to prevent fraud.

MEDIEVAL PENNY

Date: 1302-10

Period: Medieval
(Edward I 1272-1307)

From: Galata Coins Ltd.
Park House Albert Rd.
Wolverhampton
(Purchase 1988 : £8.00)

Measurements: 20mm

Weight: 1.3 gm (originally 1.89 gm as 240 pennies
= 1 pound of silver)

Materials: 92.5% fine, or sterling silver

Location: S2

SIHC: 1.7

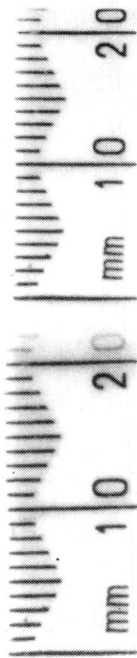

Photo: Frank Power

00002—

Description: Tiny, almost black coin, irregular circular shape, wafer-thin. Obviously silver.

Condition: Poor, distinguishing features almost erased; needs magnifying-glass and reference to Catalogue. (The photograph is an improvement on the original!)

Distinguishing Marks: Obverse: head with long hair and crown.
Rim: EDWAR.ANG.DONS.R.
Reverse: Long cross: CIVITAS.LONDON (Mint)

Possible identity: Silver coin

Reference Books: J.J. North: Coinage of Edward I & II (1965). Seaby & Purvey: Coins of England Vol.1 (1989) See the British Numismatic Journal for highly specialized articles on dating etc. Close scrutiny of exact letter-shapes, crown-ornament etc. gives our more precise date than merely dates-of-reign.

Museums: Birmingham Museum & Art Gallery, like most local Museums, has a representative collection of coins, but also organizes a Coin Opinion Service for collectors.

Data: This coin was one of a massive 14th century re-coinage. From Saxon times to 1272 the only English coin was the silver penny. This coin can connect lessons on Edward I's castle-building, Welsh wars, manorial farming and the English medieval wool-trade. The current price of silver is always a good index of comparison with earlier ages when 1lb=£1.

STONE FIGURE

Date: unknown

Period: Medieval?

From: Derbyshire Museums
               Loans Service. Box 507A

Measurements: Height: 75mm

Weight: 272gm

Materials: white stone

Location: M2

Exit Date:

SIHC: 1.1

Photo: Frank Power

00086—

Description: A crouching figure in gritty white stone, dressed in cloak and hood, with fat, round face and beady eyes. Holding a pot?

Distinguishing Marks: None

Condition: Poor, indistinct detail

Possible identity: Doll or toy? Witchcraft??

Reference Books: Ronald Sheridan & Anne Ross: Grotesques and Gargoyles (1975) Arranged by: Giants, Glaring creatures, Nightmares, Beaked heads, Biting creatures, protruding tongues' etc.

Data: This small figure is the ultimate Mystery Object. No museum seems to know what it is or for what purpose it was made. Though similar to many curious church carvings, this figure appears to be free-standing, with no evidence of breakage from a wall or other carving and is more rudimentary and crudely worked than more usual examples (hardly carved at all in any strict sense.) Otherwise, it might be compared with the more famous and legendary Lincoln Imp, a stone carving in the Angel Choir of Lincoln Cathedral. This was a horned demon figure released by the Devil, but vanquished by Lincoln's angels and turned to stone. This has become the popular emblem of the City. A plaster cast of the Imp is available from the Past Times catalogue. Children will gladly invent their own stories about any such mystery object. Their guesses will be as good as most others!

MACE

Date: ?

Period: Medieval?

From: Derbyshire Museums
Loans Service
Box 507A

Measurements: Head only:
Diameter 70mm
With haft:
312mm long

Weight: 544gm

Materials: Iron head, new wooden haft

Location: M2

Exit Date:

SIHC: 1.8

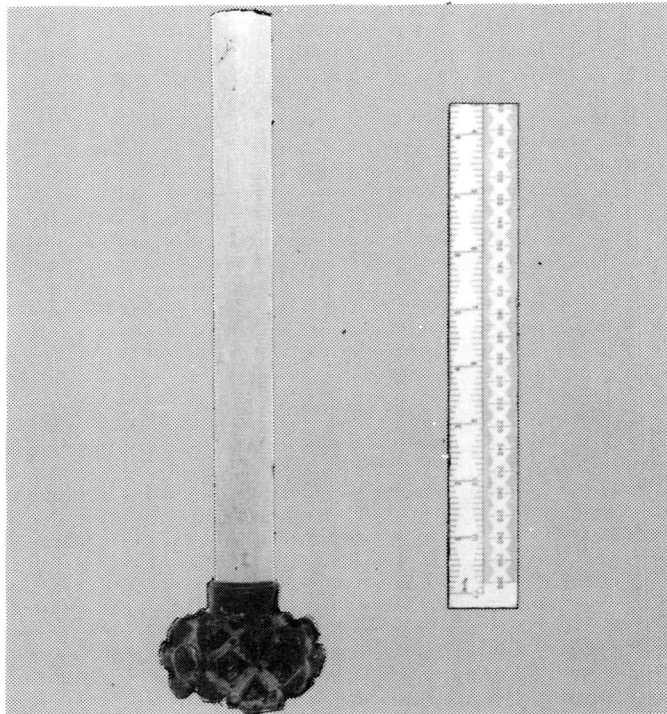

Photo: Frank Power

00082

Description: Round, knobkerry type hollow iron head with deeply segmented pattern of square-diamond and triangular knobs in groups of four. New wooden handle.

Distinguishing Marks: None

Condition: Poor, metal rotting and broken.

Possible identity: Obviously a truncheon-type weapon. Not as obvious without a handle?

Reference Books: Claude Blair: European and American Arms (Batsford,1963)

Museum: The Royal Armoury, Tower of London

Data: Maces were popular medieval weapons for close combat. Warlike bishops especially, like Odo of Bayeux and Geoffrey of Coutances used them because swords were sinful. The Bayeux Tapestry shows Bishop Odo wielding his mace at the Battle of Hastings. This is a suspiciously small example of its type, possibly a personal item of self-defence, or the law-enforcement equipment of a village constable?

MEDIEVAL ARROW-HEAD

Date: 13th-14th century

Period: Medieval

From: Derbyshire Museums Loans
Box 507A

Measurements: Length: 62mm
Width: 13mm

Weight: 1/2oz: 15gm

Materials: Iron

Location: M2

Exit Date:

SIHC: 1.8

ARROW HEAD

Photo: Frank Power

00079

Description: Narrow, sharply pointed iron arrow-head with 4mm socket for shaft and two long, in-curving barbs.

Distinguishing Marks: None

Possible identity: Obvious

Reference Books: E.K. Milliken: Archery in the Middle Ages (1967)

Museums: Collections of medieval bows are non-existent. There is doubtful, late 14c bow at Canons Hall, nr. Richmond (Yorks). Crossbows at Royal Armoury. Arrows at V & A and the Museum of London.

Data: We find archers protrayed in the Bayeux Tapestry's record of the Battle of Hastings but these use short Norman one-piece wooden bows. The longbow was a later invention, first recorded in Henry III's Assize of Arms (1252). Edward I used archers tactically in his wars with Scotland, deploying bowmen skilfully with men-at-arms and cavalry. Villagers were compelled by law to pratice regularly at their village Butts - football as an alternative was illegal. The greatest victories of the English archers were at Crécy (1346) and Agincourt (1415). Their 6ft bows were of yew, their clothyard shafts were flighted with goose-feathers. This type of iron arrow-head was known as a bodkin. The longbow declined in use after the Wars of the Roses and introduction of hand-guns. Henry VIII encouraged the continued use of bows and arrows, as the Mary Rose wreck proves, but Elizabeth I ordered their withdrawal from service.

MEDIEVAL BROADSWORD

Date: 15th century

Period: Late Medieval

From: Derbyshire Museums
Loans Service : Box 507A

Measurements: 603mm long
483mm blade
45mm wide

Weight: 900gm

Materials: Tempered steel

Location: M2

Exit Date:

SIHC: 1.8

Photo: Frank Power

Description: Polished steel blade, chased on one side with two narrow central rows of dashes and shallow curves. Other side: curves then dashes, with St. Andrew's cross central. Iron pommel, lacking wooden grip, rectangular section, forked toward blade and top.

Distinguishing Marks: decoration only. V-shaped hilt (rather than traditional cross and roundel) suggests possible Oriental origin to some curators.

Condition: Excellent. Still moderately sharp

Possible identity: Obvious, but is it a weapon for war, self-defence or hunting?

Reference Books: R. Ewart Oakeshott: The Sword in the Age of Chivalry (1981); Howard Loftus Blackmore: Hunting Weapons (1971); H.R. Ellis Davidson: The Sword in Anglo-Saxon England (1962); H.L. Peterson: Daggers and Fighting Knives of the Western World (1972)

Museums: Royal Armouries, Tower of London; for first-hand visual evidence, see monumental effigies in churches and medieval art.

Data: The medieval sword was not a crude chopping weapon, but a well-balanced, superbly crafted device. Derived in Europe from long Celtic Iron Age swords, used by Roman auxiliaries, and Saxon and Viking immigrants, a knightly sword weighed 2-3lb, with 30" straight-edged blade, 2" wide, (made in Seville, Milan, Augsburg, Cologne, Bordeaux.) and 6-7" hilt. Because knights travelled widely, origins of swords found are impossible to trace. Dating also is vague, within 50 years. Stages of development: 1000-1350: designed to attack mail; 1350-1500: against plate. Ours is evidently a smaller, more unusual weapon, possibly as illustrated by Peterson (op.cit), a knight's long sword-like dagger or braselard.

MEDIEVAL CANNON BALL

Date: 15th century

Period: Late medieval

From: Derbyshire Museum Loans
Service Box 507A

Measurements: Diam: 120mm

Weight: 2726gm

Materials: Iron stone

Location: M1

Exit Date:

SIHC: 1.8

Photo: Frank Power

00088

Description: A crude, stone-like iron ball, gritty and pitted.

Distinguishing Marks: None

Possible identity: Less difficult than date - which battlefield?

Reference Books: Lesley & Roy A.Adkins: Thesaurus of British Archaeology (1982); R.C. Clephan: Ordnance of the 14th. and 15th. centuries, in: Archaeological Journal, 68, 1911

Museums: Try your local castle.

Data: Gunpowder was used by Edward III in his 14th century Scottish wars and at Crécy (1346). Canon, *gonnes* or *bombards* were were made of bronze, later of flat, overlapping iron bars held together by iron hoops and set on a wooden bed. Cannon were not cast until the 17th century; early dart-firing *vases* were breech-loaded, firing iron *quarrels* or bolts, later stone balls - very inaccurately. Guns made little difference to the outcome of medieval battles like Crécy and Agincourt. Early cannon often exploded, killing their *gynours* - James II of Scotland was killed by "a piece of mis-framed gune that brake in the shuting". Giant muzzle-loaders like Mons Meg at Edinburgh weighed 4 tons and threw stone shot weighing 300 lb (136kgm). (A favourite name for big guns, Roaring Meg broke the Cavalier defence of Goodrich Castle in 1646). Small hand-guns were also used. The increasing use of guns as siege weapons caused some modification of defensive walls in castles and towns; gun-ports or shot-holes are shaped differently from earlier arrow-loops. Guns were placed on an embrasure or platform in the wall, opening on a circular hole with vertical slots above and below. The expense of cannon broke the power of the baronage and took one step more towards the employment of professional national armies.

LADY'S STIRRUP

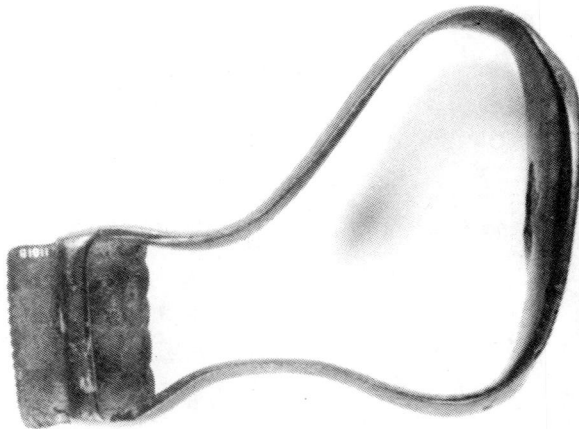

Date: 16th century

Period: Tudor

From: Derbyshire Museums Loans
Box 118B

Measurements: Length: 132mm
Width: 100mm

Weight: 8 1/2oz: 264gm

Materials: Iron

Location: M2

Exit Date:

SIHC: 3.4

00084

Description: Irregularly-shaped, strap-like wrought iron object, smoothly polished, with tooth-edged slot for a strap.

Distinguishing Marks: none but shape and wear.

Condition: Bottom of stirrup is worn to a hole.

Possible identity: Ask pony enthusiasts. Why Lady's? - check weight?

Reference Books: Medieval Catalogue of London Museum (1940 o.p.)

Museums: Museum of London, London Wall, EC2

Data: Ancient writers make no mention of stirrups, though an Assyrian sculpture of 853 BC shows one. Originating in China in the 5th century AD, they are first known to have been used in Europe in the 6th century, when they were used by Anglo-Saxons. By the 12th century they were in common use. Early models were simple triangles, as shown in the Bayeux Tapestry. Looped stirrups, ring-stirrups and square ones with a flattened footrest are found in the early Middle Ages. Stirrups gave the rider a firm seat making the wielding of longer swords and lances possible. They became more elaborate from the 14th century, with a tendency towards an asymmetrical projection on one side - as seen in our own example. In the 15th century a steel shoe-shape or soleret was used in England. The type illustrated here resembles a German box-type, used in the 17th century - later than the Museum's dating. Other archaeological finds of iron horse furniture include horseshoes, spurs and horses' bits.

– 127 –

LEATHER WINE BOTTLE

Date: 16th century

Period: Tudor

From: Derbyshire Museums
Loans Service (Box 118B)

Measurements: Height: 280mm
Diameter: 122mm
Thickness: 3mm

Weight: 18oz: 560gm

Materials: Thick leather. Probably ox-hide

Location: M2

Exit Date:

SIHC: 2.6

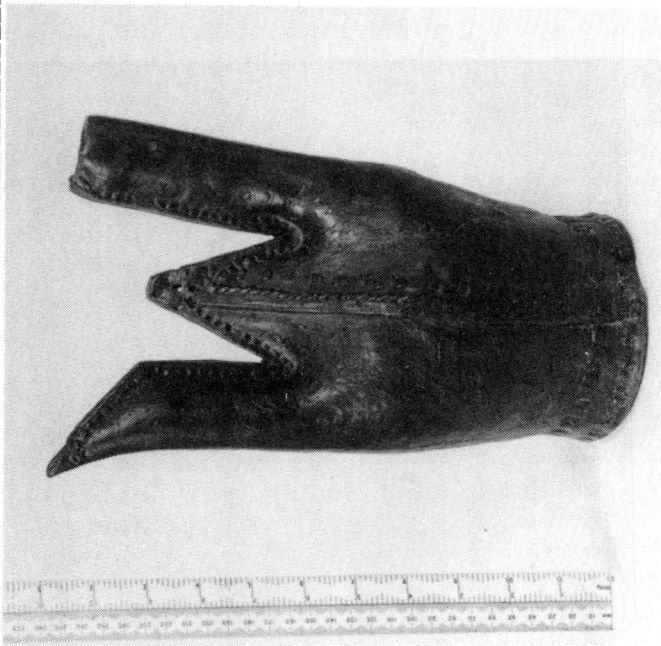

Photo: Frank Power

Description: Three-pronged bottle of thick hide, with vertical spout (33mm diameter) and integral shaped handle. Middle seam and joints stitched with leather thong. Double strapping at recessed bottom.

Distinguishing Marks: None. Modern fakes have a flat, not recessed base and stitched-on handles.

Condition: Fair - leaks

Possible identity: Obvious. Contents?

Reference Books: Oliver Boyd: Blackjacks and Leather Bottles (1921)

Museums: Northampton City Museum (Keeper of Leathercraft for details) ; Walsall (W. Midlands)

Data: Like wood (treen) and horn (See 00092) leather was a natural material domestic ware, cheap, light and unbreakable when glass and earthenware were rare. (Medieval potters were metalworkers). Thick, rigid ox-hide was moulded, wet, into shape and proofed inside with pitch. Tanners were numerous in medieval and Tudor times. Their London liveried company combined with the Horn Workers, but was short-lived, from 1476-1562. Leather containers included water-bodgets, buckets for fire-fighting, bottles, black jacks or bombards, mugs and jugs. Any great country house used hundreds of these leather goods, some painted, with family crests and ornamental shapes, as pistols and heads; even the humblest homes owned several leather containers. English tanners were most productive European workers and The Old Leather Bottle was a popular inn-sign. Earthenware pots were imported from c1500 with a late 16th century increase in cheap pewter tableware. Manufacture of leather bottles ceased at the end of the 18th century but they continued in use, especially by farmers and harvest workers well into the 20th century.

TUDOR KNIFE AND FORK

Date: 16th (or 17th?) century?

Period: Tudor or Stuart.

From: Derbyshire Museums
Loans Service Box 507A

Measurements: Knife: fragment: 140mm
Bone handle, broken at first rivet
Original length: 198mm
Fork: length: 152mm

Weight: uncertain (mounted)

Materials: Iron and bone

Location: M2

Exit Date:

SIHC: 2.6

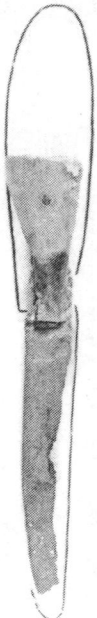

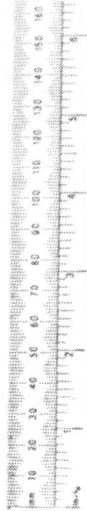

Photo: Frank Power

Description: Thick, clumsy fork, heavily pitted and rusted. Three-pronged, one broken at tip, middle prong very sharp. Knife blade incomplete. Mounted on plastic sheet

Distinguishing Marks: none

Condition: Poor, badly corroded.

Possible identity: Puzzle as to class of owner and date of objects.

Reference Books: C.T.B. Bailey: Knives and Forks (1927); Peter G. Smithurst: The Cutlery Industry (Shire Album 63)

Museums: Sheffield City Museum

Data: During the Middle Ages only the nobility used special knives for cutting their food. A pair of knives for the table is found in a will of 1370. The common people used their all-purpose working knives, with the points as prongs to pick up meat. The earliest reference to a fork is found in a will of 1463 but fingers were used until the 16th century. Forks were an Italian fashion, described by English travellers and brought home to be ridiculed. They do not appear as usual table-ware until the early 17th century, when rich folk carried a personal set in a sheath on their belts. (A later date for these utility items than the Museum suggests?) Pepys refers to his plate spoons and forks in 1664, when table-knives became rounded at the end - Louis XIV made pointed knives illegal as potential weapons. The number of prongs on a fork may be 2, 3 or 4 - these do not signify date. Whole sets of cutlery were not commonplace until the 18th c when Sheffield machine-stamped silver handles became popular. Knife-blades were often made wide to permit the eating of peas!

HORN SPOON

Date: 16th century

Period: Tudor

From: Derbyshire Museums
Loans Service
Box 118B

Measurements: Length: 202mm
Width: 50mm

Weight: 1oz + : 35gm

Materials: Animal horn

Location: M2

Exit Date:

SIHC: 2.6

Photo: Frank Power

00092

Description: Yellow, shiny, semi-transparent, with long pointed handle. Deep dessert-spoon size, slightly rough texture from wear.

Distinguishing Marks: Wear only.

Condition: Fair; handle mended in two places

Possible identity: Obvious

Reference Books: Paula Hardwick: Discovering Horn (1981)

Museums: Bewdley Museum, Hereford-Worcester

Data: Horn, bone and antler were in common use from prehistoric times; a horn spoon at Edinburgh dates from 1500 BC. and ladles, beads, spatulas, combs etc. are found in **Bronze Age** barrows. Pliny, Caesar and Viking authors refer to common horn drinking vessels, used as chalices in primitive Saxon churches. Cheap and easily available, horn was worked by travelling tinkers, into powder flasks, laminated boxes, handles, scoops, ink-horns, bobbins and buttons. The laws of King Ine c700AD refer to the craft of Horner, by the 17th century 700,000 horns were used annually by 24 Master Horners at London, Sheffield and York. There was great demand for English horn from abroad and materials were imported from Africa. Spoons of our type were moulded, other objects were turned or pressed. A will of 1418 lists a pair of knives with unicorn handles - probably Arctic narwhal (whale) - a charm against poison. From the 18th century, manufacture moved to Aberdeen, Bewdley, Birmingham, Bradford and Kendal, continuing today at Gloucester and Worcester.

TUDOR SHOE

Date: c1500

Period: Tudor

From: Derbyshire Museums
Schools Loan Service
Box 507A

Measurements: Length 132mm
Width: 60mm

Weight: 23gm

Materials: Leather

Location: M2

Exit Date:

SIHC: 3.3

SHOE FRAGMENT

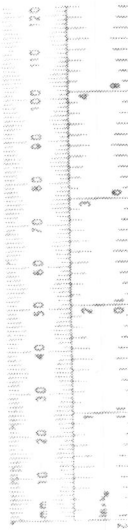

Photo: Frank Power

Description: Soft brown-black leather sole and upper, a small but complete backless shoe with original stitching

Distinguishing Marks: None

Condition: Slightly hardened and cracked by age still flexible. Shrunken with age? Hole in toe.

Possible identity: Child's shoe?

Reference Books: Doreen Yarwood: English Costume (1958)

Museums: The Shoe Museum, Street (Somerset), Museum of Leathercraft, Northampton

Data: The blunt toe dates this shoe to the 16th century. Medieval shoes had been long-pointed, some looped to the knees, until prohibited by Act of Parliament. Most fashionable Tudor shoes were cut low at the back, high at the instep, with no heel or fastenings. Women's shoes were similar to men's. Blunt toes themselves became extravagent in style during Henry VIII's reign, bulging 9-10" across, with cuts and slashes to show coloured linings. Heels were added in Elizabeth I's reign, to hold feet in stirrups. Buckles became fashionable in the 18th century, shoe-laces and different left-right shoes in the 19th. Shoes were made locally at first, by town gilds but by 1630 the craft began to be centred on Northampton. (See 00036) It is difficult to tell the original size of this shoe because of probable shrinkage.

ELIZABETHAN PURSE

Date: 16th century

Period: Elizabethan

From: Derbyshire Museums
Loans Service
Box 118B

Measurements: 140mm long
140mm wide

Weight: with plastic mount: 140gm
purse only: 70gm

Materials: silk, metal thread, beads

Location: M2

Exit Date:

SIHC: 3.4

Description: An embroidered purse in faded gold and green with small tassels.

Distinguishing Marks: Pattern, said to be Bullion work.

Possible identity: Obvious, modern aspect

Reference Books: George Winfield Digby: Elizabethan Embroidery (1963); V & A Museum: Guide to British Embroidery (1970); J.L. Levinson: Catalogue of English Domestic Embroidery, 16-17th century (1938)

Museums: Whitworth Gallery, Manchester; Birmingham City Museum and Art Gallery; Bolton Museum of Fine Arts; Hastings Museum; Lady Lever Gallery, Port Sunlight, Wirral; Hardwick Hall, Chesterfield.

Data: After a 13-14th century peak of ecclesiastical embroidery, a second phase, domestic and secular, flowered in Elizabeth I's reign. Using herbals and natural history as models, working in silks and metallic threads on linen, some work was professional - splendid costumes for masques and pageants. More was domestic work, clothes, curtains, coverlets and soft furnishings, embroidered by ladies at home - Mary Queen of Scots and Bess of Hardwick were expert needlewomen. Much survives - not outworn hangings or richly jewelled fabrics, dismantled and re-used but personal objects, jackets, gloves, cushions, nightcaps and purses for sweetmeats, gifts of money and small devotional books. Our example is typical in size, shape and materials (as illustrated by Digby: op.cit: Plates 1 and 2). Worked in tent-stitch, Gobelin- and buttonhole-stitch, some in raised and couch-work. Materials were gold and silver bullion, coloured silks, sequins and seed pearls, taffeta-lined, with silk tassels, fringes and plaited drawstrings. Purses are frequently mentioned in wills, probate inventories and other documents.

CIVIL WAR MUSKET BALLS

Date: 1643-5

Period: Stuart : Civil War

From: Monarch Antiques
Glastonbury.
Purchase @ 50p each

Measurements: diameter : 15mm

Weight: 21gm (each)

Materials: Lead

Location: H1

SIHC: 1.8

Photo: Frank Power

00081

Description: Six irregular spheroids, 3 smaller (pistol?), 3 larger.

Distinguishing Marks: Mould marks around middles.

Possible identity: Would modern children think of marbles?

Reference Books: Antony Baker: A Battlefield Atlas of the Civil War (1986); L.& F. Funcken: Arms and Uniforms (1972)

Museums: Museum and Art Gallery, Basingstoke; Alton House, Hants; Littlecote House, Berks; Naseby Battle and Farm Museum, Northants.

Data: The first (c1400) clumsy, short-barrelled hand-guns were effective up to 10m. Culverins and hackbuts (weight 30kg) needed two men to fire. With the arquebus, forges made longer, stronger barrels for single-handed firing. Muskets, weighing 10 kgm, were supported on a forked stand, muzzle-loaded and smooth-bored, fired by a pivoted length of slow-burning match. Powder was carried in leather flasks or bandoliers of wooden tubes. Loading, priming, firing, cleaning and reloading took 5 mins. and 34 drill movements! In rain the match went out. Spring-loaded wheel-locks, striking sparks from flint, made it possible to fire carbines and pistols from horseback. Flintlocks were invented c1625 and issued to the British army from the end of the 17th century. Breech-loaded percussion weapons, with rifled barrels for greater accuracy, were invented c1836. Basing, or Loyalty House, where these musket-balls were found, was Royalist stronghold of Catholic Marquess of Winchester. Twice attacked by Waller (1643-4), Basing fell to Cromwell's cannon (1645), was plundered and demolished.

No: 00049

Date:　　Original 1701, Replica 1983

Period:　William III

From:　　Purchase: Past Times @ £3.95

Measurements:　　140 x 83 x 6mm

Weight:　77gm

Materials: Printed paper and card

Location:　　H1

SIHC:　　1.1

THE
SCHOOL
OF
MANNERS.
OR

RULES for Childrens Behaviour:

AtChurch,at Home,atTable, inCompany,inDifcourfe,at School,abroad, and among Boys. With fome other fhort and mixt Precepts.

By the Author of the *Englifh Exercifs.*

𝕿𝖍𝖊 𝕱𝖔𝖚𝖗𝖙𝖍 𝕰𝖉𝖎𝖙𝖎𝖔𝖓.

L O N D O N.

Printed for *Tho. Cockerill*, at the ThreeLegs andBible-againft Gro-cers-Hall in the *Poultrey*, 1701

Description: A pretty little book in modern binding with colourful reproduction dust-jacket. 64 pp. of black print with tiny woodcut pictures. First 12 pp. are modern Introduction, explaining provenance.

Distinguishing Marks: Dated title-page.

Condition: Brand-new reproduction

Possible identity: Self-explanatory

Reference Books: Joyce I. Whalley: Cobwebs catch Flies : Illustrated books for the Nursery and Schoolroom, 1700-1900. (1974).

Museum: Victoria and Albert Museum, London.

Data: Courtesy books were popular amongst the nobility during the Middle Ages. (Courtesy = behaviour suitable to a court, as in curtesy.) These instructed boys on the proper conduct of a page or courtier, including The Babees Book (1475) and The Book of Nurture (1545). The tone is set by a 15th century book "to teche every man to serve a Lord or Mayster". Later books - there are many 18th century editions - are intended for ordinary schoolchildren. Written by John Garretson, a Latin master, in parallel English and Latin, on behaviour at school, church, and table. Shocked by Long and troublesome observation of Children's Rudeness, the author blames parents for this. Others blame teachers! Children must speak only when spoken to, address their parents as Sir and Madam; never laugh aloud, only silently smile. At table they must not criticize the food, using two fingers and thumb of the left hand as forks (See 00091) to pick up meat. They must eat slowly, throw no food under the table, pick their teeth only behind a napkin. In the living-room they must not spit - except in the corner! In the street, they must not rush about, nor jeer at pupils of other schools.

GEORGIAN SHOE BUCKLE

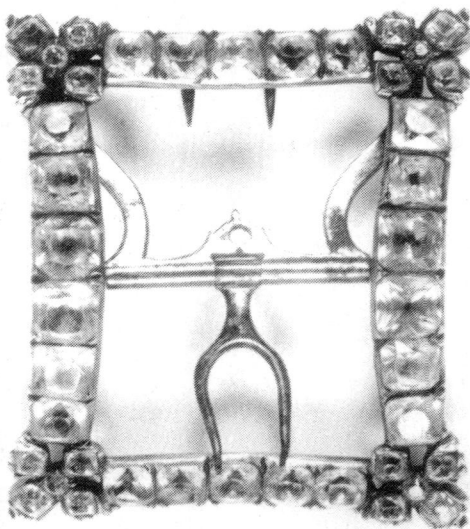
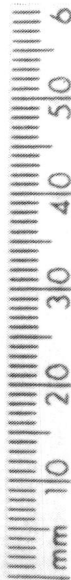

Date: c1727

Period: Georgian

From: Hartlebury Museum Loans

Measurements: 52mm x 47mm

Weight: 28gm

Materials: Silver or plate; paste or imitation diamonds.

Location: M3 (school safe)

Exit Date: 1st April 1989

SIHC: 3.3

00099

Description: Rectangular buckle with arched frame, mounted with closely-set, facetted pastes increasing in size towards centre. All sides slightly curved with four-part rosettes at corners in elaborate claw setting. Sharp, swivelled prongs on tongues, each side of middle bridge.

Distinguishing Marks: None

Condition: Good

Possible identity: Belt-buckle? - children may be unfamiliar with shoe-buckles? Man's or woman's?

Reference Books: Bernard and Therle Hughes: Georgian Shoe Buckles (1976)

Museums: Street Shoe Museum, Somerset

Data: Hartlebury Museum cites Hughes (op.cit): For about 150 years from mid-17th to end of the 19th century, a man's social position could be determined by the quality of his shoe buckles ranging from the diamond-studded gold of the dandy to the sober silver of the merchant or the craftsman. Buckles were attached to the shoe's two straps or latchets and was removable, kept from shoe to shoe, like a brooch or other jewellery. The frame's arched shape, for the instep, identifies a shoe buckle. The forked tongue on the chape, shaped like a pitchfork, dates this as an early Georgian example; in the 17th century the shoe-strap was held by a single sharp spike. So important were buckles throughout the eighteenth century on both men and women's footwear that they reflect each change in fashion, both in their design and ornament. Nineteenth century boots and shoes were fastened by laces or buttons. (See 00036 and 00037)

Date: 1747

Period: Georgian
(George II 1727-60)

From: Miss Emily Stubbington (Gift)

Measurements: 250mm x 305mm

Weight: 426gm

Materials: Card and paper

Location: H2

SIHC: 2.1

Photocopy

THE

A R T

OF

C O O K E R Y,

Made PLAIN and EASY;

Which far exceeds any THING of the Kind ever yet Publiſhed.

CONTAINING,

I. Of Roaſting, Boiling, &c.
II. Of Made-Diſhes.
III. Read this Chapter, and you will find how Expenſive a French Cook's Sauce is.
IV. To make a Number of pretty little Diſhes fit for a Supper, or Side-Diſh, and little Corner-Diſhes for a great Table; and the reſt you have in the Chapter for Lent.
V. To dreſs Fiſh.
VI. Of Soups and Broths.
VII. Of Puddings.
VIII. Of Pies.
IX. For a Faſt-Dinner, a Number of good Diſhes, which you may make uſe for a Table at any other Time.
X. Directions for the Sick.
XI. For Captains of Ships.
XII. Of Hog's Puddings, Sauſages, &c.

XIII. To Pot and Make Hams, &c.
XIV. Of Pickling.
XV. Of Making Cakes, &c.
XVI. Of Cheeſecakes, Creams, Jellies, Whip Syllabubs, &c.
XVII. Of Made Wines, Brewing, French Bread, Muffins, &c.
XVIII. Jarring Cherries, and Preſerves, &c.
XIX. To Make Anchovies, Vermicella, Ketchup, Vinegar, and to keep Artichokes, French-Beans, &c.
XX. Of Diſtilling.
XXI. How to Market, and the Seaſon of the Year for Butcher's Meat, Poultry, Fiſh, Herbs, Roots, &c. and Fruit.
XXII. A certain Cure for the Bite of a Mad Dog. By Dr. Mead.

BY A LADY.

L O N D O N:

Printed for the AUTHOR; and Sold at Mrs. Aſhburn's, a China-Shop, the Corner of Fleet-Ditch. MDCCXLVII.

[Price 3s. ſtitch'd, and 5s. bound.]

00097

Description: Tattered book, originally stitched (@ 3s.= 15p) not bound. (@ 5s.= 25p) Cover and many pages missing.

Distinguishing Marks: Dated on title-page: MDCCXLVII Note bookseller's address at a china-shop.

Condition: Poor, needs re-binding.

Possible identity: Obvious

Reference Books: The Science Museum offers a comprehensive booklist on Domestic Appliances and Cookery Books, English Heritage publishes four books on Food & Cooking in Britain, with details of cookery methods, utensils and recipes. See also: Rachel Field: Irons in the Fire, A History of Cooking Equipment (1984); Museum: The Science Museum, London: Domestic Appliances Gallery shows cookers from spits to gas and electricity stoves.

Data: Earlier cookery books include two 15th century examples edited by T.S. Austin (Early English Text Soc.1888) and A proper Newe Booke of Cookerye (1558). The Lady was Hannah Glasse, whose intention was "to instruct the lower sort"; she condemned the extravagence of French cooking. Hannah wrote several cookery books and The Servants' Directory or Housekeeper's Companion (1770); The Art of Cookery went into several editions. She is reputed to be the cook who started her recipe for hare soup with "first catch your hare". (And for shepherd's pie ....?) Her publications pre-date Mrs. Isabella Beeton's more famous plagiarism, the Book of Household Management (1861: published in a facsimile edition by Cape in 1968) by more than 100 years. Old houses, like Erddig (NT:Clwyd) and Aston Hall, (Birmingham) preserve remnants of 18th century domestic economy and servants' hall.

No: 00098

Date: 1762

Period: Georgian
(George III 1760-1820)

From: Hartlebury Museum Loans

Measurements: Diam : 17mm

Weight : 3.5gm

Materials: Silver

Location: H3

Exit Date: 1st April 1989

SIHC: 1.1

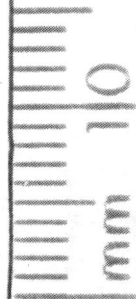

ACTUAL SIZE

1 cm

mm 10

Photo: Frank Power

00098

Description: A small silver coin, milled edge, king's wreathed head.

Distinguishing Marks: Obverse: Georgius III: Dei Gratia Reverse: Figure 3 and crown: 1762 *Mag. Bri; Fr. et Hib. Rex* (note medieval claim to French crown).

Possible identity: Unfamiliar coin to children - not even "Threepenny bit".

Condition: Good

Reference Books: Peter Seaby & Frank Purvey: Coins of England and the United Kingdom (current edition); Helen Farquhar: Regal Charities 2nd Series: The Maundy, in: Jnl. & Proc. Br. Numis. Soc. 2nd ser.16-20) W.Charlton: Maundy Thursday observances and the royal Maundy Money, in Trans. Lancs. & Ches. Ant. Soc. Vol.34.(1917)

Museums: Usher Art Gallery, Lincoln has coins, including Maundy Money.

Data: Maundy Thursday, the day before Good Friday commemorates the Last Supper, when Christ washed his disciples' feet, saying: "A new commandment (Latin *mandatum* becomes maundy) I give unto you. - Do as I have done for you." (St. John 13: 34) The early Church observed this annual act of humility, Pope, kings, nobles and prelates ceremonially washing poor men's feet. Later converted into a money payment; in England Henry IV made the number of recipients the same as the years of his age. (In 1989 the Queen gave 63 Maundy purses to couples at Birmingham Cathedral) Until 1662 the Royal Bounty was in silver pennies; after Restoration each recipient was given a set of silver 4d, 3d, 2d and 1d. pieces (total face-value 4p). Monarchs continued to wash feet until William III gave the task to the Lord High Almoner; a custom abolished in 1754. Seaby's Catalogue illustrates sample Maundy sets for each reign after the Restoration.

Date: 1781

Period: Georgian

From: Gift: Mr. Geoff Walker (Teacher)

Measurements: 8" x 11"

Weight: 653gm

Materials: Paper, cardboard, hide

Location: H2

SIHC: 1.3

Photocopy

THE

Law of Tythes.

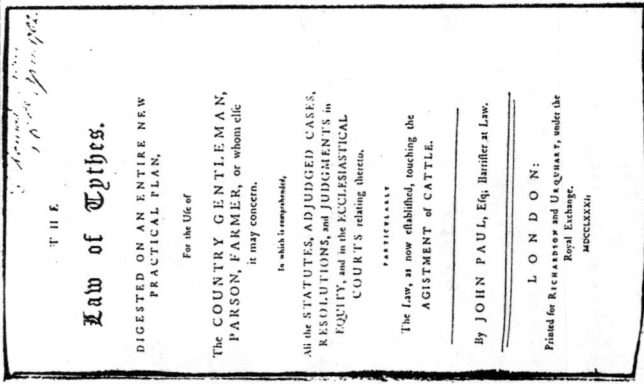

DIGESTED ON AN ENTIRE NEW
PRACTICAL PLAN,

For the Use of

The COUNTRY GENTLEMAN,
PARSON, FARMER, or whom elfe
it may concern,

In which is comprehended,

All the STATUTES, ADJUDGED CASES,
RESOLUTIONS, and JUDGMENTS in
EQUITY, and in the ECCLESIASTICAL
COURTS relating thereto.

‧‧‧‧‧‧‧‧‧‧‧‧

The Law, as now eftablifhed, touching the
AGISTMENT of CATTLE.

By JOHN PAUL, Efq. Barrifter at Law.

LONDON:

Printed for RICHARDSON and URQUHART, under the
Royal Exchange.

MDCCLXXXI.

00071

Description: Old leather-bound book.

Condition: Poor - binding decayed, pages yellowed and stained

Distinguishing Marks: Title-page dated: MDCCLXXXI use to teach Roman numbers.

Possible identity: Self-explanatory, as a book; subject unfamiliar!

Reference Books: John West: Village Records, Chapter V: Land Tax and Tithe Records. (1983)

Museums: Many great tithe barns survive in villages, usually monastic, some smaller parish barns: NT sites include: Ashleworth (Glos); East Riddleston Hall (Yorks); Great Coxwell (Berks); Buckland Abbey (Devon); West Pennard (Som); Bredon (H-Worcs).

Data: Tithe = one-tenth. Tithes were literally one-tenth of every medieval farmer's produce, both grain and cattle, owed to the local church as tax. Originally paid in kind, later commuted to money payments, this compulsory obligation dated from the time of the Saxon king Offa (787AD). There was a continual resistance to tithe payment, much of which passed into the hands of lay rectors after the Reformation. This came to a head during the agrarian revolution of the 18-19th centuries. As this book shows, tithe was a profitable cause of specialized litigation. From 1836-60 a series of local Tithe Commutation Acts were passed, parish by parish, for almost 12,000 English villages. These substituted a standard money rent based on a price index in place of miscellaneous exactions. The records of Tithe commutation are stored in County and Diocesan Record Offices; the Awards provide an extensive land-use survey of almost three-quarters of England and are based upon large scale parish maps, usually surveyed c.1840.

– 149 –

SUGAR NIPPERS

Date: Georgian?

Period: 18-19th centuries

From: Mrs. Elizabeth Buxton
(Great-grandparent) Gift.

Measurements: Length: 241mm

Weight: 328gm

Materials: Steel

Location: H1

SIHC: 2.6

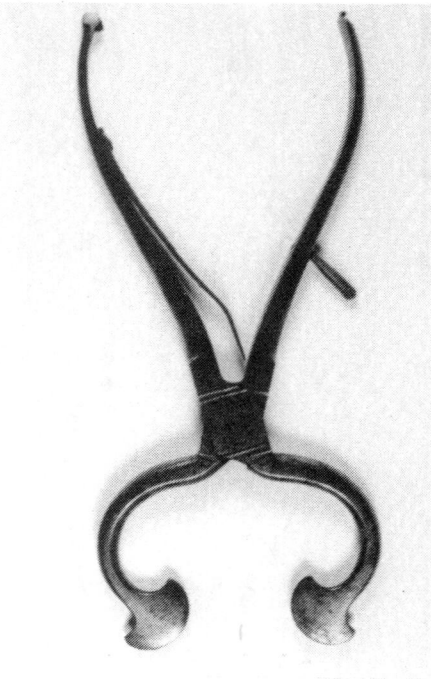

Photo: Frank Power

Description: A neatly made Mystery Object, scissor-shaped with long curved handles, well sprung, and small, broad crescent-shaped blades

Possible identity: What could this tool cut?

Condition: Excellent; metal slightly blackened with age - no rust

Distinguishing Marks: chased pattern by hinge. Small spike or distance piece on handle protects knuckles.

Reference Books: J.Seymour Lindsay: Iron and Brass Implements of the English House. (1964) illustrates identical example on pp. 207-9; Geoffrey Warren: Kitchen Bygones, a Collector's Guide (1984); Doreen Yarwood: The British Kitchen (1981) Illustration:pp.37-8.

Museum: Hartlebury Museum (H-Worcs): Sheffield Museum

Data: Sugar is a comparatively modern commercial product. The Greeks and Romans had none, using honey instead. Sugar was used medicinally, or as a delicacy in India c100BC, the Arabs brought sukkar to Egypt, Spain and Sicily. Crusaders introduced it to Britain - earliest references occur in the 14th.c. By 1500 there was a flourishing overland trade from the East to Venice; tropical sugar-cane growing became a colonial incentive. (More sugar was used with the introduction of tea and coffee in 17th.c.) Supplies of sugar were moulded in wooden conical loaves, 3ft tall, weighing 14lb. (Sugar-loaf is a shape which gave its name to mountains and hills all over the world.) Surviving cutters, some mounted on wooden blocks, are usually Victorian, but continue in production (though not in much use?) into the 1930s. Decorative glass sugar crushing rods were also used at table. This, like the shaving mug (See 025 and 040) is an object which outlived its use, surviving in production as a curio. Decorative chasing on the hinge denotes a late 18th century example.

GEORGIAN COIN

Date: 1799

Period: Georgian (George III)

From: Gift: Mr. H. Withers

Measurements: 31mm

Weight: 14gm

Materials: Copper

Location: H2

SIHC: 1.7

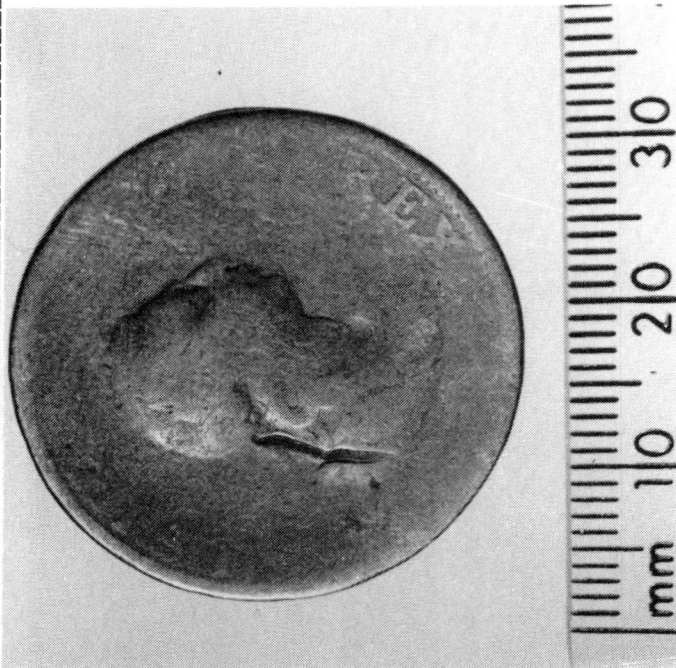

Photo: Frank Power

Description: Smooth, defaced copper coin, like a pre-decimal penny.

Distinguishing Marks: Draped bust : G...IUS III REX : Reverse: Britannia figure and ..99 The edge of this coin has a distinctive grained or safety edge to prevent forgery.

Condition: Very poor

Possible identity: Coin or token

Reference Books: Peter Seaby and P.F. Purvey: Coins of England and the UK (Vol.1:19th Edn. 1982)

Museums: Hereford City Museum (for replicas); Westair also uses metals, not plastic

Data: This coin can be identified in Seaby's Catalogue (p.232, No:3778) as a George III halfpenny of 1799. It is a useful exercise in deduction from flimsy evidence. How many English kings are there who numbered III? How many with initial G? Which reigns have any date ending in ..99? Which period imitated a classical tradition? Which Georgian king faces right on coins? Then check the coin Catalogue. Medieval English pennies (00002) were silver and 240 weighed 1lb or £1. Minted until the reign of Charles II, they steadily decreased in weight. In 1672 halfpennies and farthings of copper were coined, and copper pennies and twopenny Cartwheels (40mm diameter) were minted from 1797. During the second half of the 18th century, little silver or copper was minted, resulting in commercial production of trade tokens (00032). The first copper pence were minted by steam presses in 1797. Tokens became illegal, reappearing in industrial areas during 1811, but were suppressed by 1816, when new coinage was introduced. These were the first official token coins - silver coins worth less than their face-value.

WORCESTER TRADE TOKEN

Date: 1811

Period: George III

From: Gift; Miss M. Henderson

Measurements: 33mm diam

Weight: 31gm

Materials: Bronze

Location: H2

SIHC: 1.7

Photo: Frank Power

Description: Thick, bronze coin-like object, similar in size and weight to pre-decimal penny. Milled edge. Engraved inscriptions around edges.

Distinguishing Marks: Obverse: Worcester City coat-of-arms and motto: *Civitas in Bello in Pace Fidelis.* Reverse: Worcester City and County Token 1811 : Value One Penny

Condition: Excellent

Possible identity: Coin or token?

Reference Books: Jim Newmark: Trade Tokens of the Industrial Revolution (Shire Album: 1981); J.R.S. Whiting: Trade Tokens (1971); P. Matthias: English Trade Tokens (1962); A.W. Waters: Notes on 18th century Trade Tokens (1954)

Museum: Hereford-Worcester County Museum, Hartlebury.

Data: Trade-tokens came into use during periods when volume of trade exceeded the ready supply of low denomination silver coins as small change. This happened in three main periods: 1648-72; 1787-97 and 1811-17. Tokens were first issued by traders and shopkeepers, as 1/4d, 1/2d and 1d pieces during the reign of James I. At first they were made of lead, later in 17th c. of copper and brass. Their issue was taken up by corporations and banks; we find workhouse pennies, town pieces as illustrated, inn- and coffee-house tokens and mail-coach halfpennies. There were also political tokens, patriotic farthings, radical and satirical pieces. Bearing the name and address of the issuer, and in many industrial cases, pictures of his factory or shop, tokens are found widely circulated across Britain. They fell into disuse at the end of the 18th century, when the government began to issue a copper 1d and 2d coinage.

CRYSTAL PALACE SOUVENIR

Date: 1851+

Period: Victorian

From: Dr. John Fines (Gift)

Measurements: Diam. 134mm

Weight: 109gm

Materials: china

Location: H2

SIHC: 1.1

Photo: Frank Power

Description: A pretty little circular dish with serrated edge and floral decoration. Gilt letters: A Present from the Crystal Palace.

Distinguishing Marks: Reverse: Made in Germany.

Condition: Excellent

Possible identity: Obviously a commemorative gift, but Crystal Palace will be unfamiliar. Children can compare family Presents from Bognor.

Reference Books: Cape's Jackdaw No.43: The Great Exhibition (1968); J.R.C. Yglesias: Life & the Great Exhibition (1964); J. Kamm: Joseph Paxton and the Crystal Palace (1967)

Data: In 1851, Queen Victoria's husband Albert, Prince Consort, planned an international Exhibition of inventions and manufactured goods despite vigorous opposition in Parliament. Joseph Paxton, the Duke of Devonshire's gardener, designed a prefabricated Crystal Palace, using 32 miles of iron pipes, 72ft. girders and 18,000 panes of glass. Built for £170,000 in 22 weeks on 18 acres around trees in Hyde Park. Gaily painted Halls displayed wares of 14,000 exhibitors from America, Russia, Canada, India and Europe - more than half from Britain or her colonies. A 24-ton block of coal stood at the entrance, there were stuffed elephants, models of bridges, lighthouses, and dockyards, the Koh-i-Noor diamond, calculating machines, furniture, textiles and the Folkestone Express. Boilers drove steam-ploughs, printing presses and ships' engines. 6,000,000 visitors came by rail excursions from all over England; 1m. gallons of soft drinks and 2m. buns were sold; 170 Gold and 2,918 Silver Medals were awarded. In 1854 the Palace was moved to Sydenham, but was destroyed by fire in 1936. Many relics are in the V & A Museum. The Exhibition was a monument to the Industrial Revolution and Victorian bad taste.

GLASS PHOTOGRAPH

Date: c1860

Period: Victorian

From: Gift: Mrs. Emma Skinner (Grandparent)

Measurements: 70 x 84mm

Weight: 70gm

Materials: Glass, frame is pinchbeck, alloy of copper and zinc.

Location: H2

SIHC: 3.1

Photo: Frank Power

00048

Description: Photograph of an elderly woman in bonnet and shawl, printed on glass, opaque black backing, oval gilt mask and another glass, held together by a finely scrolled narrow soft-metal frame.

Distinguishing Marks: Full sleeves, low-waisted gown and bonnet offer dating evidence, though reference to type of photograph is more exact.

Possible identity: What type of photograph?

Reference Books: Margaret Haller: Collecting Old Photographs (1978); Lee D. Witkin & Barbara Lund: The Photograph Collector's Guide (1981); Helmut & Alison Gernsheim: History of Photography (1969/1982)

Data: Photography (Greek), means light-writing. Niepce (1822) printed pictures on glass but changed to zinc. Daguerre (1837) printed daguerrotypes on silver-coated copper plates, a more practicable process. The collodian wet plate was faster (2-20 secs), developed in portable darkrooms on the battlefields of the American Civil War and Crimea. It also made cheap personal photographs possible. Our example is an Ambrotype, (1855-67) a sixpenny (= 2 ½ p) portrait made fashionable by J.E. Mayall (1860), using collodian and a simple non-print process. It is in fact a negative print on the lower glass - Herschel had shown that weak b/w negative on opaque backing, reverses. Confused with daguerrotypes, which they replaced, ambrotypes have dull grey surface, not Daguerre's shiny silver. *Relievos* gave a 3D effect. Despised by expensive photographers as art for the millions, Ambrotypes were exhibited in the Great Exhibition. (See 096). A famous woman photographer, Julia Cameron (1815-74), photographed Darwin, Tennyson and Browning. Lewis Carroll (Charles Dodgson), author of Alice in Wonderland was an enthusiast. In 1838 William Fox Talbot printed on silver-chloride paper, making cheap popular cameras possible (0093).

VICTORIAN SMOOTHING IRON

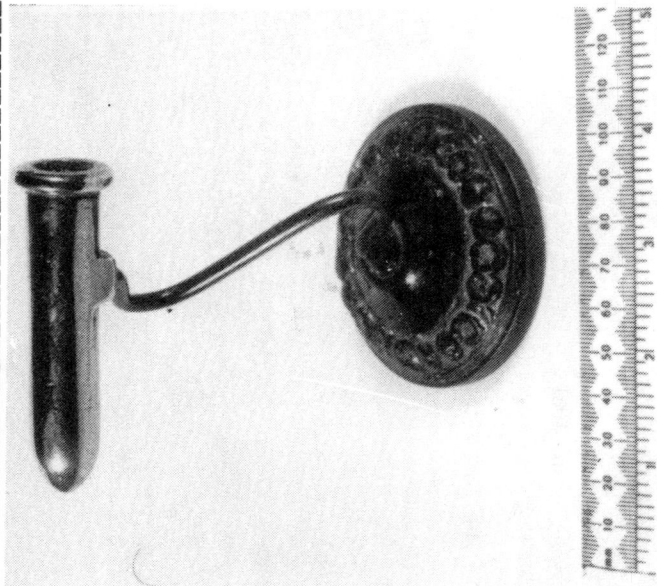

Date: c.1880+

Period: Victorian

From: Miss Jean Abbiss,
Wolverhampton: Gift.
Belonged to her grandmother.
c.1936; "in the family a long time"

Measurements: Ht: 110mm; base: 72mm;
head: 80mm

Weight: 198gm 98gm

Materials: Head: brass;
Base: cast-iron;
Stand: bent iron-rod

Location: S1

SIHC: 2.5

Photo: Frank Power

Description: One of an identical pair of mysterious shape. Bullet-head of cast brass, approx. 2mm thick, with 4mm lip, hollowed to full depth (72mm), mounted (screw-thread) on S-bend (iron rod), to circular cast-iron base, hollow underneath. Used recently as mantel-shelf ornaments.

Condition: Excellent, highly polished. Missing part from hollow head?

Distinguishing Marks: Number 3 (8mm) on underside of base; rose-pattern on rim.

Possible identity: Tool? Gadget? Mounted bullet?

Reference Books: David de Haan: Antique Household Gadgets; J. Seymour Lindsay: Iron & Brass Implements of the English Home (1970); Dorothy Hartley: Water in the English Home: The Laundry (1964).

Museums: Castle Museum York: gave precise identity and book-references. See also Shugborough (Staffs) and Hartlebury (H-W).

Data: A smoothing iron, for ribbons, lace, small caps etc. Heated by insertion of a hot iron slug - probably on a rod-with-handle for easy handling (now missing). Sometimes referred to as an Italian iron, this is not a goffering or crimping iron, which produced a fluted, corrugated effect. Miss Abbiss remembers how, when she was a little girl, as late as 1936, her grand-mother, Mrs. Adelaide Collins, regularly used this iron on maids' caps taken in as washing from Wolverhampton houses.

OIL LAMP

Date: c1880

Period: Late Victorian

From: Loan: Mrs. R. Waylett

Measurements: 788mm tall

Weight: 3.6kg

Materials: Brass-plated iron and glass

Location: H2

Exit Date:

SIHC: 2.3

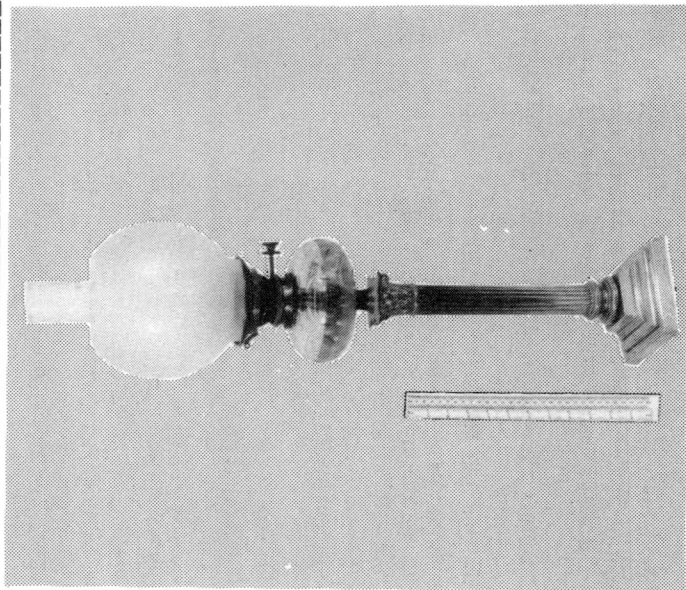

00042

Description: A fine example of a Victorian Corinthian table twin-burner oil-lamp with glass oil reservoir, modern replacement glass chimney and globe. (Corinthian from Greek order of brass column.)

Distinguishing Marks: On burner control: No.2 Hinks Lever. On base: J. Hinks & Son 1781

Condition: Excellent working order, giving adequate reading light.

Possible identity: Obvious; oil function unfamiliar to children? **Reference Books:** Cecil A. Meadows: Discovering Oil Lamps (Shire Album 145); Victorian Shopping: Harrods Catalogue 1895 (David & Charles Reprint 1972); Mrs. Beeton's Book of Household Management (Facsimile Edition 1968)

Museums: Castle Museum, York

Data: In the 18th c. (1784) a Swiss chemist, Aimé Argand, revolutionized lamps by inventing an air-controlled wick and smokeless glass chimney. Until c1845 domestic lamps burned animal fats, whale-fish- and vegetable-oil. Camphine, made from turpentine, was the first substitute, but tended to explode. Safer, cheap paraffin came into use c1860. Oil lamps were used downstairs, as table models, bracket lamps and standard floor-lamps. Candles were usually taken to bedrooms. Victorian catalogues advertize a wide range of lamps; prices range from 6 shillings (30p) to £5.00 (An identical model to our illustration sold at 10 shillings (50p). A similar range is found in the Army & Navy Stores Catalogue of 1907, alongside new gas and electrical fittings. An ordinary house would have several lamps; Mrs Beeton lists their cleaning, trimming and refilling amongst the duties of the footman, in smaller households the housemaid. Very large estates employed a Lamp-boy.

CHILD'S BUTTONED BOOTS

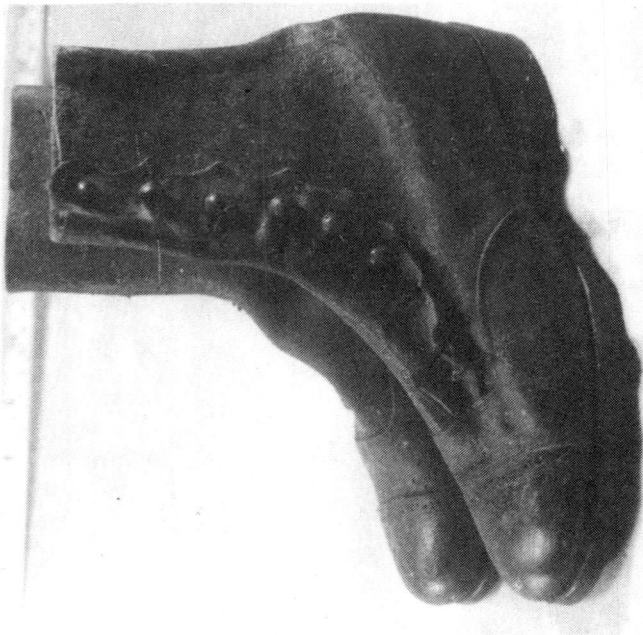

Date:	c1880
Period:	Mid-Victorian
From:	Mr. Andrew Barnett Retired Headmaster (Gift)
Measurements:	Length: 215mm Height: 195mm heel to top
Weight:	18oz/560gm
Materials:	Leather
Location:	S1
SIHC:	3.3

Photo: Frank Power

Description: A neat, small pair of boots, with worn uppers and newly repaired soles and heels. Heavy toe-caps; originally stitched, repaired by nails. 16 round buttons on outer side of each boot.

Distinguishing Marks: Stamped 13 on sole

Condition: Fair, leather soft, but flaking

Possible identity: Obvious; buttons unfamiliar

Reference Books: June Swann: Shoes (Batsford 1982) and Shoemaking (Shire,1986)

Museums: The Shoe Room, Central Museum, Northampton - the largest boot and shoe collection in the world, - useful Information sheets.

Data: Boot and shoe-making had become centred on Northampton by 1630. With the introduction of sewing machines c1850 manufacture, which had been on a domestic cottage outwork basis moved into factories. In 1859 a widespread strike against increasing use of machinery caused shoemakers to move to Leicester, which captured much of the trade. Mechanization caused vast output from c1888, based on Norwich and Strafford. Throughout the 19th century local bootmakers also continued working. Commercial Directories list 3 or 4 in small villages; Bentley's Worcestershire Directory for 1841 names 682 from all over the county, the next largest retail craft after grocers and taverns and 13% of all distribution trades. The size (13) of these Victorian boots matches the trainers of a modern 8-year old at Yew Tree Infants school, Dudley, but hers weigh only 7oz. The Deputy Headmistress's size 4 sandals are the same length, but weigh only 5oz. Victorian photographs show most classes of people as more solidly shod than they are today, except for very poor, barefoot children. Excellent clogs were still worn by pupils in Lancashire schools in 1943.

NEEDLEWORK SAMPLER

Date: 1883

Period: Victorian

From: Loan: Mrs Anne White

Measurements: 280 x 280mm

Weight: (unframed) 62gm

Materials: Canvas and wool

Location: S2

Exit date:

SIHC: 3.2

Photo: Linda Burridge

00026—

Description: A square of coarse canvas cross-stitched with alphabet in alternate coloured wools, red and faded blue. Stitched by Adelaide Port, aged 9 in 1883. Modern frame and glass.

Distinguishing Marks: Child's name, age and date.

Condition: Fair, but faded and stretched

Possible identity: Purpose more difficult than identity for modern children. Standard of child's needlework incredible today.

Reference Books: Pamela Clabburn: Samplers (Shire Publications, 1980) F.G. Payne: Guide to the Collection of Samplers and Embroideries. (National Museum of Wales Cardiff, 1939); Christine Stevens: Samplers from the Welsh Folk Museum's Collection. (1987); A Calendar for 1989 (by S P Publishing Ltd) offered 13 beautiful examples (12" x 16", with notes) from the large collection at the Fitzwilliam Museum, Cambridge.

Museums: Blaise House Museum, Bristol; Castlegate Museum, Nottingham; Gawthorpe Hall, Padiham, Lancs; V & A Museum, London; Strangers Hall, Norwich; Whitworth Art Gallery, Manchester. Modern commercial patterns available.

Data: Samplers originated in the 16th century, before printed pattern books. They were used to teach children needlework, and educate them in Geography, Nature and moral virtues. 17th century specimens are long and narrow, becoming square in the 18th, with birds, trees and verses. Numerous Victorian examples are stereotyped in form, often crude, in coarse wool and simple stitches. Pattern and instruction books can also be found. Some survive from the original City & Guilds examination syllabus. Many homes had sewing machines by 1870-80 but handwork was still common until quite recently.

– 167 –

CUT-THROAT RAZOR

Date: c1880

Period: Late Victorian

From: Family collection: Harry West

Measurements: 168mm

Weight: 50gm

Materials: Blade: hollow-ground steel.
Handle: black celluloid.
Box:: Cardboard

Location: H2

WARNING: **DESTROY THE DANGEROUS EDGE OF THE BLADE BY GRINDING FLAT, BEFORE CLASS-ROOM USE.**

SIHC: 3.4

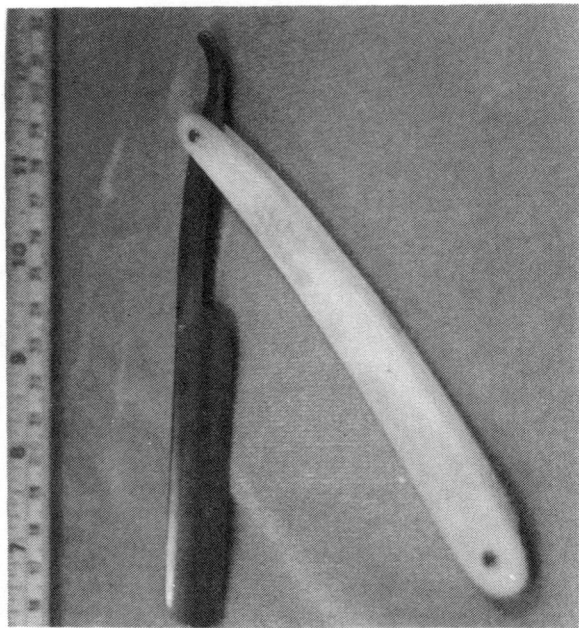

Description: Typical open razor of pre-war pattern, kept in original cardboard box.

Distinguishing Marks: Crown and Sword Razor: Made in Germany ; ERN 116 Crown and Sword trade-mark stamped on handle.

Condition: Fair - still very sharp but rusts easily

Possible identity: Children may not connect the blade with shaving.

Reference Book: Gail Durbin: Wig, Hairdressing & Shaving Bygones (Shire Album 117)

Museums: Sheffield City Museum (razors collection); Museum of London (reconstruction of barber's shop)

Data: Bronze and iron razors are found on prehistoric and Roman sites. Blades were flat, until the early 19th century, when hollow-grinding was introduced. Handles were of bone, ivory or mother-of-pearl; celluloid, an early plastic, was used from c1868, as in the case of the illustration. In 1870-80 machine-grinding shifted production from Sheffield to Germany. Blades, set by barbers, were honed daily on leather strops. Until the 20th century men shaved less often than today, often going to the local barber only once a week. Catalogues (1895) advertise open razors from 1-5 shillings each (5 - 25p). Wealthier customers kept a case of seven razors, each day of the week engraved for daily use. Safety razors were patented in 1876 in America, 1887 in England, at first a short hollow-ground blade, replaced by Gillette's wafer-thin razor-blade from 1903. Many old soldiers in 1939 still used open, cut-throat razors. Electric razors were first sold c1930. Shaving paraphernalia included badger-hair brushes, mugs, stands, mirrors and strops - now collectors' items.

JUBILEE PLATE

Date: 1887

Period: Victorian

From: Pupil loan: Gerald Simms

Measurements: Width: 242mm

Weight: 575gm

Materials: White china

Location: H3

Exit Date:

SIHC: 1.1

00027—

Description: An octagonal plate for Jubilee Year 1887. Black and white pictorial pattern, picked out with touches of red, yellow and gold.

Distinguishing Marks: On back: Rd. No:63164 Adhesive price ticket: 1089; £4.50. See also Data (below)

Possible identity: Explicit

Reference Books: Dorothy Marshall: Victoria(1972); Elizabeth Longford: Victoria RI (1966) and Lytton Strachey: Queen Victoria (1988).

Data: This is an Imperialist plate! Considerable text: Victoria, Queen and Empress, Jubilee Year 1887 (i.e.Golden = 50 years) Pictures of Her Majesty the Queen and HRH the Prince of Wales (later Edward VII - the Queen's husband, Albert, had died in 1861). The world map shows The British Empire, on which the sun never sets, coloured red, with time-differences, e.g: Cape Town: 1 hr.14 mins. Fast; Ottawa: 5hrs.3mins Slow etc. The coats-of-arms of Australasia, Canada, Cape Colony and India surround Brittania with 6 colonial costumed figures in black and white and the punning motto: *Ubi Virtus, Ibi Victoria.* There are two vignettes of Canadian voyageurs on the Nile and Australians in the Soudan. Statistics give the Empire's total population as 305,347,924, its area as 9,101,699 sq.mls and a its annual balance of payments in the red, with Exports: £390,018,569 and Imports £295,967,583. See also the Queen's Diamond Jubilee (60 years) portrait. (00080)

WILLCOX & GIBBS SEWING MACHINE

Date: 1888+

Period: Victorian

From: Loan: Miss Joan Simms

Measurements: Base: 432 x 530mm
Machine: 242mm

Weight: 7,000gm

Materials: Wood and iron

Location: H4

SIHC: 2.4

Photo: Frank Power

00047

Description: A heavy iron, hand-cranked sewing machine in full working order, screwed by original wing-nut to modern wooden base. All parts screw home well, the machine is capable of easy repair

Condition: Excellent, smoothly running working order.

Distinguishing Marks: Patent-plates and makers' dated name plate.

Possible identity: Obvious, though possibly an unfamiliar form to children.

Reference Books: David de Haan: Antique Household Gadgets and Appliances (1977)

Museums: Hartlebury Museum (H-Worcs). The National Needle Museum, Redditch (H-W)

Data: A brass medallion on the machine identifies its makers as Willcox and Gibb Sewing Machine Co., New York. Patents, recorded on the top of the sewing-table, list applications by J.H.A. Gibb, Willcox & Cableton for 1871-1888 and by Willcox & Gibbs (1888). Also, almost illegible, are patents for France, Germany and, by Royal Letters Patent, England. The makers' names are repeated here, adding New York, London and Paris. The owner, hoping for a treasure, discovered in an antiques book that the British market was flooded by these cheap, mass-produced machines at the turn of the century. Victorian Shopping (Harrod's Catalogue for 1895), a David & Charles Reprint (1972) illustrates almost identical machines, priced from 16s. (80p) to £2 12s. 6d. (£2.62) Isaac M. Singer built the first successful domestic sewing machine in 1858, improving on the invention of Elias Howe (1846). Singers also introduced the new scheme of Hire Purchase. This was the first of the new modern household appliances which changed domestic life in the 1900s.

GLOVE STRETCHERS

Date: 1880-90

Period: Victorian/Edwardian

From: Gift: Mrs. Emma Skinner

Measurements: 178mm

Weight: 21gm

Materials: Ivory; metal spring and rivets.

Location: H1

SIHC: 3.4

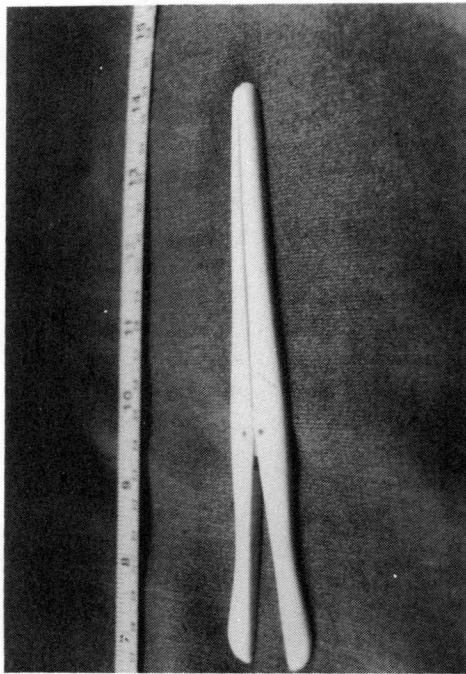

Photo: Linda Burridge

00035

Description: Smooth, white scissors- or forceps-shaped object, tapering to point; tightly sprung flat-sided arms. Outer faces smoothly turned and polished. Blades are riveted to interior spring.

Distinguishing Marks: None

Possible identity: Children guess "tweezers, scissors or tongs". A useful mystery object, correctly identified and demonstrated by a Stourbridge 5-year-old, whose Nan had showed her a similar pair. A useful Antiques Fair buy.

Condition: Excellent

Reference Books: Victorian Shopping: Harrods Catalogue (1895) (David & Charles Reprints 1972) page 190.

Museums: Hartlebury Museum, Hereford-Worcs.

Data: It will be difficult for modern children to appreciate a society in which no respectable woman, including many of the working class, would think of leaving the house without hat and gloves. Similarly, the author's father, a miner's son, in 1900, was not allowed to leave the house without his cap! This was a society too, which not only washed its gloves, but bought - in their thousands - a special tool to stretch washed gloves into shape. Victorian and Edwardian Catalogues list dozens of glove-stretchers, made of ivory, ebony, boxwood, tortoiseshell, xylonite and silver. Prices range from 2s. (10p) to 30 shillings (silver - £1.50) Key questions for deducing possible use of this object: Will it withstand heat?; Will it pick things up?; Does it seem to operate more strongly on opening or closing?; If it is a stretching instrument, what is the size of the opening to be stretched? The popularity of glove-stretchers is perhaps revealed by their numerous survivals at Antique Fairs - though it must be said that most of these are in mint condition - unused?

SCHOOLROOM SLATE

Date: c1889 (School centenary)

Period: Victorian to 1920s

From: Inter-school loan by
Red Hall Junior School,
Lower Gornal, Dudley
(W. Midlands)

Measurements: 330 x 229mm
Frame 10mm thick

Weight: 684gm

Materials: Wood and slate

Location: S1

Exit Date: 21.10.89

SIHC: 1.5

Photo: Frank Power

Description: Schoolroom slate of early Board School days, framed in wood. One side has etched lines, alternately wide (30mm) and narrower (23mm) apart, for writing practice, main line for words, upper and lower lines for pothooks and tails of letters. Other side has 32 rows of 20 squares (8mm) for sums.

Distinguishing Marks: Paper ticket No:685

Condition: Poor - broken

Possible identity: Children familiar with replicas? - available, e.g. at St. Julians Craft Centre, Shrewsbury, or modern kitchen/gift shops.

Reference Books: For children: Jean Morgan: Great Grandma's Schooldays (Macmillan Detectives,1988)

Museums: Several museums now offer a period participation classroom, e.g: Hartlebury (H-W); Shugborough (Staffs); Armley Mills Industrial Museum, Leeds. See also 0034.

Data: Like so many Victorian relics, slates remained in use for a surprisingly long time. The author remembers using them as a pupil in 1933 (just before the school phased them out.) A usual (comparatively lenient) punishment was to be stood in the corner with a pile of 6 slates held on top of the head! As a young Headmaster, the author's grandfather was threatened by a caned boy who "made as if to throw his slate at my head". Written on with a squeaky grey slate-pencil and cleaned with a a smelly rag (on which you spat - day by day!) the slate obviously did not preserve children's work from day to day. Inspectors often demanded more paperwork as evidence. For local data on older schools, refer, wherever possible to the Log Books, or, in the case of C.E. (earlier National) Schools to any surviving Parish Magazines, which sometimes paraphrase HMI Reports.

INFANT'S SCHOOL CERTIFICATE

Date: 1896

Period: Victorian

From: Loan by Mr. E. Williams

Measurements: 228 x 178mm

Weight: 303gm

Materials: Paper, card, wood

Location: S1

Exit Date:

SIHC: 3.4

Photo: Linda Burridge

Description: An attractive coloured certificate, on parchment-type paper. Awarded by Liverpool Council of Education, to William Williams, a scholar in the Infant department of St. Catherine's School, for regularity and punctuality of attendance and general good conduct during the year 1895. Modern frame and sealed surface.

Distinguishing Marks: Picture of Jesus with children. Motto: *Suffer little children* ....: Printer's name: E.J. Arnold & Son, Schools Stationers, Leeds. (survived until 1989); President of Council's signature: J. Sephton, MA.

Condition: Excellent

Possible identity: Obvious (Dated)

Reference: W. Hewitt: Liverpool Council of Education, a Notable Educational Experiment. (1928)

Museums: Liverpool Museum of Labour History: Education gallery, and Edwardian classroom.

Data: Education in Liverpool, as elsewhere, was administered, during and after the period of this Certificate, by a local Education Committee. Minutes (from 1848) are available at the Local History Library. From 1878, a Diocesan Board administered Church schools. The Council of Education which made this award was a philanthropic body whose Reports survive from 1885-1965. The Council's objectives were to elicit and enlist the sympathy of parents and the co-operation of people at large. They aimed "not to supplant the present system", but to fill up gaps and spare the public money where this can be done, by procuring the assistance of parents. This has a very topical ring today! St. Catherine's school no longer exists, it may have stood on the site of the present University Senate House in Abercrombie Square. The C. E. Teachers' College was, until the 1960s, St. Catherine's.

QUEEN VICTORIA PORTRAIT

Date: 1897

Period: Victorian

From: Gift: Mr. William J. West

Measurements: 580 x 710mm

Weight: 3175gm

Materials: Paper, wood, glass.

Location: S1

Exit Date:

SIHC: 1.1

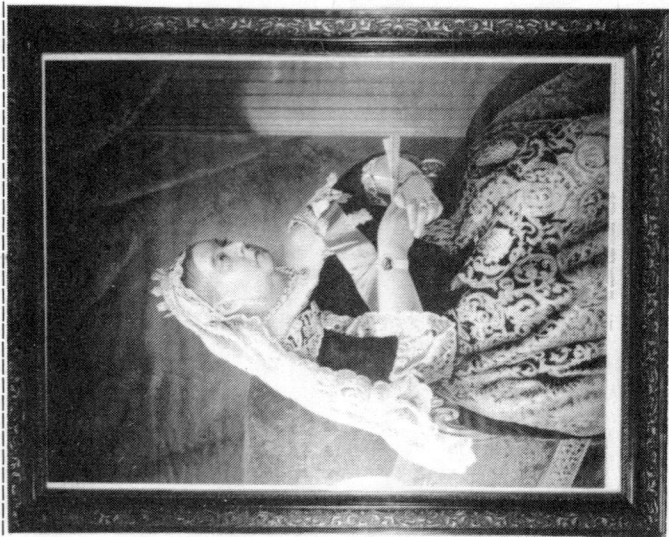

Photo: Frank Power

Description: A framed coloured photographic print of Queen Victoria, made for her Diamond Jubilee (60 years) in 1897.

Distinguishing Marks: Title: H.M Queen Victoria Born: May 24, 1819; Ascended the throne: June 20, 1837. Bottom left: Photo by Hughes & Mullins, Ryde IoW.

Condition: Very good, unfaded colours

Possible identity: Children recognize the Queen, but get the name wrong. (Queen Victory or Elizabeth I) Relationship to the present Queen usually unknown.

Reference Book: Dorothy Marshall: Life & Times of Victoria (1972)
More revealing is any of the many contemporary biographies, e.g: Anon: Our Noble Queen (Nelson,1899) - ingratiating but factual!

Museum: Osborne House, E.Cowes, Isle of Wight

Data: Grand-daughter of George III (see 093) and daughter of the Duke of Kent, Victoria succeeded two uncles, George IV and William IV in 1837, aged 18. She reigned for 63 years, until her death on January 22nd, 1901. Succeeded by her son Edward VII, she is the present Queen's great-great grandmother. In 1840 she married a cousin, the German Albert of of Saxe-Coburg, her Prince Consort. He attempted a liberal, progressive influence but was never popular, though his Great Exhibition of 1851 was a great success (00096). Albert died in 1861 and the Queen never ceased mourning, withdrawing from public appearances for many years to become very unpopular as the Widow of Windsor. She won the people over by sheer staying power and was created Empress of India in 1876. So many of her daughters and nieces married so many of the now lost crowned heads that she also became known as the Grandmother of Europe.

SHOE-HORN AND BUTTON-HOOK

Date: 1880 - 1914

Period: Victorian-Edwardian

From: Gift: Mr. K. Harris

Measurements: 235mm

Weight: 36gm

Materials: Ebony and steel

Location: H1

SIHC: 3.4

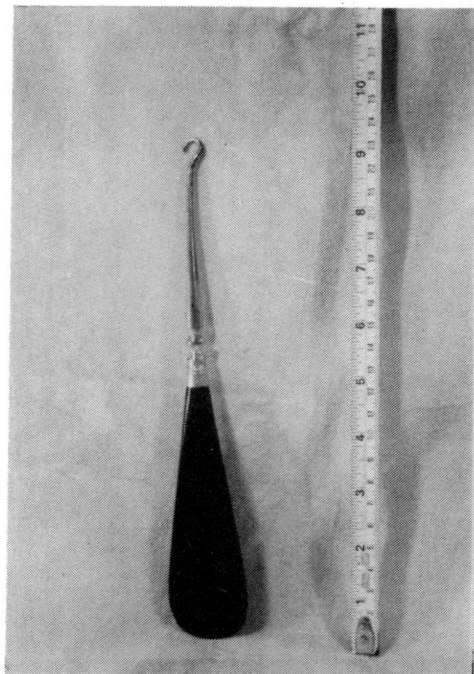

00037

Description: A two-ended instrument, half scooped in smooth black material, half in polished steel.

Distinguishing Marks: Marked EBONY

Condition: Excellent

Possible identity: Shoe-horn may be familiar, hook is difficult - some think of crochet or knitting.

Reference Books: Sue Brandon: Buttonhooks and Shoe-horns (Shire Album 122); Jackie Booker: Button-hooks. A Guide for the Collector (1982)

Museums: The Gallery of English Costume, Manchester; Blaise Castle House Museum, Bristol; Northampton Central Museum; The Buttonhook Society (Sec: Paul Moorehead, 222 Bishopsgate, London EC2 M4JS publishes a bi-monthly Newsletter, The Boutonneur)

Data: Buttons were in use in the 14th century and stiff Tudor doublets probably needed buttonhooks. The first printed reference to buttons is from 1611. Dating, before the 19th century is difficult and few examples survive. Men wore buttoned boots c1830s, setting a later women's fashion in the 1880s (See 00036). Bodices and gloves were also tightly buttoned. Victorian shopping Catalogues, as in other cases (See 00035), illustrate a wide variety of mass-produced shoe-horns and button-hooks, with a wide variety of materials, including silver. Shoe-horns or shoe-lifts were in use during Elizabeth I's reign and inns kept their own for the use of travellers. Softer shoes in the 17th century caused a decline in their use and most surviving examples date from Victorian times, using horn, silver, brass, ivory and ebony. Modern, plastic shoehorns are offered in most shoe-shops.

ROW OF PENNIES

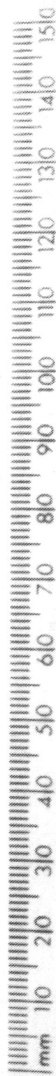

Photo: Frank Power

Dates: 1870-1967

From: Gift: Mr. H. Withers, Galata Coins, Wolverhampton

Weight: 14gm each

Location: H2

Period: Modern. Victorian to present

Measurements: Uniformly 30mm

Materials: Bronze

SIHC: 1.7

Description: Six pre-decimal pennies from successive reigns.

Distinguishing Marks: Royal titles and heads ; Dates on reverse.

Condition: Poor to almost mint condition.

Possible identity: Pre-decimal values and size unfamiliar to children.

Reference Book: P.J. Seaby & P.F. Purvey: Standard Catalogue of British Coins 1984

Museums: Try any Antique Fair. Some dealers give pre-decimal pennies away. A useful, large bag need cost no more than £1.

Data: The coins are pennies of: Victoria (1870 and 1896); Edward VII (1908); George V (1921); George VI (1937); Elizabeth II (1967). Left-right-left alternation of royal profiles reveals a missing right facing head between 1921 and 1937. This indicates the Abdication of George V's son, Edward VIII in 1936, (though oddly, he reversed the tradition by showing his preferred left profile.) Note persistence of royal titles: Dei Gratia and Fid. Def., but the omission by 1967 of (Britt. Omn.) Reg (in 1954), in deference to Commonwealth countries and Ind. Imp., after 1949. Copper pennies were first issued in 1797 (See 00093), adopting a familiar size and pattern in 1825 under George IV and William IV (dated on the obverse). Britannia appears on all early tails, but her lighthouse comes and goes. The date sometimes has a letter to denote a mint, e.g. H=Birmingham in 1912, 1918-19). A lighter, bronze coin was introduced with the Victoria bun penny of 1860 (as shown here). This was redesigned in 1895 with an "old head" of the Queen. The coinage was decimalized in 1971 with the issue of smaller 2,1 and ½ new pence (though 10 and 5p pieces were introduced in 1968 and the 50p piece in 1969. Farthings were demonetized in 1960, the old halfpenny in 1969, the new ½ p in 1986.

SHAVING MUG

Date: c1900+

Period: Edwardian

From: Mrs. Margaret F. West (Gift)

Measurements: Height: 102mm
Diameter: 83mm

Weight: 327gm

Materials: Moulded pot.

Location: H1

SIHC: 3.2

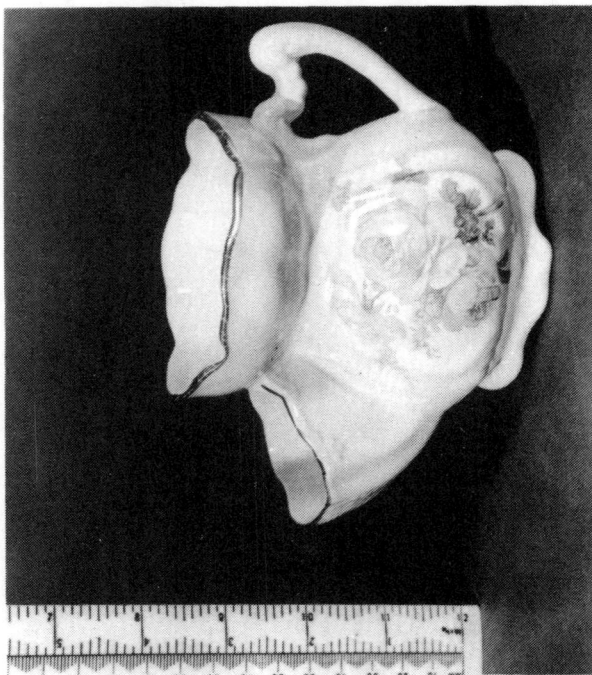

Photo: Frank Power

Description: A tubby little shaving mug, primrose tinted, floral decoration

Distinguishing Marks: Base-stamp: James Kent. Old Foley

Condition: Good, signs of wear on base indicate age.

Possible identity: Unfamiliar to children; cf. similar moustache cups.

Reference Books: J.P. Cushion: Pocket Book of English Ceramic Marks (1959); G.Godden: Encyclopedia of British Pottery and Porcelain Marks (1968); Gail Durbin: Wig, Hairdressing and Shaving Bygones (1984).

Museums: Stoke-on-Trent City Museum; Gladstone Pottery Museum, Longton, Staffs.

Data: Shaving mugs date from c1840, used by barbers and in the home. The mug holds hot water, (brought by servant or hotel boots in a brass jug), with upper ledge and drain-holes for soap and large lip for insertion of the shaving brush. Mugs were colourfully decorated, with floral patterns, pictures of famous towns and resorts (often Foreign made). They were moulded ware, painted by hand. A firm's back-stamp on a mug's base can be precisely dated by reference to books of ceramics marks. *England* denotes 1891+; *Made in England* is 1914+. Hieroglyphics, numbers and letters, are piece-marks, identifying the worker who decorated the mug at piece-work rates. Kent's firm was founded in 1897 and still trades under the same name after several changes of owners. Unfortunately, the archives of most Staffordshire potteries have been destroyed; only larger concerns, like Doulton, kept their own art-studios and designers, so pattern-books are rare. Smaller companies bought in ready-made patterns. The *Old Foley* pattern of shaving-mug is still in production, so that our example may well be a reproduction, more recent than Victorian.

COLUMBIA PHONOGRAPH

Date: 1900+

Period: Victorian/Edwardian

From: Loan: Miss K. Francis

Measurements: 310 x 203 x 160mm (Case)

Weight: 11,000gm

Materials:

Location: S2

Exit date:

SIHC: 2.8

Photo: Frank Power

Description: A heavy machine mounted on a wooden case, interior spring mechanism (Case hinges to open), domed wooden lid, carrying handle and crank-winder to screw into aperture on side of case. An aluminium cylinder (44mm diameter) is driven by a leather band. Soundbox, with diamond stylus, runs along concealed worm-drive, activated by same cogs which rotate cylinder. Levers operate brake and clutch mechanisms. Detachable wooden horn fits soundbox. Black iron frame has ornate floral painting, similar to sewing machines of the same period.

Condition: Still works.

Distinguishing Marks: Scroll label in gold: The Graphophone. On back, black-and-gold medallion: The Graphophone and Columbia Co. were awarded the Grand Prize at the Paris Exposition of 1900: cites patents May 7th 1886 - March 20th, 1897 for Columbia Phonograph Co, New York, London, Paris, Berlin

Possible identity: With cover, keeps children guessing - treasure-chest? sewing machine? Without cover uncertain - ironing-machine?

Reference Books: J. West: Telltale (1990); H. Thomas: Thomas Alva Edison (1959)

Museums: Woolstaplers' Hall Museum, Chipping Campden (Glos); National Sound Archive, London SW7

Data: Edison invented the phonograph in 1877 as an office dictaphone. Its immense popularity as entertainment surprised him - the office machines were a commercial failure. Prototypes were driven by batteries, water-power and treadle, early cylinders cut on tin foil; the first recording Mary had a Little Lamb. Discs, which replaced cylinders, were invented in 1894. The Army & Navy Stores (1907) offers models @ 30s. (£1.50), Gamages (1913) @ 3s.6d. (18p)! They also list disc-players.

CORONATION CUP (EDWARD VII)

Date: 1902

Period: Modern Edwardian

From: Loan: Mr. Daniel Skeath

Measurements: Height: 70mm
Diameter: 70mm
Saucer: 134mm

Weight: 220gm

Materials: Fine bone china

Location: H2

Exit Date:

SIHC: 1.1

Photo: Frank Power

00039

Description: A dainty cup and saucer in white bone china with gilt trim and commemorative inscription. Originally one of a set of 12.

Distinguishing Marks: Crown and royal cipher ERVII: 1902. When the (empty!) cup is held to the light, a photographic transparency of the King is seen.

Possible identity: Coronation is not mentioned

Reference Books: K. Middlemas: Life and Times of Edward VII (1972)

Museum: Central Museum & Art Gallery, Stoke-on-Trent; Waxwork tableaux at Warwick Castle.

Data: Edward VII (b.1841) was only son of Victoria and Prince Albert. After nominal attendance at three Universities, the Prince of Wales was sent to the Army in Ireland. A sexual exploit with an actress shocked his father, who died of typhoid in the same year. Victoria despised her weak-willed son, who, as heir for 60 years, became a compulsive glutton, gambler and womaniser. Gross and jovial, he involved the Crown in repeated scandals. His Queen, Alexandra, daughter of Christian IX, the impoverished King of Denmark, was elegant, deaf and long-suffering, taking a lifelong interest in hospital charities. Edward succeeded in 1901, his coronation postponed during an attack of appendicitis. His many royal relationships in Europe - the Kaiser and Tsar were nephews - influenced British foreign policy. His dislike of the Kaiser and Entente Cordiale with France set the scene for World War I, three years after his death. Edward gave his name to a more elegant, worldly era than the earlier Victorian mood. His eldest son, Albert, Duke of Clarence, mentally unstable, died in 1892; Edward VII was succeeded by the Duke of York in 1910 (039, 045)

SCHOOL ATTENDANCE MEDAL

Date: 1905

Period: Edwardian

From: Loan: Mr. H. Munn

Measurements: Diam: 38mm

Weight: 21gm

Materials: plated nickel alloy

Location: H1

Exit Date:

SIHC: 3.1

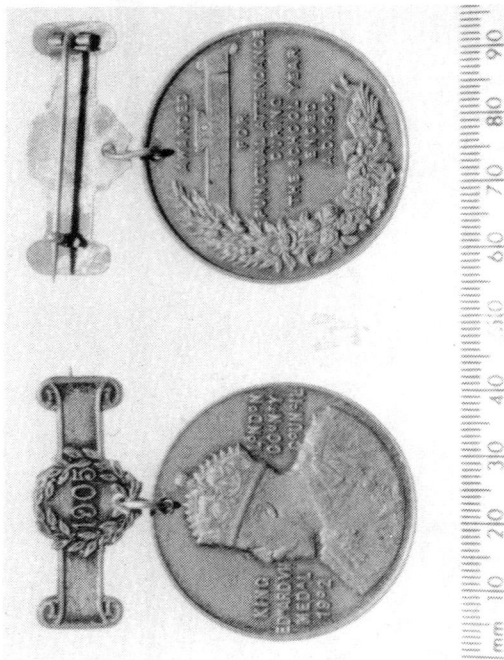

Photo: Frank Power

00033——————————————————

Description: A silver-coloured medal and clasp, lacking ribbon, clearly stating its function as an LCC School Attendance Medal of 1905.

Distinguishing Marks: Obverse: King Edward VII Medal 1902: London County Council : Reverse: Awarded to: R.Munn for punctual attendance during the school year ended AD 1905 ; Clasp: laurel wreath, 1905.

Condition: Fair - slightly scuffed.

Reference Books: Eric Jackson: A Short History of the LCC (1965); S. McLure: 100 Years of London Education, 1870-1970 (1970).

Museums: Museum of the History of Education, Leeds

Data: Counties, including London County Council, (LCC) founded in 1899, became Education Authorities by provision of the 1902 Education Act. London was reorganized as the Greater London Council in 1965, incorporating 31 London Boroughs with the Cities of London and Westminster. Under the GLC 20 Greater London Boroughs administered their own schools, and an Inner London Education Authority controlled 10 central boroughs. The GLC was abolished in 1986 - there is no London County - and ILEA will be disbanded in March 1990. State education became compulsory after the original 1870 Education Act, attendance being enforced by truant officers, local byelaws and the courts. Registers were a fetish - a post-war Headmistress remembers that in case of fire, teachers' first care must be for registers, her own priority being the Log Books. Victorian attendance medals and books as prizes for regular timekeeping and good conduct are fairly commonplace family relics. Our example was awarded to the lender's grandfather. Educational records of LCC are accessible at GLC Record Office, County Hall SE1 and will be transferred to the City of London

PHONOGRAPH CYLINDER AND BOX

Date: 1908+

Period: Edwardian

From: Personal, family collection; Original owner unknown.

Measurements: Length: 115mm
Diam: 65mm

Weight: 71gm

Materials: Shellac

Location: H1

SIHC: 2.8

Photo: Frank Power

Description: An almost exact cylinder, actually a slightly truncated cone, imperceptibly wider at one end. Grooves much as on a modern disc.

Condition: Good, but fragile. Plays clearly

Distinguishing Marks: Title printed in white on top rim. Soldiers in the Park; Band No.51 Other end: International phonograph and Indestructible Record Co. Ltd. Petit's Patent Box: has Thomas A. Edison's name and photograph; National Phonograph Co., Orange N.J: USA Patent dates 1900-08

Possible identity: Obvious, as stated on box.

Reference Books: Many facsimile editions by City of London Phonograph: Edison Bell Phonograph Co.1905 Catalogue (1965); Edisonia Ltd. 1885 Price-list (1966); Catalogue of Edison Phonographs & Accessories 1909 (1981) also: Sydney H. Bayley: List of all Edison Blue Amberol Cylinder Records (1978).

Museums: The National Sound Archive, 29 Exhibition Road, London SW7 2AS

Data: Thomas Alva Edison, (1847-1931) born in Ohio, invented the first sound-recording process after 1877. He was also involved in the development of light-bulbs, telephone, cameras and electric generators. The recording described here still works. For the Phonograph machine to play this cylinder on, see 00043. Even empty cylinder boxes are highly priced by dealers! These cylinders take very unkindly to central heating and should be kept cool and dry. Beware of the slightly truncated cone shape, as offering the mis-named cylinder to the machine by the imperceptibly narrower end causes breakage.

GEORGE V PICTURE POSTCARD

Date: 1911

Period: Modern

From: Gift: Miss M. Roberts

Measurements: 140 x 89mm

Weight: 7gm

Materials: Light card

Location: S2

SIHC: 1.1

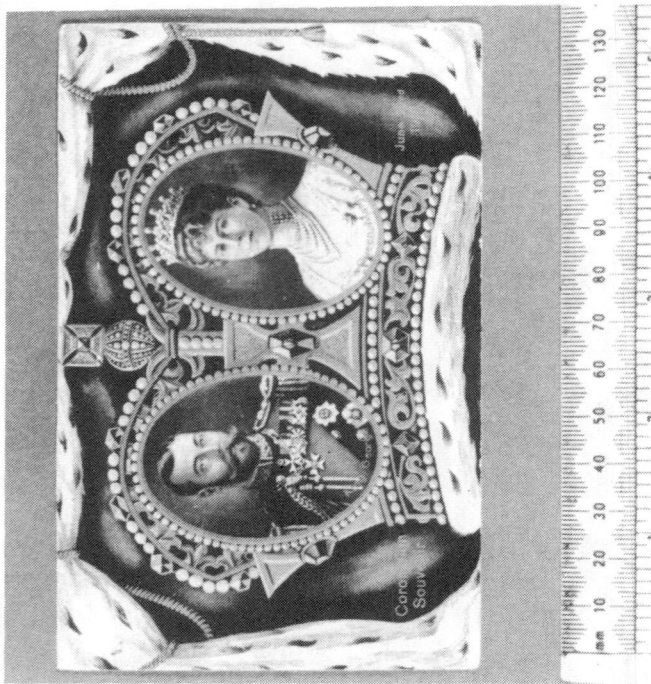

Description: Coloured postcard commemorating Coronation of George V and Queen Mary in 1910, sent to Miss M. Roberts at Prescot in 1911

Distinguishing Marks: Published by Raphael Tuck and Sons, Art Publishers to their Majesties the King and Queen. Biographical notes; postmark AU 11 (August 1911). Pencilled message from seaside. Front as shown in picture: Coronation Souvenir

Reference Books: Denis Judd: The Life and Times of George V (1973)

Museums: See Royal waxworks at Madame Tussaud's.

Data: By a persistent accidental English royal tradition, George, Duke of York and a naval officer, became king as second son, after the death of the Duke of Clarence, and married his elder brother's fiancé, Princess Mary of Teck. He reigned from 1910-36, a staid, gruff man who restored a dependable air of respectability to the Crown, after the raffish behaviour of his father Edward VII. George V reigned during the First World War, changing the Royal family's German name of Guelph to the present house of Windsor. During the 1930s the King established the tradition of a Christmas radio broadcast. Unlike his son and successors, George V never went on overseas goodwill visits; he loathed abroad (and even Bognor, which was the subject of the King's only two-word, memorable epithet!) The Silver Jubilee of 1935 was a joyful holiday for schools. He worried about the trendy clothes and irresponsible behaviour of his eldest son, David, Prince of Wales. Remembered as an affectionate grandfather by the Queen, George V was feared by his son, who succeeded him as Edward VIII, but abdicated in the same year, 1936 in favour of his younger brother, the Duke of York. (George VI, the present Queen's father.) Queen Mary, an avid collector of jewels and antiques lived on as Queen Mother until 1953.

FRENCH STEEL HELMET

Date: 1915-16

Period: Modern: First World War

From: Mrs. Jacqueline Ivell (Gift).

Measurements: Diam: 230mm
                Length: 280mm

Weight: 650gm

Materials: Steel

Location: H1

SIHC: 1.8

Photo: Linda Burridge

Description: A rather small steel helmet, painted olive-green, with leather interior cap; strap missing.

Distinguishing Marks: Badge: RF (Republique Francaise) and grenade

Condition: Scratched and dented, not in war, but by teachers' Courses!.

Possible identity: Military use obvious, but shape and nationality less familiar to children.

Reference Books:

Museums: The Museum in the market place of Ypres has relics, models, diorama etc. of the Western Front.

Data: The helmet belonged to Mrs. Ivell's great-uncle, Gaston Masdebrieu, a soldat, poilu or private soldier in the French 366th Regiment of Infantry. He served with his brothers Valentin and Louis and won the Croix de Guerre and Medaille Militaire. Other souvenirs of his service include several faded sepia photographs of French soldiers in the trenches, with pencilled notes. These place Gaston in the French sector of the Artois front during the Anglo-French offensive of Summer 1915. His 4th Squadron, 3rd Platoon was dug in, facing Souchez and Vimy Ridge; several photographs are labelled Labyrinth. This was a massive German fortified section of deep trenches, a maze of barbed wire and underground passages, site of terrific fighting between French and Germans during 1915. The pictures show German trenches of the first and second line, captured by his regiment. In this offensive and the corresponding British push to the north around Ypres, the French lost 192,000 men, the British 60,000. Gaston returned, badly wounded, Louis was gassed and Valentin was lost in September 1916, during the murderous battles of Verdun. The only record of his death was: *Disparu*, and a certificate: *Mort pour la France.*

1914-1945 WAR MEDALS

Date: 1918-1945

Period: Modern; World Wars I-II

From: Teacher's collection

Measurements: 35mm diameter

Weight: 130gm (altogether)

Materials: Silver, bronze, nickel, silk ribbons

Location: H6

SIHC: 3.2

Photo: Frank Power

Description: Three British medals, mounted on a single bar or brooch, with pin. One is heavy silver, the second bronze, the third nickel.

Distinguishing Marks: Medal 1: Head of George V Britt Omn Rex et Ind Imp; Reverse; horseman, 1914-1918 Medal 2: Angel obverse. Reverse: The Great War for Civilization, 1914-1919. Both rims engraved with soldier's number, rank, name and regiment. Ribbons: (1) Orange stripe, bordered blue-black-white (2) Rainbow. Medal 3: Head: George VI Reverse: The Defence Medal 1939-45, coat-of-arms.

Condition: Fair - ribbons grubby.

Reference Books: John West: Telltale (1990)

Museums: Royal Hampshire Regiment's Museum, Southgate St., Winchester.

Data: These medals were awarded to the author's father. The data on the rims are: 42422/PTE/A.T.WEST/2ND BN. Hants Regt. (i.e: a Private soldier of the Second Battalion of the Hampshire Regiment). Alfred having volunteered at 16 in 1914, his angry father got him out, but he went again next year and served doggedly on the Somme. He always said that his platoon officer once wrote him down for the Military Medal, but was blown up immediately after. He was always disappointed that his delayed service did not qualify for the full set of three medals - Pip, Squeak and Wilfred, (the first two here plus the Mons Star of 1914.) Having served in the occupation army for two years, he returned an ardent pacifist with a scholarly command of German language and literature. Still shell-shocked, he told his son terrible tales of the trenches. In old age he remembered only the comradeship of the Western Front, regularly attending regimental Remembrance parades at Winchester. The Defence Medal was for service with the Observer Corps in 1942-4.

BOX BROWNIE CAMERA

Date: 1916-1953

Period: Pre-war

From: Gift: John F. Skeath

Measurements: 146 x 88 x 101mm

Weight: 467gm

Materials: Wood, cardboard, imitation leather, tin, metal fittings

Location: S1

SIHC: 2.8

Photo: Frank Power

00094

Description: A neat rectangular black box covered in leatherette. Circular aperture on front end, various metal fittings in chrome metal and small glass view-finders top and side, red window at back for numbered film. Metal plate identifies: No.2 Brownie, Model E, made in USA by Eastman Kodak Co.Rochester N.Y.USA. Opens at back to release inner tin casing with spools at each end, connected to outer winder; corresponding lens-aperture in wooden front.

Condition: Excellent working order. Dust and oil occasionally.

Distinguishing Marks: Makers' labels and US Patents listed Apr 14, 1903 - Mar 22, 1916

Possible identity: Probably unfamilar as a camera to modern children.

Reference Books: Peter Johnson: Phillips Guide to Tomorrow's Antiques (1987)

Museums: British Photographic Museum, Totnes (Devon)

Data: In 1884, George Eastman, a New York banker, founder of the Kodak Company, invented roll-film on celluloid and, in 1888, a cheap box camera, sold for £1 or 5 shillings (25p). The Brownie sold more than 100,000 in the first year, to become the most popular camera of the 1920-30s. Kodak (a meaningless name, chosen as easily pronounced in any language) introduced send-away commercial processing, when most amateurs developed and printed their own 120 film. The simple lens and rotary shutter of this 1930s model still produce prints on 120 film, available from local photography shops. Brownies were still sold during the 1950s, but in 1963 Kodak introduced the revolutionary Instamatic, with simple cartridge-loading. This saw the end of the box-camera; thousands were thrown away, they are now low-priced collectors' items.

CIGARETTE CARD

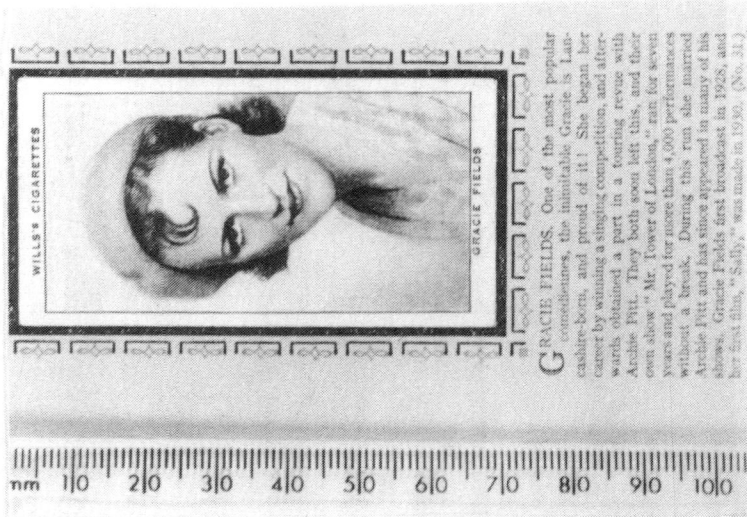

Date: 1934

Period: Pre-World War Two

From: Antique Fair (Album:£2.00)

Measurements: Album: 350 x 180mm
Card 70mm x 38mm

Weight: 2gm

Materials: Light card with adhesive back

Location: S2

SIHC: 3.2

Photo: Frank Power

WILLS'S CIGARETTES

GRACIE FIELDS

GRACIE FIELDS. One of the most popular comediennes, the inimitable Gracie is Lancashire-born, and proud of it! She began her career by winning a singing competition, and afterwards obtained a part in a touring revue with Archie Pitt. They both soon left this, and their own show "Mr. Tower of London," ran for seven years and played for more than 4,000 performances without a break. During this run she married Archie Pitt and has since appeared in many of his shows. Gracie Fields first broadcast in 1928, and her first film, "Sally," was made in 1930. (No. 31.)

Description: A typical cigarette card from a page of Wills's 1d. (Old) Penny (= 0.42p) Album for 50 Radio Celebrities. Shows Lancashire singer-comedienne, Gracie Fields. Album's text as printed on adhesive back of card

Condition: Good

Distinguishing Marks: Wills Cigarettes, artiste's name and biography. The album has 3 celebrities per page.

Possible identity: Modern children will be more familiar with similar modern trade-cards, e.g. for tea.

Reference Books: Frank Doggett: Cigarette Cards and Novelties (1981). London Cigarette Card Co's: (annual) Catalogue of Cigarette Cards (1988: £6.50) and: Catalogue of British Trade Cards (1988: £3.95); Murray's: 1988 Guide to Cigarette Card Values.

Museums: The British Museum will one day inherit the largest (more than 1 million) private collection in the world, as the first cigarette cards Museum. Rochdale Museum has Gracie Fields memorabilia.

Data: Cigarette cards were the greatest collecting craze of pre-war years. Small boys hung around tobacconists' doors to beg customers for cards, mint-new from the packet, or swopped grubby doubles with their friends. Sets were usually 32 cards, with an album for one old penny. Some firms, like Kensitas, produced luxury sets such as Flags of All Nations on silk; Peter Scott painted Players' Wildfowl. Most series, eg: Dickens's characters, motor-cars, Royalty, Medals etc. were very informative. A Lancashire lass, Our Gracie, star of music-hall, radio and British films, recorded on the Rex label, broad comic songs like The biggest aspidistra on one side, tremolo Sally-type songs on the other. She fell into disgrace with the patriotic British public for escaping to America, saving her Italian husband from internment.

GEORGE VI PICTURE POSTCARD

Date: 1937

Period: Recent past (Pre-war)

From: Gift, Miss M. Roberts

Measurements: 90mm x 148mm

Weight: 7gm

Materials: Thin card

Location: H2

SIHC: 1.1

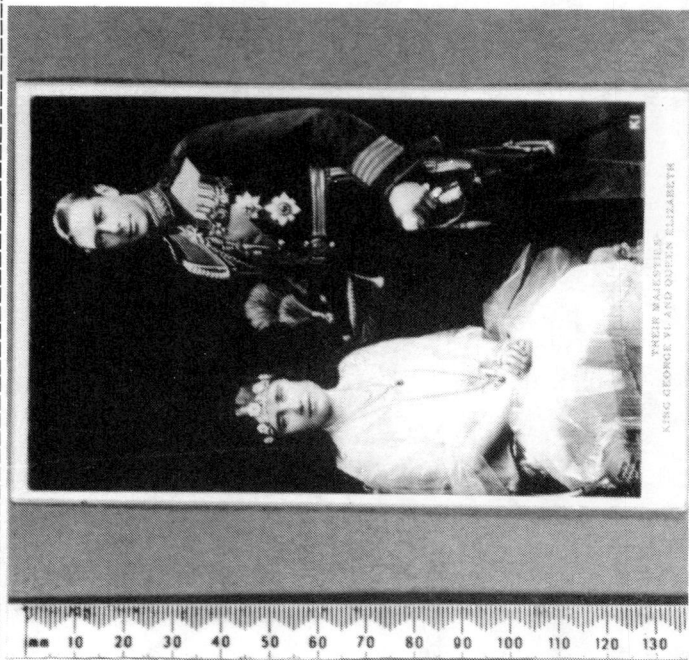

KING GEORGE VI AND QUEEN ELIZABETH
THEIR MAJESTIES

Photo: Frank Power

Description: A finely coloured photograph of Their Majesties King George VI and Queen Elizabeth, almost certainly a Coronation souvenir. The King wears the uniform of a Marshal of the RAF.

Distinguishing Marks: Valentine's Post Card, printed in GB (Trade mark); This is a real photograph

Condition: Excellent; unfaded and unused

Reference Books: Stanley Gibbons Postcard Catalogue (5th Edition 1987); Keith Middlemas: George VI (1974)

Museums: Polesden Lacy, Surrey; Osborne House, IoW; The Royal Mews, London.

Data: George VI (1895-1952) was second son of George V. As Prince Albert, said by his family tutor to be a scatterbrain, he was educated at Osborne Naval College (where he was 68th out of 68 cadets), at Dartmouth and Trinity College, Cambridge. He served at the naval Battle of Jutland, then as an air cadet at Cranwell. As Duke of York, he was keenly interested in boys' welfare, Summer camps and a tennis player of All England championship standard. He married Lady Elizabeth Bowes Lyon, youngest daughter of the Earl of Strathmore in 1923. A shy man, with a painful stammer, he never expected to become King, until his elder brother, David Prince of Wales, abdicated as King Edward VIII, in 1936. The new King and Queen never left London during the German Blitz and set an example of quiet family life with their daughters, Princess Elizabeth and Margaret Rose. The King opened the Festival of Britain in 1951, but died suddenly in the next year. His widow survives him as Queen Mother, now 90 years old and great-grandmother of Princes William and Henry.

CORONATION (GEORGE VI) SHAVING-MUG

Date: 1937

Period: Modern

From: Gift: PTA evening

Measurements: Height: 108mm
Diameter: 77mm

Weight: 362gm

Materials: Plain white china

Location: H1

SIHC: 1.1

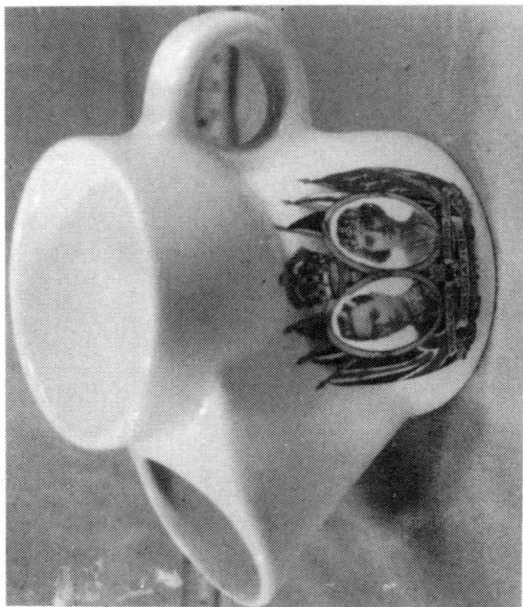

Photo: Linda Burridge

00040

Description: A simple commemorative mug of a cheap white pattern, with coloured emblem applied as a Coronation souvenir.

Distinguishing Marks: No potter's marks; Coronation date and data as shown.

Possible identity: See Cards 00025 and 00046

Reference Books: Mary & Geoffrey Payton: Observer's Book of Pottery and Porcelain (1973)

Data: This item may cause teachers some surprise, considering its relatively late date as a shaving mug. This is not unusual - mugs have been made continually from Victorian times to the present day. It would be a useful local survey to enquire from children which of their elderly relatives can remember last using an open razor (00028) or hotwater from a shaving mug - and at what dates. Grimwades of Stoke-on-Trent were still making mugs for use in the late 1930s. Is this item then, only an ornamental Coronation souvenir? There are many more old-fashioned inventions and utensils which continue in daily use long after a more modern development had taken place - 78 rpm gramophone records were produced - with brand-new wind-up machines for playing them -alongside LPs, stereo and hi-fi, until the end of the 1950s. Continuing production of pen-nibs and fountain-pens since the invention of the Biro is a similar example. Another interesting line of discussion is the Royal aspect of this item and so many more family relics. What does this tell us about ordinary people's views of the relative (commercial?) importance or popularity of the English monarchy.

CIVILIAN RESPIRATOR (GAS-MASK)

Date: 1938-9

Period: World War Two

From: Birmingham City Museum
Schools Loan Service

Measurements: Length: 240mm
Diameter: 85mm

Weight: 320gm

Materials: Rubber, canvas, micah, metal,
chemicals, wadding

WARNING: DO NOT ENCOURAGE CHILDREN
TO WEAR THIS RESPIRATOR : ITS FILTER
CONTAINS ASBESTOS!

Location: M1

Exit Date:

SIHC: 1.8

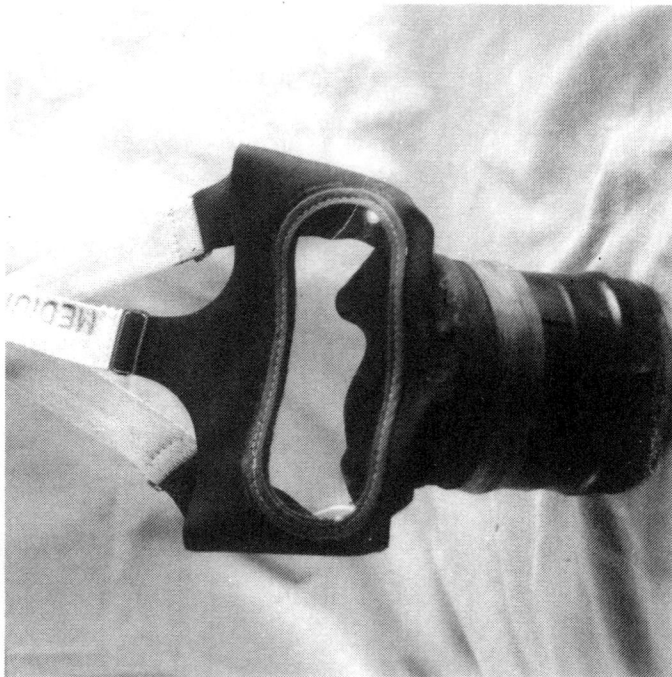

Photo : Linda Burridge

00008

Description: Black rubber face-mask with transparent window and canvas straps. Fastened to the snout by a rubber band, is a metal drum, with perforated green base. A white filling is visible.

Condition: Mint condition - unused

Distinguishing Marks: Size Medium on strap; On face-mask: 9192; HENLEY 6-38 Z. On rubber band: POPPE LOT 3056 19.8.39

Reference Books: Barbara Nixon: Raiders Overhead (1943) Tom Harrison: Living through the Blitz (1978)

Museums: Birmingham City Museum; Coventry City Museum & Art Gallery

Data: It is difficult now, to recall the near-panic apprehension of air-raids in the pre-war years. The fear was almost as great as the more recent fear of nuclear warfare. There was widespread conviction, spread by writers like H.G. Wells, that "the bombers will get through"; a fear confirmed by savage Japanese attacks on China, Italian bombing of Abyssinians, German practice in the Spanish Civil War - and RAF punitive raids in the Middle East and NW Frontier of India. Most of all, people feared gas attack - familiar to some old soldiers of 1918. During 1936-39, successive crises over Hitler's spreading power in Europe made air-raids seem more and more probable. Notice that this civilian respirator was made in 1938-9, when 38,000,000 were issued in square cardboard boxes. A special line for children 2-5 came in a Mickey Mouse box! At the outbreak of war, it became illegal not to carry your gasmask everywhere. There were, supposedly, special masks for farm-horses and dogs. In fact, gas was never used in air-raids on England. Which was just as well, as the respirators were full of asbestos filters. DO NOT TRY THEM ON!

BABY'S RESPIRATOR (GAS-MASK)

Date: 1939

Period: World War Two

From: Birmingham Museum
School Loans Collection

Measurements: Length: 558mm
Width: 356mm

Weight: 3636gm

Materials: Metal, canvas, rubber

Location: M1

Exit Date:

SIHC: 1.8

Photo: Linda Burridge

00009

Description: A metal frame, holding a rubberised canvas bag with drawstring. A micah window is rigidly rivetted to a black rubber surround. To the right of the bag is a rubber concertina pump fastened to a perforated metal drum; these are joined to the bag by an L-shaped rubber tube.

Condition: Very slightly perished and very grubby. Smells horrible!

Distinguishing Marks: Several official stamps: On pump: WD broad arrows and NBR Co.1939 On bag: L&BR Co.1939; Lot 90 L74, On reverse of frame: A brass plate reminding the parent that this appliance is Government property, to be kept in good condition and returned to Local Authority when no longer required. On rubber strap: L & BR Co: Apr.1939, and Lot 127:L226

Reference Books: Arthur Marwick: The Home Front (1976) John Simkin: Contemporary Accounts of the Second World War (1984)

Museums: Museum of London, London Wall; Derbyshire Museums Loans Service.

Data: Surely one of the most gruesome relics of any war, fortunately never to be used, as there were no gas attacks on Britain. It has been alleged that panic-issue of gasmasks was an attempt at peace-at-any-price by Government, to frighten voters into acceptance of further negotiation with Hitler. As any child will ask: "What if Baby was more than 20" long?" Prams were available with tin roofs and a chimney.

DAILY MIRROR (1939)

Date: 4th September 1939

Period: World War Two

From: Teacher's personal collection

Measurements: Length: 365mm
Width: 300mm

Weight: 70gm

Materials: Paper

Location: H1

SIHC: 1.7

Daily Mirror

BRITAIN'S FIRST DAY OF WAR: CHURCHILL IS NEW NAVY CHIEF

POLES ATTACK

"BREMEN IS CAPTURED"

Petrol Will Be Rationed

The King to His People

Photo: Frank Power

00007 —————————————

Description: Recognizably the same Daily Mirror as today, though without present-day colour and priced One Penny (= 1/2p), now 20p.

Condition: Fragile; yellowing, edges tattered.

Distinguishing Marks: Dated and explicit

Reference Books: Benn's Press Directory. Willings's Press Guide

Museums: The British (Newspaper) Library, Collindale, London.

Data: The Daily Mirror was the most popular wartime newspaper, especially amongst the Forces. It was an early tabloid, often critical of authority, with a reputation for cheerful, cheeky good humour. Note how prominently Churchill is featured, though not yet P.M. The King's message (p.3) urges "his people to stand calm and united". There is news of rationing of Pool, (one-brand only) petrol - no amount given, but priced at 1s.6d (7 ½ p) a gallon. Pictures show Londoners calmly queuing for underground air-raid shelters after Sunday's first sirens - a false alarm, and the first war-wedding, of a private soldier and ATS girl. Parents are encouraged not to worry about their evacuated children and most people are carrying gasmasks. A final Don't Worry instruction advises readers not to listen to rumours or spread information. "Enemy ears are listening to you - Even if a bomb falls in your street - Keep smiling!" Jane's famous soft-porn cartoon-strip too, becomes warlike!

ARP WARDEN'S HELMET

Date: 1940

Period: World War Two

From: Birmingham Museum
Schools Loans Service

Measurements: Length: 305mm
Diameter: 253mm

Weight: 1136gm

Materials: Steel, leather, rubber

Location: M1

Exit Date:

SIHC: 1.8

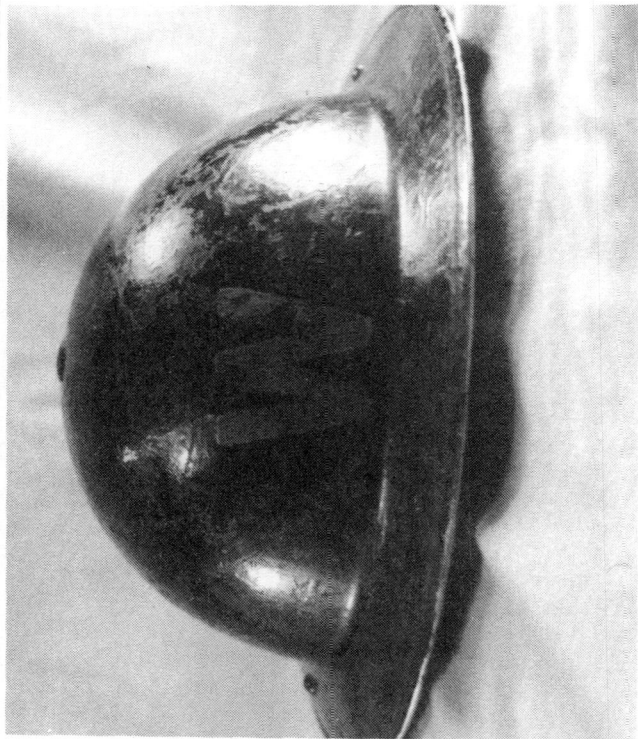

Photo: Linda Burridge

Description: A normal British military steel helmet, painted black. Inside is a rubber and canvas headband, with rubber shock absorbers.

Condition: Paintwork badly scratched but serviceable.

Distinguishing Marks: White-painted **W** (= Warden), front and back.

Reference Books: Staffordshire LEA: Staffordshire in Wartime 1939-1945. Local History Source Book No.8 (1970); Arthur Marwick: The Home Front (1976)

Museums: Imperial War Museum, London; The Museum of London, London Wall; Helston's Theme Park includes Britain in the Blitz a vivid recreation of a wartime street.

Data: As early as 1935, Government issued an Air Raid Precautions Pamphlet; the ARP service was set up in 1937 and mobilized during the Munich crisis of 1938. By March 1939, 1½ million men and women had volunteered for Civil Defence. During September under-table shelters and stirrup-pumps were issued, 400,000 pets put down and 13,000 women and children evacuated from London. The Blitz did not begin until August 1940; during October 200-500 tons of German bombs were dropped on London, with 30,000 dead in September-November. The Auxiliary Fire Services (AFS), ambulance crews and Air-raid wardens (hated at first for their rigid enforcement of blackout - "Put that light OUT") coped magnificently. 1½ million Londoners were homeless by May 1941, by June 2 million houses had been bombed (60% in London). Bristol, Coventry, Southampton, Liverpool, Exeter still bear the scars of bombing - as do Dresden, Berlin, Hanover, and, most of all, Hiroshima and Nagasaki.

DAILY MIRROR (1940)

Date: 16th August 1940

Period: World War Two

From: Teacher's collection

Measurements: Length: 385mm
Width: 293mm

Weight: 31gm

Materials: Paper

Location: H1

SIHC: 1.7

This page is reproduced by permission of
Mirror Group Newspapers

Photo: Frank Power

00078

Description: Reduced in size from 24 pages to 12 since the first day of the war (cf 0007), but still the same tabloid as before - and since. The headline refers to the height of the Battle of Britain.

Condition: Fragile; slightly yellowing.

Distinguishing Marks: Headline and date

Reference Books: John West: Telltale (1990). Len Deighton: Fighter (1977)

Museums: Battle of Britain Museum, Hendon.

Data: France conquered by May 1940, the Germans occupied most of Europe, including Denmark, Norway and the Channel Islands. Hitler expected Britain to make peace. His Operation Sealion, the plan for invasion by sea was never realistic, but Hitler's deputy, Goering aimed to destroy any possibility of RAF resistance. His Eagle Attack - the Germans insist that this was never a Battle - first attempted to cripple the RAF's south-eastern airfields and lasted for 3 months. The Battle reached a climax on 15th September (Battle of Britain Day), when 200 Spitfires and Hurricanes and 500 German aircraft contested the sky above London. Both sides exaggerated their kills - the final British claim for day reported here was 182 Germans shot down - now officially recognized as 75. The Luftwaffe claimed 101 RAF aircraft destroyed (in fact 47 - not 27!). As September ended, the weather deteriorated and German invasion was indefinitely postponed. Air-attack turned to night-raids on cities like London, Coventry, Liverpool and Southampton. Churchill's tribute to Fighter Command: "never in the field of human conflict was so much owed by so many to so few" was hard-earned by very young, exhausted pilots. Merely by staying intact Fighter Command had won the Battle of Britain.

– 219 –

WAR WEAPONS WEEK BADGE

Date: 1940

Period: World War Two

From: Birmingham Museum
Schools Loans Service

Measurements: Diam: 30mm

Weight: 4gm

Materials: Painted tin (red, white, black),
steel pin

Location: M1

Exit Date:

SIHC: 1.8

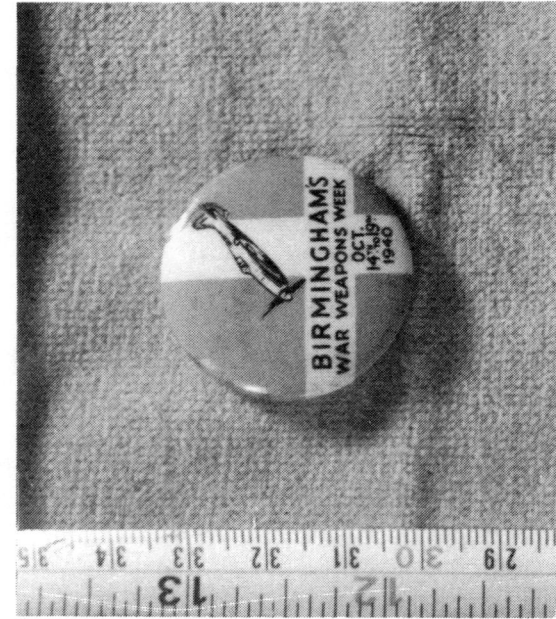

Photo: Linda Burridge

00024

Description: A typical modern lapel-badge (though not plastic). Painted pattern and words as seen on photograph. (Today, for the same price one would get self-adhesive paper!)

Condition: Good

Distinguishing Marks: As seen: Dated October 14th-19th 1940; Birmingham identity

Possible identity: Self-evident: donor's badge

Reference Books: Frank R. Setchfield: The Official Badge Collectors' Book from the 1890s to 1980s (1986)

Museums: Birmingham Museum

Data: Large-scale local collections were a regular feature of wartime Britain, with Wings for Victory, War Weapons Weeks, Aid to Russia and Spitfire Funds a speciality. Civic programmes included military parades with bands, set targets, concerts and usually an excitable, Garden Fete atmosphere. Thomas Fattorini Ltd.made tens of thousands of these badges from 1940-41, including luminous blackout badges. Other wartime efforts included the removal of many beautiful sets of Victorian railings and ornamental wrought-iron gates from parks, stately homes and simple town terraces, as salvage for recycling as war material. People were also persuaded to give up their aluminium pots and pans to be made into Spitfires.

PIECE OF ANTI-AIRCRAFT SHRAPNEL

Date: 1941

Period: World War Two

From: Family collection of
Mr. and Mrs. F.E. Roberts,
17, Columbia Rd., Prescot
(Lancs) : Gift

Measurements: Length: 80mm
Width: 25mm

Weight: 43gm

Materials: Steel

Location: H3

SIHC: 1.8

Photo: Frank Power

Description: A very sharp, jagged, irregular-shaped piece of metal. Smooth on the inner and outer surfaces, almost crystalline or laminated between.

Condition: A broken fragment, slightly rusted.

Distinguishing Marks: None

Reference Books: Peter Lewis: A People's War (1986); Arthur Marwick: The Home Front (1976); Bombers over Merseyside; the Authoritative record of air-raids on Liverpool (1943) at The Labour History Museum, Liverpool (From Liverpool Post & Echo)

Museums: Walker Museum & Art Gallery, Liverpool

Data: This sharp fragment whizzed through a home's roof-top skylight during a noisy German air-raid on Liverpool, 9 miles away. No bombs fell nearby, this is a fragment of British anti-aircraft shell, sometimes as dangerous as German bombs! Grandmother Mrs Roberts took this as a personal affront - "It might have hurt someone!" From Saturday August 17th 1940, when the first bombs fell on Caryl Street, until the height of the Blitz in May 1941, 2,715 Liverpudlians were killed and 2,293 seriously injured. There were also heavy casualties on other parts of Merseyside - Birkenhead and Wallasey. 120,000 homes were destroyed. In the late 1960s the painted walls of schools' basement swimming pools - used as air-raid mortuaries - still showed the shadow of grim headings Dead Males; Dead Females etc. An Emergency Committee was given considerable powers, meeting 3 times a day. By 1943, the City's recovery was said to be remarkable.

WARTIME UTILITY LABEL

Date: 1941+

Period: World War Two

From: Birmingham Museum
Schools Loan Service

Measurements: 45mm x 82mm

Materials: Coarse cloth

Location: M1

Exit Date:

SIHC: 3.3

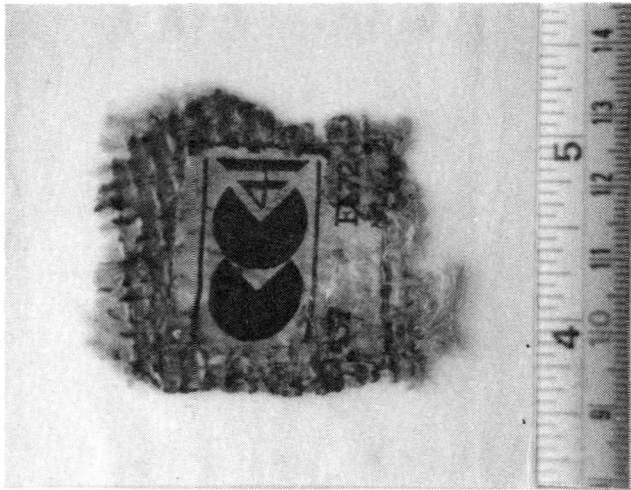

Photo: Linda Burridge

00015

Description: A fragment of cloth, mounted for display, to show the wartime Utility label.

Condition: Fragmentary, but clearly readable.

Distinguishing Marks: Two segmented circles, Cs or cheeses, (Civilian Clothing) and 41 (1941)

Reference Books: Raynes Minns; Bombers and Mash (1980)

Museums: The Victoria & Albert Museum, London (Gallery 40) has a large collection of Utility clothes, some on display. See also The Geffrye Museum, Kingsland Road, Shoreditch, London E2

Data: In 1940, the Government passed a Limitation of Supplies Order, restricting production of luxuries - cosmetics, razor-blades, paper-clips, cups, buckets, kettles, prams, clocks, toys, in fact, almost all useful, everyday items - to save precious raw materials. Clothes and bedding went on points or coupons. In Autumn 1941, the Utility scheme recruited top designers to make furniture and clothing of simple, economic design. The first Utility designs were pots and pans, then textiles, lastly, in 1942, furniture, only 22 items in three designs. Furniture permits were issued for newly-weds, bombed-out families and expectant parents. Units were allocated (6 for a dining table, 5 for a bed etc). By May 1942 80% of all clothing produced was Utility-wear. Some Utility goods were clumsy stuff, some was clean-cut and well-proportioned. It is still possible to find pieces of furniture at antique fairs and junk shops, branded with this CC41 mark.

ARP IDENTITY CARD

Date: 1940-42

Period: World War Two

From: Birmingham Museum
Schools Loans Service

Measurements: Length: 102mm
Width: 77mm

Materials: Light card, pink, printed

Location: M1

Exit Date:

SIHC: 3.1

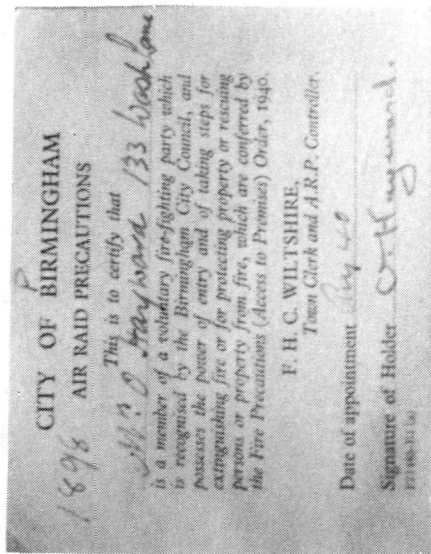

Photo: Linda Burridge

00016

Description: As seen in photograph

Condition: Clean

Distinguishing Marks: As seen. Note Birmingham identity, Town Clerk as Air Raid Precautions Controller. Stamp shows Mrs. Hayward's later training in fire-fighting. Dated August '40 and 19/8/42 FG

Possible identity: self-evident: Dated

Reference Books: Raynes Minns: Bombers and Mash (1980). Barbara Nixon: Raiders Overhead (1943). Tom Harrisson: Living through the Blitz (1978). Jane Waller & M. Vaughan-Rees: Women at War (1987)

Museums: Cobbaton Combat Vehicles Museum, Chittlehampton (N.Devon) has Home Front and Mums at War sections.

Data: Much local archive material - leaflets, committee minutes, instruction manuals etc. survives in Reference Libraries, on air-raid precautions, food rationing, Home Guard, evacuees and the home front in general. The main force of the Blitz was from 1940 until Summer 1941, when ordinary people of London, Birmingham, Coventry, Liverpool, Southampton etc. were genuinely in the front line and more civilians (45,000) died than soldiers. Women played a vital part in civil defence, factories and women's services; they were conscripted from December 1941. Feminists, never there, now complain that women's liberation by war service was a "con", over-rated by wartime propaganda. This is not so, as many elderly male ex-soldiers and factory workers remember.

78 rpm GRAMOPHONE RECORD

Date: 1940-41

Period: World War Two

From: Gift: Mr. W.H. Skinner

Measurements: Diameter: 257mm (whole disc)

Weight: 218gm

Materials: Shellac

Location: H1

SIHC: 2.8

Photo: Frank Power

00006

Description: Typical 1940s 10" gramophone record of Vera Lynn on the blue Decca label. Recorded electrically at 78 rpm: *When the Lights go on again*

Condition: Reasonable, though scuffed surface; no cracks - playable

Distinguishing Marks: Title, artiste and band all clearly marked. Most important, as dating evidence, is the serial no. (F8241). Use this by reference to printed discographies, to find exact (to the day) date of any record.

Reference Books: Brian Rust: Discography of Historical Records on cylinders and 78s (1979; See also sleeve notes to EMI's (HMV) LP of Vera Lynn - Hits of the Blitz (1962); Eric Thomas Bryant: Collecting Gramophone Records (1978); Nance Lui Fyson: Growing up in the Second World War. (1981); Vera Lynn: Vocal Refrain (1976)

Data: The popular songs of World War II were never as memorable as those of the 1914-18 war. They vary from over-optimistic numbers: *We're going to hang out the washing on the Seigfried Line*, immediately before Dunkirk! to wives' nostalgia over *A lovely weekend* in *Room 504*, for the nightingale which sang in Berkeley Square, a longing for the end of war when *There'll be bluebirds over the white cliffs of Dover* or this reference to wartime blackout. Oddly, the most popular British soldiers' song of all - *Lilli Marlene* - was taken from the Germans. Vera Lynn - now Dame Vera - travelled to Burma and other war-theatres to entertain troops and was, justifiably, the British Forces' Sweetheart.

Date: 1945

Period: World War Two

From: Pupil's collection
Christopher Guyver. Loan

Measurements: Length: Ribbon: 76mm
Star: 44mm

Weight: 19gm

Materials: Inferior bronze alloy

Location: H2

Exit Date:

SIHC: 3.2/1.8

Photo: Frank Power

00011———————

Description: Two campaign Stars, engraved on the obverse, blank on reverse

Condition: Good

Distinguishing Marks: Crown: GRI VI: France and Germany Star/1939-45 Star. Unlike earlier British medals, the reverse sides are blank, and there is no engraving of the soldier's name, rank, regiment or number. The adoption of an almost identical Star for each wartime campaign is also mediocre.

Ribbons: Narrow blue-white-red and broader navy blue-red-RAF blue.

Reference Books: Donald Hall: British Orders, Decorations and Medals (1973); E.C. Joslin: British Orders, Decorations and Medals (1976) (gives valuations); Observers Book of British Awards and Medals

Museums: Royal Hampshire Regimental Museum Southgate Street, Winchester.

Data: The 1939-45 Star was given for separate campaigns like Dunkirk, Narvik, Dieppe and the Battle of Britain. (Aircrew wore a bar, or rosette on ribbon only.) Medals were awarded for 6 months in an operational area, including Merchant Navy. The France and Germany Star was awarded for service in France, Belgium, Holland and Germany, from D-Day (6th June, 1944) to VE Day (8th May, 1945). Other identically shaped Stars were engraved for Aircrew Europe (with a bar, or rosette when ribbon only is worn - the only rare example); Africa; the Pacific; Burma; the Atlantic and Italy. Civilian services gained the Defence Medal and 1939-45 War Medal. Only the Canadian Defence Medal is silver. Bomber Command survivors rightly resent the absence of their own campaign medal.

No: 00012

GERMAN MEDAL (IRON CROSS)

Date: 1939-45

Period: World War Two

From: Pupil's collection,
Christopher Guyver. Loan

Measurements: Length: 100mm
Medal: 50mm; 4mm thick
Ribbon: 50mm long; 32mm wide

Weight: 35gm

Materials: Lightweight alloy Certainly **not**
iron

Location: H2

Exit Date:

SIHC: 3.2

Photo: Frank Power

00012

Description: Ribbon has a broad (18m) scarlet stripe, bordered by narrow white and black stripes (3mm each). This is gathered in a ring-swivel mounted to the medal. This is a Pattée (not Maltese) cross of black with silver-coloured border in relief.

Condition: Good, but has a generally tawdry appearance, plastic-like finish.

Distinguishing Marks: Obverse: centrally, a swastika in relief, 1939 below. Reverse: Blank, except for the date: 1813

Reference books: R.J. Wilkinson-Latham: Collecting Militaria (1975); Brian Leigh Davis & Malcolm McGregor: Badges & Insignia of the Third Reich (1984); Alec A. Purvis: Collecting Medals & Decorations

Museums: St.Peter's Bunker Museum, Jersey has a comprehesive collection of German militaria from their occupation in World War Two.

Data: At first a Prussian, not a German military medal, white, black-bordered ribbon. (Vice-versa when awarded to non-soldiers). Founded by Frederick William III in 1813 for the Napoleonic War. Revived in 1870 by Kaiser William I for the Franco-Prussian War and again by Hitler in 1939 (with red-black-white ribbon as shewn). Many fakes are made in Spain and imported into Britain. There were many variations of the Iron Cross - with oak leaves, swords, diamonds, the Grand Cross, Knight's Cross etc. Regrettably, many modern English children are fascinated by this type of Nazi rubbish.

– 233 –

POST-WAR IDENTITY CARD

Date: 1951

Period: Post-war Britain

From: Birmingham City Museum
Schools Loans Service

Measurements: Length: 128mm
Width: 167mm

Weight: 7gm

Materials: Light card, pale blue

Location: M1

Exit Date:

SIHC: 3.1

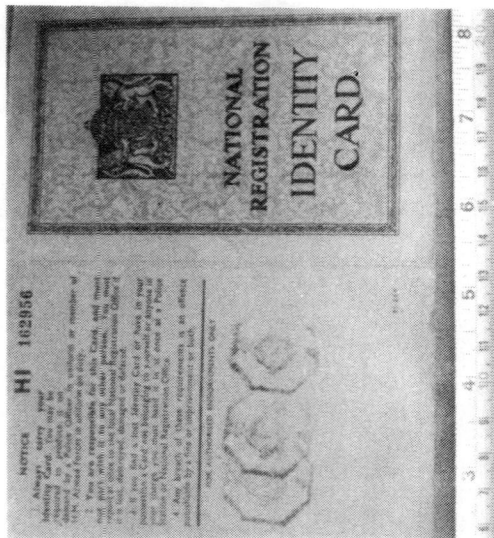

Photo: Linda Burridge

00010—

Description: Clearly labelled as a National Registration Identity Card, with particulars of owner, Amy G. Beddon, 7, Second Avenue, Birmingham.

Condition: Clean.

Distinguishing Marks: Royal coat-of-arms on front, date-stamp:20 Ju 51.

Reference Books: Arthur Marwick: The Home Front (1980)

Museums: Birmingham City Museum

Data: In April 1939, the Military Training Act conscripted 20-21 year-old men for 6 months. In August, an Emergency Powers (Defence) Act gave government power to make regulations without reference to Parliament. At the outbreak of war, a National Service Act called up men aged 18-41. Three weeks later, a National Register was set up, with Identity Cards to be carried at all times. This was intended to catch German spies and Army deserters. During the first few months of the Phoney War police road-blocks were set up to check people's cards. For a short time too, all cinemas, theatres and dance-halls were closed and more people were killed in blackout road accidents than in air raids. Notice from the date of this card how, like the Ration Book (00076) Identity cards remained in use for several years after the War. As in the case of the 1914-18 licensing laws, Government's emergency powers always die hard!

POST-WAR RATION BOOK

Date: 1953

Period: Post-war Britain

From: Gift from John Slater HMI

Measurements: Length: 127mm
Width: 110mm

Weight: 15gm

Materials: Light card and paper 26 pages

Location: SI

SIHC: 1.3

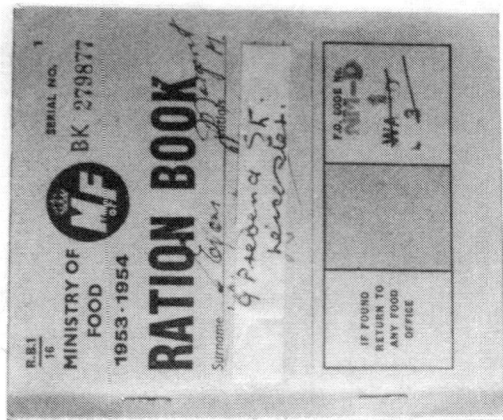

R.B.1
16

MINISTRY OF FOOD

M F

SERIAL NO. BK 279877

1953-1954

RATION BOOK

Surname

IF FOUND RETURN TO ANY FOOD OFFICE

Photo: Linda Burridge

00076

Description: a buff-coloured, stapled booklet, labelled Ration Book 1953-1954

Condition: Fairly clean, almost unused.

Distinguishing Marks: Ministry of Food emblem. Issued to Margaret M. Evans; Leicester address. Interior: different pages for Tea, Cheese, Meat etc. and personal Points for sweets, jam and tinned food. This customer is registered at Worthington Ltd., London Road, her only grocer's shop.

Reference: Raynes Minns: Bombers and Mash: 1980

Museums: Birmingham City Museum

Data: Food rationing began in January 1940. Each person was allowed 12oz sugar, 4oz butter, 8oz bacon or ham a week. This was more than pre-war average per-head consumption – as with may of more healthy foods, the poor fared better on war time rations! Free or cheap milk was issued to mothers and children. Meat (1lb, except offal), was rationed next, and an off-white National Loaf was produced. Families registered with one grocer and one butcher and could not use ration coupons elsewhere. During 1941 food became scarcer when German submarines and bombers sank 221 merchant ships. Unrationed food went under the counter and a Black Market developed in rationed food and coupons. Next cheese (1oz), jam (8oz), milk (2 pts), eggs (2), and sweets (4oz) were rationed, also soap at 4oz a month! Amounts varied from time to time, with occasional treats for Christmas or extra sugar for jam-making. Lord Woolton, at the MoF, advertised the delights of potato pie, dried egg and tinned whalemeat. Much welcome American food, such as Spam, arrived on Lend-Lease. As this book shows, rationing continued long after the War; some foods became even scarcer and bread was rationed for several years after the war.

ELVIS PRESLEY SINGLE

Date: 1962-3

Period: Recent Past

From: Gift: Andrew Jennings

Measurements: 173mm

Weight: 36gm

Materials: plastic

Location: H1

SIHC: 2.8

Photo: Frank Power

Description: A typical 45 rpm RCA singles recording of Elvis Presley, with the Jordannaires, singing *Kiss me Quick* and *Something Blue.*

Distinguishing Marks: Serial No: RCA1375; Make in England by Decca Record Co. Etc. Unlike earlier 78s (see 00006) these discs are dated.

Possible identity: Well-known

Reference Books: P, Gambaccini: Guinness Book of Hit Singles (since 1952); E. Presley: Elvis in his own words (1977); W. Licfe: Life and death of Elvis Presley (1977); N. Slominsky: Biographical Dictionary of Musicians (1988); W. York: Who's Who in Rock Music (1982).

Museums: The National Sound Archive in London has a Pop Curator, with collections of Presley discs, film, videos, archives and reference books.

Data: Born 1935 in Tupelo (Miss.), employed as a mechanic and furniture repairer, Elvis began by singing cowboy ballads with guitar. His first record was Mystery Train (1954); from 1957-1977 he was supreme genius of rock-and-roll, making millions of discs and 20 chart-toppers; his songs were in the charts for 1131 weeks. A highbrow receiver refers to his 'hallucinogenic monotone' and 'rhythmic pelvic gyrations' giving rise to his nickname, 'Elvis the Pelvis'. Kiss me Quick rose to No.14 in 1963, in the charts for 10 weeks. His records, some of which he wrote, films and stage act, were immensely popular; songs written about him include 'Elvis for President!' He died in Memphis in 1977, his funeral the scene of riots and mob hysteria. A Bill before Congress proposed his birthday (8th Jan) as a national holiday. His reputation has been damaged by adverse biographies written by his bodyguards. His house in Memphis is now a shrine.

QUEEN ELIZABETH II JUBILEE MUG

Date:	1977
Period:	Modern
From:	Mrs. B Cattermole (Gift)
Measurements:	Height: 93mm Diameter: 83mm
Weight:	225gm
Materials:	Fairly heavy china mug
Location:	H1
SIHC:	1.1

Photo: Frank Power

00038

Description: A typical Royal souvenir mug in white china with portrait heads of Queen Elizabeth and the Duke of Edinburgh and floral decoration.

Distinguishing Marks: On Back: 1977: Jubilee Year; On Front: The Queen's Silver Jubilee, 1952-1977.

Condition: Good

Possible identity: Obvious

Reference Books: J. and J. May: Commemorative Pottery 1780-1900 (1972).

Museums: City Museum & Art Gallery, Stoke-on-Trent has a Commemorative pottery collection – as have many ordinary families.

Data: Queen Elizabeth II was born in 1926, elder daughter of the Duke and Duchess of York and granddaughter of the reigning King, George V (See 00045). She was third in succession to the throne but with the abdication of her uncle Edward VIII in 1936, her father became King George VI (See 00040 and 46) and she succeeded him in 1952. As Princess Elizabeth she served briefly during the War as an ATS officer and received a thorough training in constitutional History. In 1947 she married a distant cousin, Lieut. Philip Mountbatten, a Naval officer, member of the Greek royal family. The Queen has 4 children, Charles Prince of Wales heir to the throne, (b. 1948), Anne, Princess Royal (b. 1950), Andrew, Duke of York (b. 1960) and Prince Edward (b. 1964) and, (in 1990) 6 grandchildren. She is Queen of 48 Commonwealth countries. Her Silver Jubilee was celebrated in 1977, her Golden Jubilee would take place in 2002, her Diamond Jubilee in 2012, when she would be 86 – 8 years older than Queen Victoria in the 60th year of her reign. Like Victoria, her youthful succession raises occasional rumours of her possible abdication in favour of the Prince of Wales, who otherwise, like Edward VII (See 00039) will be an elderly man on natural succession.

Wordsley Gate

Frees Coalbourne Brook, Wordsley, Old-swinford, Hollowayend, Pedmore and Heath Gates and bars.

day   Mo.   187
Produce the ticket or pay the toll

Corbyns Hall Gate

Frees Princes End, Queen's Cross, Pensnett, Brettell Lane, Kingswinford, Nether Trindle, Tipton, Round Oak, and Corbyns Hall gates and bars.

day   Mo.   187
Produce the ticket or pay the toll.

Kingswinford Gate

Frees Princes End, Queen's Cross, Pensnett, Brettell Lane, Kingswinford, Nether Trindle, Tipton, Round Oak, and Corbyns Hall gates and bars.

day   Mo.   187
Produce the ticket or pay the toll.

CHAPTER FOUR : RECORDING AND RETRIEVAL

In this Chapter we analyse the standardised record card which was used to catalogue our small collection in the last Chapter. One of the most significant museum developments in recent years must be the organization of MDA (*Museum Documentation Association*) at Cambridge. This grand design has begun to enlist all the Museums in Great Britain, each with an MDA registration number, to programme their individual collections as part, eventually, of a vast nation-wide data bank. The boundless possibilities of such a resource, in the however distant future gives us pause to think about our own tiny retrieval system in schools. Without intending any ludicrous comparison with MDA, our own cards have included as many of their fields as possible, and the author is grateful for the patient advice and help received from Mike Budd and his colleagues at Cambridge.

Amongst the essential objectives of thorough documentation, MDA lists:-

'Providing clear proof of ownership of all material in your care; ensuring that as much relevant information as possible about items in your care is captured and held permanently; ... preventing duplication and revealing gaps in the collection which might be filled by more active collecting (Chapter Three has fulfilled this task admirably for our tiny sample collection!); providing detailed descriptions for the police in the event of theft; finding desired items promptly whenever required and ensuring that losses are promptly identified.'

To ensure the ongoing value of our classroom collections, we too must devise a standardised form of cataloguing, labelling and card-indexing for each new item. This will be most helpful of all in ensuring the possible retrieval of loan items, from parents, pupils and museums, which may come and go from time to time. As we have seen in Chapter One, as much as 50% of our long-term collection at any given time may be in hands other than the schools'. We shall in fact, require two aids, one the catalogue cards as shown, the other some form of index to facilitate cross-reference from card to card, period to period and object with object. Let us look first at the familiar card:-

FRONT OF CARD:

1: Accession Number: Give each new item a consecutive accession number. Keep these separately listed in an uptodate Museum Register, with brief identification, for quick reference. The Register should also give: date received: received from: basic description and initial store.

Our collection must perforce be catalogued and numbered in accession order, even though a multitude of periods and topics will follow one another in haphazard, non-chronological order. (It is possible, but unwise, to attempt to accede by periods, setting a series of blank numbers (1:000 for fossils; 2:000 for Prehistoric; 3:000 for Roman etc.) Something unusual will always turn up to demand the insertion of a 1a or 2a series.)

2: Photograph: Take a clear 4" x 4" black-and-white photograph of each new object, being careful to include a ruler as a scale for the picture. Attach each photograph to the front of an 8"x5" index-card, for central storage in a special box. This becomes the classroom catalogue of our collection. Coloured transparencies are an additional option.

2a: Drawings: Pupils make their own drawings of each item in their notebooks, being encouraged too, to attempt extrapolations of incomplete objects; to these pictures they add their own written descriptions.

3: IDENTIFICATION **4: DATE** **5: PERIOD**

6: SIHC CLASSIFICATION 1.00-4.00: This is an MDA classification for Social and Industrial History Collections, published in full by the Association @ £4.00. Its main headings are:

> **1.00: Community Life**
> **2.00: Domestic & Family Life**
> **3.00: Personal Life**
> **4.00: Working Life**

These sections can be extended to classify each section more precisely (e.g. 1.21 Business organizations etc) but for our own small collection, time may permit taking the record only to its primary level. This simple classification is forecast by discussion of any object's **Main Features** and **Possible Identity** (11 and 15, below). Enthusiasts however, may wish to extend this as far as the tertiary stage (e.g. 2.61: Recipe and Cookery Books; 3.36: Girls' Costume; 2.81: Toys etc.), so our specimen cards attempt this more precise classification. (see below for further details of SIHC).

7: Obtained from: Here we introduce children to the important concept of **provenance**. This has direct bearing on the possible authenticity of any item. Often we shall not be able to trace the origins of a loan or gift, beyond the last-known owner. Museum objects, or well-authenticated items, like dated coins or medals, usually - though not always - have a more reliable provenance.

8: Measurements: **(i) Weight:** **(ii) Materials:**

Entries **6-8** should be made first, at the same time as the drawing and photograph. These data complete our objective view of the artefact; we then turn to a more general investigation, leading to a more detailed description, based upon observation and research.

9: Location: Retrieval is the most vital part of any resources collection. This is only too familiar to those of us who know the *exact* item we need for the next lesson, which *was* in the large cardboard box under the stairs, or that thick red book on one of the lower shelves. The catalogue therefore, must show the exact location of each item in several different places, described in Chapter Three. Our examples have used the codes H = History Room or, in Primary schools, Classroom and M = Museum. Consecutive numbers identify separate places in each location, so that H1 = less valuable items on display and open access in the classroom. ; H2 = a locked case in the classroom for fragile objects; H3 = the relative safety of the stockroom or locked cupboard and S1 = the school safe. Similarly, for the author's collection, M1 is Birmingham Schools Liaison Service, M2 is Derbyshire's Resources Centre and M3 is Hereford and Worcester's Hartlebury Museum (John West Boxes). To these we should add A = Home address as an additional reminder on all loans' cards. This entry should be backed up by a Loans Book's list of lenders' addresses, for return and future access.

10: Exit date: Mainly used to record the return of loans to their owners, **Exit** will also be entered for breakages and losses. It will be as well to back this entry up with an exit form on which the owners acknowledges safe return of the loan.

BACK OF CARD:

11: Main features: These one-word characteristics, usually alternatives, are applicable to any item. They can be programmed for computer record and identification, or used as the basis of a simpler form of optical coincidence-card system, or merely as simple alphabetical index cards in a box. Suggested features might include:

Natural	OR	Man-made
Immobile		Portable
Inexpensive		Precious
Simple		Ornate
Runctional		Ornamental
Industrial		Domestic
Impersonal		Personal
Outdoor		Indoor
Mechanical		Non-mechanical
Mass-produced		Hand-made
Authentic		Fake
Facsimile		Replica
Dated		Undated

This list of **Main Features** can be duplicated as 'boxes' attached to each card or notebook page, ready-made to be filled in as shown on pages 40 and 330. Most of these features will suggest the types of reference books to which we will refer for confirmation of our own ideas. These are recorded, with notes of data found.

The same format can be printed separately as cue-cards, to act as prompts in children's classroom identification activity, such as 'Twenty Questions' or 'Animal, Vegetable or Mineral'. For this purpose the card can be combined with a similar offprint of the Possible Identities of 15 (below).

12: **General Description**: This must be a *brief* description of what is immediately obvious about the object. At first, we should encourage children to record only what they actually see, not what they guess or think they know already. Describe any obvious mechanism or moving parts. Is there any cutting edge, hinge, lever- or screw-action? Is there a handle, cover, stand or feet, mounting or apertures? Is there a pattern, complete or incomplete? Does the object appear to be free-standing or portable? Some of these points have been suggested as **Main Features**.

13: Condition: Does the item appear to be complete, as-new, broken or fragmentary? Suggest any obviously missing parts.

14: Distinguishing Marks: Note separately any distinguishing marks or clues, especially any pattern, lettering, engraving, hallmarks, patent-plate or other dating evidence. Note any apparently foreign influence. (e.g. Oriental appearance, *Made in Germany* etc.).

15: Possible identity: This is the MDA's *simple name,* using less highly qualified guesswork. If we think we already *know* what the object is, enter our first suggestions here, and under (1) above. At this stage, the teacher should avoid *telling* the class what they need to know, but will accept all reasonable ideas. These will usually be too limited, prompting further research — for example: "a sort of fossil" or "a tool of some kind". In some of the more conjectural cases, the children's first impressions may even be misleading - as for example, identifying the Roman lamp (00063) as a teapot! We can encourage them to choose from the a readily available list of the following suggestions:

Fossil	Weapon
Coin	Medal
Gadget	Tool
Garden Tool	Carpentry tool
Needlework	Jewelery
Ornament	Commemorative
Pottery	Clothing
Furniture	Electrical
Bottle	Toiletry
Toy	Musical
Plate/dish	Cooking utensil
Newspaper	Postcard
Photograph	Picture
Document	Book
Label	Advertisement

Like the **Main Features** listed in broader terms above (11), this list can be used to prompt ideas for a Twenty Questions session, and may also have separate index cards prepared for each simple name.

These first conjectural steps should be productive of much useful oral discussion and note-making. The preliminary set of entries (**4-14**), completes our introductory, visual check of the object but leads us on to research into reference books and museum collections, before we can come to a final conclusion.

16: Reference Books or Catalogues: Give full details of author, editor, publisher, date and, if necessary, the Library where the book is available for reference.

17: Museum Collections: Give the address and type of collection, with dates of any letter or visit, Catalogue references and picture postcards etc.

18: Additional Data: Here we add notes of information found in reference books and museums. These, with all the above facts, should now enable us now to complete entries 3-5 with some confidence.

Preparation of a complete set of record cards gives us a comprehensive *Catalogue* of our collection. Here we must emphasise that our function, methods and objectives in making and keeping such records are slightly different from those of museum curators. Our catalogue provides, not only a reliable record of the scope and whereabouts of individual items in our growing collection; it also embodies a teaching strategy and modes of guidance to pupils. Our use of **Main features** for example and the conjectural guesswork of **Possible identity** are deliberately designed to prompt children's oral discussion. We aim, at two distinct levels, on the catalogue cards and projected into pupils' notebooks, to inculcate motives of curiosity and methods of investigation, as well as disciplines of professional recording.

Another method of classification can be incorporated with whatever software or system we choose. For this, we can use a simplified level of the SIHC classification, which we borrowed from MDA, to add to our own record card. For this information we are further indebted to WMSIHCRU (West Midlands Social and Industrial History Collections Research Unit), particularly to Michael Vanns, the Unit's Secretary, and John Crompton of the Black Country Museum, where the West Midlands Area Museum Service bases the organization of its Social & Industrial History Collections Research Unit. Their printed booklet offers proforma record sheets for member museums to enter entire collections on different themes and activities. These afford a useful set of guidelines for teachers too.

WMSIHCRU's intention is not as far-reaching as MDA's, but concentrates solely on the field of Social and Industrial History. (Other active groups and other Area Museum Services are concerned with Natural History or Archaeology.) Less demanding too is the Unit's intention to amass data on *collections* of items (e.g. schoolroom, police, hobbies etc.) rather than concentrating on the whereabouts of individual specimens. In this they anticipate our own cards's entry **17** above (Museum Collections) and will eventually expand upon the simple subject gazetteers listed in Chapter One.

As we have seen, SIHC'S numerical system divides museum collections into four main sections of activity moving into and beyond a tripartite classification. As in the Dewey library subject index, each subdivision takes an additional decimal places:-

Section 1 deals with **Community Life**. It comprises sub-divisions of: 1.100: material on cultural traditions; 1.200: Community organizations (political, labour, sporting etc); 1.300: Community regulation & control (by national, regional and local government; law enforcement etc.); 1.400: Community welfare (health, sanitation etc); 1.500: Education 1.600: Community amenities, entertainment & sport; 1.700: Communications & currency; 1.800: Warfare and defence (Army, Navy RAF etc.)

Section 2 deals with **Domestic & Family Life**, including 2.100: Domestic & Family administration (household bills and other documents); 2.200: House structure; 2.300: Domestic heating, lighting, water & sanitation; 2.400: Domestic furniture & fittings; 2.500: Home cleaning & maintenance (including laundry, house cleaning etc.); 2.600: Domestic food, drink & tobacco; 2.700: Family medical; 2.800: Domestic hobbies, crafts and pastimes (including toys, music, broadcasting etc.)

Section 3 deals with **Personal Life**. This covers 3.100: Personal administration and records (certificates, diaries, portraits etc); 3.200: Personal relics, mementos and memorials; 3.300: Personal costume (not working wear); 3.400: Personal accessories (wallets, watches, purses, pens etc); 3.500: Personal toilet items; 3.600: Personal food, drink and tobacco accessories; 3.700: Personal medical & infant-raising (includes hearing aids, spectacles, etc.)

Section 4 deals with **Working Life**, under separate headings for 4.100: Agriculture, horticulture, forestry & fishing; 4.200: Energy & Water supply industries (coal, coke, oil, gas etc); 4.300: Extraction of minerals; 4.400: Extraction of metallic ores, manufacture of metals and engineering; 4.500: Management industries, (food, drink, textiles, leather goods, clothing etc.) 4.600: Construction (bricklaying, carpentry, plumbing, painting etc); 4.700: Transport & Communications (Railways, inland waterways, maritime, air transport and space technology); 4.800: Distribution, hotels & catering (includes all high street shops, from grocers to petrol stations.)

SIHC classification, *in extenso,* is obviously better suited to large-scale collections of similar objects rather than to each item in a small classroom museum of assorted objects. It is however, worth asking ourselves, of each new accession, in what type of national or regional collection any of our own specimens might be found or matched.

Next we can use our catalogue cards and their various modes of classification, whichever we have chosen or omitted to use, extending them into a form of *Index*. This involves further sorting and setting of the different fields, categories and sub-sets into which each specimen falls. We may, for instance, need to know how many different types of shoe there are in our collection; to sort out all our fossils and separate originals from replicas, or quickly refer to an index of donors and/or lenders.

More elaborate searches demand rapid cross-reference - for example, how many items can we withdraw from the collection which illustrate standards of Victorian as opposed to medieval education; which isolate the simple technology of the Romano-British kitchen, as distinct from earlier and later domestic econo-mies, or which find not only Stuart garments, but Stuart *children's* dresses. In a large collection (*and never forget that Museum loans come and go, remaining available only by adequate records*) all these demands require the availability of special index systems.

The Museums Documentation Association produces an invaluable information pack, intended only for its member-museums. This includes a catalogue of reference books on collections manage-ment, conservation, documentation etc; a handlist of the MDA's own publications; a Systems catalogue of computer documen-tations; sample catalogue forms and index cards and, most relevant of all to schools, outline notes on a basic documentation system. From this outline the following advice on index cards is gratefully taken.

MDA recommends the keeping of donor index cards, or which the following is their own example. (References such as i.1.; 8.41 etc. are the sample museum's identity numbers).

Hat
1979.32.21 **hat, top** 1979.32.22 **hat, bowler** 1980.7.3   **hat, top** 1984.127.1 **hat, trilby**

Another type of card is the Simple Name Index, such as:-

Smith, J., 4 High St, Newtown
1980.1.1   **shoes** 1980.1.2   **hat** 1982.84.1 **mangle** 1984.43   **blacksmith's tools**

We might also group together on one Period Card all our Roman items, on another Victoriana, another for fossils, and for prehistoric remains etc. With a small collection this is as far as we need to go. Given different coloured dividers, index cards of all types, period, simple name, lenders and donors can, for some time yet, be kept alphabetically in the same box without undue confusion.

However, with the availability of computers as commonplace equipment of Primary school classrooms, the natural progression to a younger generation of pupils and teachers, will undoubtedly be towards a data-base. And why not? I leave this to the experts and to MDA, with only a tentative plea that, for those of us, technological peasants, without a computer to hand, nor the skill to programme it, there *are* other steam-technology methods of multiple cross-reference across a moderately large collection. A serious failing in any modern child's total dependence on floppy discs is the possible loss of certain hand-skills, such as the ability to make a simple alphabetical index, and to sort and set manually, with reference to Venn diagrams. One fears that, like multiplication tables displaced by calculators, these skills too are in danger of falling into disuse and ignorance. Let us never forget that the professionals' academic Classification is little more than the traditional Infant method of sorting and setting writ large. Where indeed did we go from there?

Looking back on the resources boom of the 1960s, one remembers with affection, many old-fashioned experiments with punched cards and knitting needles. Best of all these systems, effectively used for years at Dudley Teachers' Centre Resources Bank, is the Anson system of OCCI (Optical Coincidence Cards Index). This simply applies a light-source to punched cards, instead of prodding them with knitting needles or bent wire. One small card, as illustrated in Fig. 2, measuring only 5½" x 6", can hold or cover up to 1,199 numerical references. The larger (12" x 11") sheet accepts 9,999 references, which is more than our entire collection will need for some years yet! A simple electric light box, as shown in Plate 1, is simply made at home or school and readily accessible in any classroom.

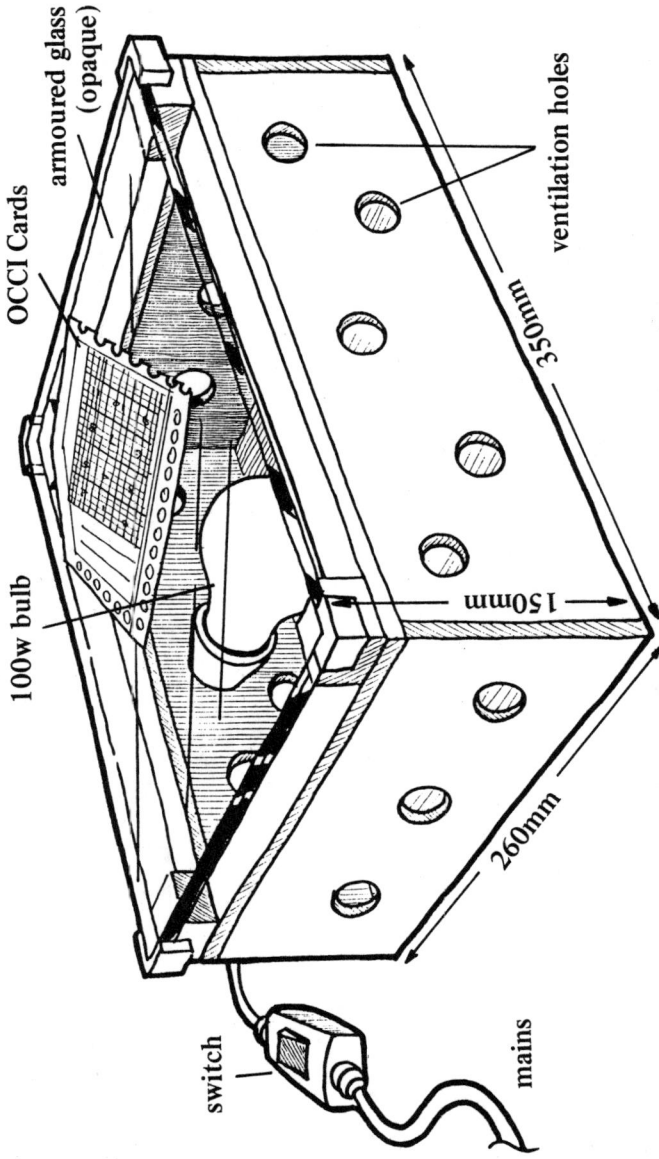

armoured glass (opaque)

OCCI Cards

ventilation holes

100w bulb

350mm

150mm

260mm

switch

mains

Plate 1 : Illustration of light-box and cards

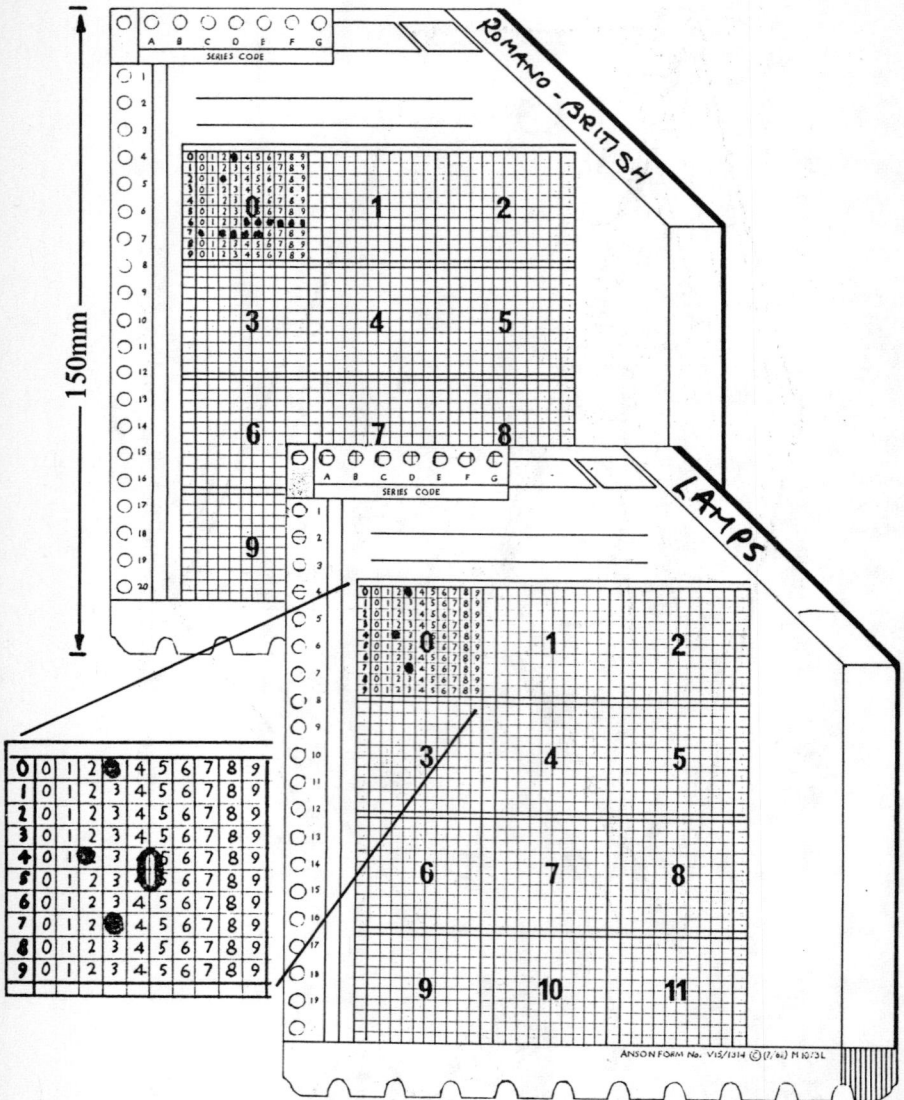

Fig 2: A pair of optical coincidence cards: to find 'Roman lamps'

It is obvious from the pair of OCCI cards illustrated in Fig 2 that if the marked accession numbers are punched out and both cards placed together on the light deck, only Nos. 3 and 73 will show light. These items are both Lamps and Roman. Had a separate card punched for Replicas been added, the light-deck would have revealed our single replica Roman lamp as No.3. On the other hand, if the Lamps card is paired again with Victorian, then only No.42 will be disclosed. By these means we can quite easily group together, for example, all those objects which record the activities of an older generation at war; which compare a soft Tudor slipper with a Victorian child's clumsy buttoned boots; which establish the child's new concept of Bronze Age or Royalty and those which will illustrate a project on Inventions.

Recording and retrieval is only one of the many activities - perhaps the most basic skill - which a classroom museum promotes. At its most mundane level, adequate record-keeping might be interpreted as a routine administrative task for the teacher. In this sense only, filling out each new record card is an *ad hoc* activity to be carried out whenever a new museum loans-case is received, or as yet another gift, loan or purchase is added to the Accessions Register. As we have seen, this also becomes a regular opportunity to involve the children themselves in oral discussion, language development, research, measurement, drawing and precise written description. Each new specimen is weighed and measured before it is placed upon the classroom timeline; reference books, museum catalogues and guides are consulted; drawings are made and notes are taken. Thus each pupil's Museums Notebook becomes a specialised and attractive set of personal records. In this sense too, the teacher's own invaluable card-catalogue becomes his/her lesson plans and preparation. The following chapter discovers what other more creative activities will also be planned, to follow - or precede - the basic skills of record-keeping.

Hard-working teachers may insist that the amount of clerical work involved in these suggestions, however desirable, makes a strong case for the employment of classroom auxiliary, non-teaching aid. The author would whole-heartedly agree. Primary schools which never enjoyed the facilities of a well-staffed Resources Centre, have for too long struggled with the inadequate provision of LEAs who never understood that Primary school History must also be a highly specialised subject. The demands of New Curriculum and LMS must set this matter right; Classroom Museum makes a case for improvement.

CHAPTER FIVE : CHILDREN AT WORK

The wealth of possible activities which emerge from classroom handling of ancient artefacts might be simply divided into parallel functions of **investigation** and **imagination** but these are not exclusive modes of activity. Much valuable content will be acquired, much formative process will be experienced as bygones are passed from hand to hand. Nor will empathy or creativity be lacking as the relics speak to us of those, long gone, who made and used them. Let us move from scientific investigation towards creative play, starting with the bold detection of fakes and forgeries.

Detective Work

"Is it a fake?" Children love the idea of a clever imitation. Indeed, there is some risk that the detection of fakes may become an obsession, spoiling opportunities for more productive tasks. Nor should we work on the assumption that mere *identification* of an object is the only museum-based activity - nor even the most important of all. Purists well may criticize the presumption of the teacher who encourages pupils to believe that they might succeed where Professor Trevor-Roper failed with the Hitler Diaries! "If," they will say, "the experts have told us what this thing is, why encourage a child to question that identity?" But *telling* often discourages curiosity and further investigation by children.

Using a classroom museum in fact demands a careful re-assessment of our whole aims as teachers. If we believe that the purpose of education is to cultivate enquiring minds, to encourage children to learn by discovery and experience, to treat documents and artefacts as evidence, not as 'facts', then we must continually encourage the questions: "Is this a real one?"; "How do we know this?" and, best of all, "How can we find out?"

Perhaps we are hoist with our own petard, causing much glee for the critical purist, when we accept that our last resort must always be provenance. Built into this concept too, must always be the acid test: "What do the experts say?" So, after all, our children's enquiring minds must still accept the disciplines of recognized authorities. Where is the harm in that?

There are many more tests and questions that children can pose for themselves. In all their work with museum artefacts, teachers will recognize the essential value of those questions to language development in oral discussion and firm definition of technical terms. Pupils can certainly be encouraged to make hypotheses and test them by using the evidence of their own eyes and their not inconsiderable powers of deduction.

What, for example, are the signs of newness on an article which should be worn and old? Why is *this* coin wafer-thin, its milled edge worn and chipped, its surface dull and smoothly indistinct, whilst *that* similar specimen is mint-fresh, its metal bright and its embossing sharply defined? Is it perhaps because the first example is a defaced counterfeit, the second a prized and unused original?

What are the significant marks of guarantee and dating evidence - hallmark, potter's stamp, patent plate or trademark - which can be checked with catalogues and reference books? How could these be forged? What are the new materials - plastic, nylon, fibre-glass and resins - which were not available in olden days? Which other materials are more likely to be older - silk, brass, celluloid, stamped tin? How important are labels which proudly announce Made in England or, more cryptically, a diamond with letters and numbers in each corner? What is the meaning of CC41? If there are rivets and fasteners on a buckle or badge, are they as old as the rest, or brighter? If there are rusted nails or screws, are they *all* rusty and, more important in a wooden surround, do the rust-marks stain the wood? What is the difference between stamped and moulded metal? If we have two specimens of the same coin, medal or casting, do they, suspiciously, show identical scars and marks of wear? All ancient artefacts bristle with clues and messages.

To assist children in their discussion a set of cues or prompt-cards is a useful device. Printed question by question on a 4″ x 3″ card, these are offered with reference to the special relevance of specific challenges to particular objects. The basic question "What is it made of?" for example, is most relevant to a scrutiny of the Roman thimble (00022) or Jorvik's pewter coins (00020); the same question becomes more searching in the case of the Victorian ribbon-iron (00001) or glove-stretchers (00035) as "Would this material stand up to heat?" The use of brass for the iron's head raises important scientific questions for older children and the ivory stretchers could never be curling tongs. Other key questions to match different specimens include:

Are there any special clues or markings?
Are there any words, numbers or symbols on it?
Is it dated?
Is it heavier or lighter than similar examples?
Is any part of it missing?
Can we find its picture in a reference book?
Does it show signs of age in rusting,wear,fragility etc?
Does it feel right?

The last question is of course the professional expert's test, too much to demand of inexperienced children? An experienced furniture expert from Sothebys once said that blatant fakes are relatively simple to detect because of their inevitable mistakes. More deceptive, he believed, were faithful copies, made by crafts-men with no intention to defraud, these then gently worn for a hundred years. His only acid test was "Does it feel right?" In this vein, no children's group, from 6 to 17 has ever failed to query the reliability of the Palaeolithic hand-axe (0004) and it is always interesting to discover their reasoning (Usually: "It isn't heavy enough" - less experienced: "It's too shiny").

Before we reach this fairly advanced stage of experience, we must adjust our expectation to meet the inexperience of other modern children who have never seen a lump of coal; who believe that ivory is plastic; who do not know what flint is; who believe that *any* smooth and shiny material is plastic; who have never seen a pen-nib, a farthing, a gramophone needle or a cigarette card.

Such inexperience has nevertheless been matched by the more sophisticated responses of Dudley Primary school children: those who collected semi-precious gem-stones - or coins - or fossils - or military models (*not* toy soldiers); one who was writing a book about the Romans; another who saw the Bayeux Tapestry in Normandy last year and preferred it to the D-Day beach-head Museum; a girl who owned a metal-detector; another whose father was a member of the Sealed Knot; the nine-year old who preferred to paint in oils rather than water-colours; the five-year-old who recognized glove stretchers, "Because my Nan showed me." Children like this are difficult to deceive.

Handling a facsimile of the American Declaration of Independence, one of those very ten-year-olds once answered the persistent query: "Is it authentic?" with the weary response: "Who would want to fake it?" The rest of the class took up this challenge by listing more than 20 answers, not only about "Who?" but also "Why?" and "How?" They appreciated too, the difference between original, facsimile, photocopy and transcript, between third- and fourth- generation copies, and between forgery and reproduction. Nor did they neglect to discuss the importance of 'those truths held to be self-evident' nor fail to explore the dramatic possibilities of rebellion. The only certainty about this dubious field is that fakes can always be relied on to stimulate heated discussion!

Older and Newer

We begin with a simple comparison of pairs, asking each group to decide Older or Newer?   Give out pairs of assorted artefacts, two to a table. Ask the children to decide which of their own pair is the older. This exercise immediately raises useful language-opportunities in discussion of what exactly we mean by 'looking older'. What are the characteristic signs of antiquity? These of course vary considerably from one class of object to another. Can we, however, begin to assume that the larger, clumsier object of one pair; the smoother more worn coin; the flimsier, more fragile fabric; the simpler, more unwieldy mechanism may be in each case, the older one? We shall learn to be careful.

Dangerous exceptions will be found - the exquisitely worked microlith or polished Neolithic celt which is less clumsy, but millennia older than the Black Country nailer's 'hommer'. In this pair, which is the decisive age-factor - metal newer than flint? Haft not lost or decayed? Signs of machine- or mass-production as opposed to handwork?

Then, how about dating evidence, explicit or deduced? Is there a date, a king's head, a patent-plate, a hallmark, diamond mark, or other clue? Can we recognize a type and order of one or the other item? How much can we be expected to know - or find out about the forms of Samian pottery, the different characteristics of parchment and paper? In a photograph or picture, is there internal evidence of costume, architecture or transport, which can be checked in reference books?

By one means or another - and it always seems unjust to me that some colleagues will dismiss these as guesswork, rather than reasoning - any group of children will usually experience little difficulty in reaching sensible conclusions. Of course, it helps if sensible, interesting pairs of artefacts are chosen. Sometimes, to create problems, we might deliberately include a fossil with a fossil replica, two very new objects or two differently dated coins from the same reign.

Trump my Ace!

Another stimulating starting-point, which appeals to the poker-players amongst us, sets children to conjecture about the *relative age* of any object. In this exercise, one artefact is given to each player (individual or group). This is kept covered, so that one group cannot see another's object. The question is: "Do you think you may have the oldest item of all?" This can of course, be played very much more subtly if, for example, unknown to the class, every item is a decimal coin (of different dates), or six different kinds of fossil. In all these games it goes without saying that we should expect a high standard of written recording of our conclusions, to be read out as a statement of our case. Whether we have the oldest object or not, we must be equally prepared to say what we have and why it is, or isn't old enough.

One in the Middle

The next step from pairs follows naturally with growing confidence. Each table now has a trio of objects and a tabulated 1-2-3-box score-card (See illustration). Their task is to arrange the three artefacts in chronological order, checked in turn by the teacher and entered on the score-sheet. As soon as each group has completed its turn, *one* object (presumably the most difficult to date!) is passed clockwise to the next table. Each new trio is re-ordered and recorded and the change-over is repeated. By combination of three from 18 objects available to 6 group-tables, we offer the opportunity week by week of 142 *different* combinations for each group.

As each box must be filled by a description at each turn, and any one easy item may be retained by a play-safe group, turn after turn, we insist on a more and more explicit description for each new entry. So fossil becomes fossilised fern, then Carboniferous fossilised seed-fern, then (perhaps! - after permitted reference to the Library) *Alethopteris lonchitica*. The main trend of all our classroom museum work has always been the circumvention of the one-word answer, insisting inexorably on a complete sentence, then upon a lucid paragraph of notes.

Twenty Questions

Make a simple cardboard screen, about 1ft high, which will divide a table in half. Sit one child behind the screen with a museum object on his half of the table. His questioner sits at the other side of the table. The class may, if not similarly engaged on other tables, sit behind the hidden half of the table, watching the state of play. The questioner is allowed 20 questions with which to arrive at the correct identification of the hidden object. Another development of the blind quest is the Infant teacher's old-fashioned feely bag, containing the mystery object which must be identified by touch alone.

Making a Classroom Timeline

From all these activities, a classroom Timeline emerges very naturally and soon becomes a regular reference point. We start with only the simplest of markers along the wall, usually major dividers: BC and AD; Our lifetime or before; Our Lives, Mum's and Dad's Childhood and Grandparents Time; The Ancient end and the Modern end. Group by group, each artefact we have discussed is placed in a hotly debated order. As soon as we have been awarded the agreed Oldest of All decision, our object is placed first on the line. (It is essential to choose a length of wall with a narrow shelf running below the soft-board - or build it! Artefacts are placed on the shelf, notes and drawings pinned above them.)

Simple *sequencing* is our first objective. *Distance* from one object to another comes next, then measured scale, step by step comes later. Finally, by reference to books, we can confidently place numerical *dates*, though we shall already have rounded up some

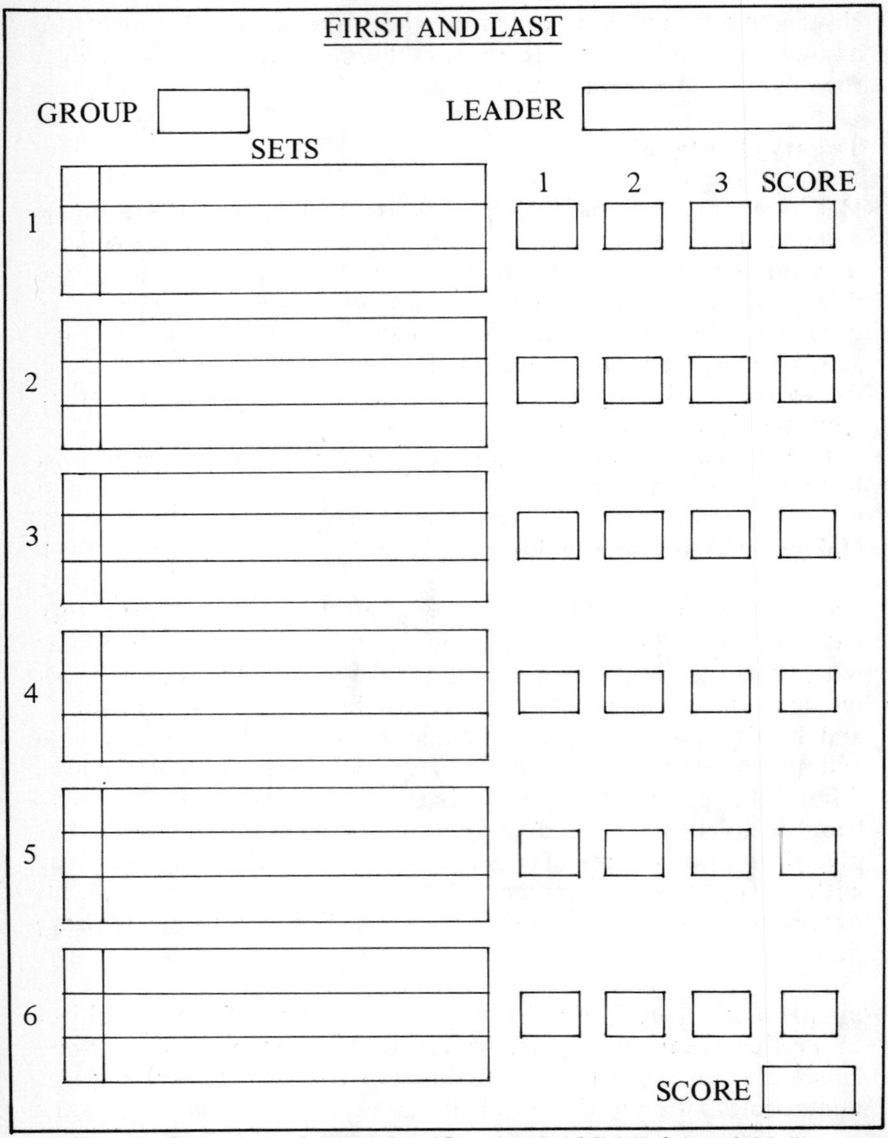

FIRST AND LAST

GROUP [ ]   LEADER [   ]

SETS

		1	2	3	SCORE
1		[ ]	[ ]	[ ]	[ ]
2		[ ]	[ ]	[ ]	[ ]
3		[ ]	[ ]	[ ]	[ ]
4		[ ]	[ ]	[ ]	[ ]
5		[ ]	[ ]	[ ]	[ ]
6		[ ]	[ ]	[ ]	[ ]

SCORE [ ]

Fig. 3: Group work card for 'One in the Middle' (pp 264-5)

useful marker-figures, such as 2000 for the Nativity, 1000 for Hastings or 500,000 for Man's beginnings. (Make full use of the junior date-freak here - she'll love it!).

Children who practice these activities become very adept at manipulating and varying their time-scales. Given one fossil only and ten 20th century items, the disproportion becomes immediately evident. What can we do? We either have one immensely long, blank scale with a solitary item at the far end and ten objects crowded in the last 1mm - or remove the fossil and re-scale the modern end. This type of situation can be endlessly repeated with carefully selected time-sequences. Children soon develop some *fairly* reliable landmarks: Fossil before Dinosaur before Man before Tools before Machines etc.

The variety of our collection creates a peculiar timeline problem by its use of replicas. At first the house-rule can be that every item is taken at face-value - the replica Roman Lamp (00003) is a Roman lamp for purposes of an initial sequencing exercise. Some children will immediately spot this anomaly and protest its inaccuracy. Each replica can then be given two token placings, then and now. Better still, we can create a special time-line on the theme of Originals and Reproductions (See pages 25-33). Be careful to distinguish between the real anachronism of replicas and the dual identity of some pictures, which in two different versions may show the same Acropolis, (or the same Grandfather) *both* then and now. Old things do not arrive neatly packaged and dated!

There is, in fact, some virtue in this necessity, for all of us, as children do, experience daily contact with old things in haphazard, non-chronological order. Emerging from the modern housing estate, we pass the 18th century mine-workings, with the ruined medieval castle standing in the distance before us. Before we reach it, we must cross Telford's New Bridge. Last of all, in the Museum showcase, we examine ancient fossils. Going home, we pass 'in accession order' the 1914-18 War Memorial, the 1870

Board School, a Civil War battlefield and a Perpendicular church. It will take a special visit, later, to see the nearby Iron Age hill-fort overlooking the Roman road, but encountered before the so-called Druid's Stone - in fact a far earlier Bronze age megalith. If we take the baby, born in 1989, we shall see her first, before visiting Grandpa (born in 1926) for tea.

Role-play and imaginative use

As all the previous activities show, the author never had a very strong suit in drama, music or other creative arts. The tendency therefore, to adopt an aggressively objective or scientific approach to the museum evidence has often been, quite justifiably, noted by his more imaginative friends. It is quite true that *the whole object* of handling ancient artefacts must not be mere identification or exercises in logic and language. We need team-teaching here, the working together of more creative colleagues to create a spirit of empathy with the past and a more imaginative use of its evidence than mere scientific scrutiny.

In self-defence, it always seemed too obvious to need belabouring, that the actual *handling* of ancient treasures will inevitably arouse strong emotions and feelings which we must discuss. To heft a palaeolithic hand-axe, so beautifully crafted to my palm jolts me, wondering, into time long past. The whole essence and meaning of vast antiquity is in the fossilised fern and sea-urchin. Once, shown round a superb classroom museum by a proud Deputy Head (every specimen was carefully labelled) I was more deeply impressed by a small girl who, pulling me quietly by the sleeve, offered me a Victorian cut-glass perfume-bottle with the single word - "Smell". There was in fact the ghost of a fragrance. We can never ignore such experience, but what do we *do,* beyond emoting?

Museums already rise energetically to this challenge by offering visiting school parties participation sessions of all sorts. At

Shugborough Mansion House in Staffordshire for example, children dress up in Eton collars and pinafores to experience a Victorian lesson from a teacher in period dress. So realistic are these lessons that it has occasionally ended in tears! In the laundry, children wear wellies, launder a sample of fabric and see it ironed by slug-iron. In the kitchen, cakes are made on an open range.

Wolverhampton Infant classrooms were always well ahead in this sort of hands-on experience. Studying Victorian laundering methods, significant comparisons were made of old and new results. The comparative efficiency of washing machine and dollies, flat-irons and electric irons - all this was safely carried out under careful teacher supervision and demonstration. In fact, normal infant school practices of house-play, dressing-up and other learning experiences lend themselves best of all to the more vigorous uses of a classroom museum.

All the possibilities of dressing-up and role playing are surely fairly obvious? It takes a teacher of genius however, - named Dorothy Heathcote, at Newcastle University - to have shown so many of us what can be done with sign and the mantle of the expert. A generation of her student teachers have helped me understand my own inadequacies. Nowadays, on a good day, the possibilities of simply a broken pair of pince-nez on a black silk ribbon can bring the owner once more to life. More hazardous operations culminate in a Victorian shaving act, complete with probationer-housemaid, brass hot-water jug, badger-brush, shaving mug and - recklessly - open cut-throat razor. In total silence, broken only by the dangerous hiss of the razor, children and teachers sit motionless on chair-edge, waiting for blood! Not quite what Dorothy had in mind, perhaps.

Story-making

We must never fail to enliven a lifeless artefact with the story of its making and its use, long ago. Some stories are ready-made to work with museum objects. The gruesome remains of our own item No: 023 (fragments of an Egyptian mummy's skull) will seem literally lifeless until we turn to the handy paperback edition of Herodotus's Histories and read his DIY mummy-making instructions:-

'Mummification is a distinct profession. The embalmers, when a body is brought to them, produce specimen models in wood, painted to resemble nature and graded in quality ...
the relatives of the dead man, having agreed upon a price, go away to leave the embalmers to their work. The most perfect process is as follows ....'

Read on - if your class have strong stomachs!

Often we can speculate on how a small find was lost by its original owner, many centuries ago. Brooches, buttons, coins and trinkets, so many tiny treasures lie unseen for so many years, until the modern archaeologist discovers them again. What could be more easily mislaid than a lady's thimble? More particularly if her town was being looted by terrorists. The historian Tacitus, writing nearly 2,000 years ago, graphically describes the Roman sacrifice of many a British town to Queen Boudicca's ferocious rebels in 62AD:

'Suetonius's numerical inferiority decided him to sacrifice the city of Londinium in order to save the province as a whole. Unmoved by the citizens' laments and appeals, the general gave the order for departure. The inhabitants were allowed to accompany him. But those who stayed, being women, old folk, or attached to their homes, were slaughtered by the enemy. *Verulamium suffered the same fate*. The natives enjoyed plundering and thought of nothing else....'

Perhaps at Verulamium, amongst the richer plunder, they overlooked a thimble? (Item no: 022).

It was once again a time of fire and sword over England when Viking pennies were first struck at Jorvik (Item no: 020). Turn our specimen in your hand, fresh from the dramatic sensory experiences of Coppergate's time-cars, as you read extracts from the Anglo-Saxon Chronicle. (Another handy paperback edition). There, the fearful monks tell our children of those violent days:-

'867 AD: In this year, the heathen host went from East Anglia over the mouth of the Humber to York in Northumbria. And there was great disturbance of the people amongst themselves. For they had thrown out their king, Osberht and accepted Aella, a man not of royal birth. It was late in the year when they set about making war against the Northmen, even so, they gathered great levies of warriors and went to attack the host at Jorvik. They stormed the city and some of them got inside. Immense slaughter was made of the Northumbrians there, some inside the walls, some outside. Both kings were slain and the English survivors made peace with the Northmen...'

Year after year the terrible saga of the Host's continual attacks are told, there for us to read.

As we see, coins, both replicas and originals will always form a staple part of any museum collection. Strangely, they are also a remarkably frequent source of stories, especially in the Bible with its widow's mite and thirty pieces of silver. The museum shop at Bath offers a useful replica of the Tribute Penny with which Jesus was tempted to make a political statement for His time. Saint Matthew's Gospel tells the story for the speechless silver coin:-

'Then went the Pharisees and plotted how they might entrap him in his talk....
"Tell us", they said to him, what do you think? "Is it lawful to pay tax to Caesar or not?"
Seeing their wickedness, He said: "Why do you tempt

me,you hypocrites? Show me the Tribute money."
So they brought him a penny. And He said to them:
"Whose is this head and superscription" "Caesar's" they said.
"Well then", He said,"Render unto Caesar those things which
are Caesar's, and to God, those things which are God's!"
When they heard this answer, they marvelled and left him,
and went on their way....'

A Dudley nailer's hommer is a fearsome object - not so much for
its heavy iron head as for its gnarled wooden handle, worn thin
and concave at the grip by generations of iron men. Their childrens' too, as the Victorian Factory Commissioners reported:-

'They make a profit and loss of the children. They make as
much as they can ... it stops their growth and they never
recover it. There is very little cruel beating nowadays. The
bad treatment is only in excessive labour, beyond what the
constitution and age of the children can bear......

Mary Humpherson, aged 12 (a poor emaciated object, filthily dirty
and in rags, very small for her age, more like a child of 9) takes up
the tale:

'Can't spell my name. I work at nails from half-past six in
the morning until a quarter before nine at night. I feel very
tired at night. There's always a pain in the middle of my
back - it begins to ache about 9 in the morning, every day. I
gets a shilling a week - give it to me Mam.....'

Billy Harthill too, aged 13, though healthy and sturdy, was stupe-
fied with work, apparently deaf from the constant hammering......
He says:

'I work at nailing from 6 in the morning until 9 or 10 at
night, with ¾ an hour for breakfast, an hour and a half for
dinner and a half-hour for tea. I work with my father and

sister - she's 15. I'm always very tired at night. Don't know my letters......'

Let the children of today grasp the battered hommer. Let them hear the story too, and remember Mary Humpherson and Billy Harthill. There are literally hundreds of these heartbreaking stories to match the museum's tangible evidence of our industrial heritage.

In a happier, middle-class vein, the very Commissioner, Richard Hengist Horne, who listened kindly to so many Dudley children's tales of hardship beyond their years, wrote a different kind of story, *The Memoirs of a London Doll* (still in print). Surely an essential accompaniment to any ancient doll we find, the tale begins:

'In a large dusky room at the top of a dusky house in one of the dusky streets of High Hoborn, there once lived a poor doll-maker, whose name was Sprat ......'

Take it from there.

Some Primary school textbooks build their themes around Museum visits, our own families' souvenirs and the stories which they tell. Macmillan's *Time Detectives* offer many valuable links between artefacts and text. Jean Morgan's *Great Grandma's Schooldays* for example, steps back in time to take a lesson from the Victorian schoolroom at Armley Mills Museum, near Leeds:-

'You will have to dress up as children in 1900. You will do the same lessons that they did. You will also have to behave like the children in your great-grandparents' day ....'

Back in our own classroom several 19th century objects take up the lessons of a Museum visit we may never be able to make, to Leeds, or Shugborough, or Hartlebury. We have in our own collection, for example, an Infant scholar's Certificate (034), an attendance medal (033), a schoolroom slate (031) and a little girl's pair of button boots (036). These can all be backed up by the continuing narrative of our own National School's log-books, with many an Object lesson to work on:-

'The Head Master writes on July 6th,1900: Albert Dallamore, a boy in Standard V was lightly caned on the back - no more than 2 stripes. He immediately threatened to throw his slate at my head. Being then further punished, he called on the biggest boy in the school to 'Come on' and attack me. The boy called on however, did not respond and A. Dallamore received a third punishment. I considered that an exceptional occurrence such as this deserved exceptional treatment. The event was rather surprising, as the boy named does not appear to be the worst in the school...'

The same Time Detective series too, in Ian and Pat Dawson's *Family in the Wars* introduces us to Grandma as Matthew Barlow's family guide to their family's treasures. Photographs, medals, newspapers, ration book and Identity card all take us back to World War Two, then, with badges, posters and personal papers into another generation and the Western Front. All these relics, and more, are documented in our local collection.

Unfortunately, not all our essential stories can be found readymade. Some we must be prepared to invent for ourselves. Handling the Palaeolithic hand-axe (004), my own imagination, much assisted by William Golding's story of *The Inheritor* created a tale of Kal the Hunter. My own story ends:-

'Kal was a hunter, the first man to walk upright. He lived hundreds of thousands of years ago, long before the priests built Pyramids and the temple at Stonehenge or wrote their Histories. He lived and died, as very few men live nowadays in faraway jungle-corners. Kal was a fierce and savage hunter. He was your earliest ancestor. And *this* was his axe.......'

Nor does it take much more imagination than the curiosity which the Columbia Phonograph (043) immediately stimulates, as the *Florida Rag* cylinder begins to play again after a silent interval of 90 years, to invent a middle-class Victorian family named Roberts, with two children, Edward and Alice. One day in 1900, their father brings home, to Laburnum Villa this very mysterious machine. We can describe the differences in their home and ours, with no car, no electricity ("So where do we plug the Phonograph?"), no television or radio, but a new-fangled telephone which can ring only Father's bank or the doctor. We can furnish the Nursery - which 7-year-old Edward now prefers to call the Schoolroom - and count the children's toys. Best of all, we can literally travel back in time, to recreate the very sound, and the excitement of that evening when Father played the first phonograph cylinder that any of us ever heard.

'This story really happened, more than 80 years ago, perhaps just before your own great-great grandparents were born. Edward died ten years ago; he was 87 when he died. His sister Alice still lives in London, in an old peoples' home. She will be 95 next month. She has forgotten all about the phonograph, which her grandson lent to us for our classroom museum. Alice watches television all day. Every now and then we can take the Phonograph out and play a cylinder or two. It still works very well and sounds no stranger than your own Michael Jackson discs will seem in 2080.'

The Area Museums Service for South East England (Ferroners House, Barbican, London EC2Y 8AA) has published a fascinating set of 42 schools' case studies, entitled *Museums and the Curriculum (1988)*. These show how teachers in Infant, Junior and Secondary schools (including GCSE projects) all over England have integrated museums visits with their studies of Drama, Religious Education, Science, History and Environmental Studies. Projects included work based upon visits to an American dolls exhibition at Stevenage, animated film-making at the National

Museum of Photography, a mock excavation at Bedford Museum, dressing in armour at the Tower of London and many more exciting ideas.

Now try the following flow-chart (p 277) for use with a collection of coins, medals, badges and tokens. As well at war-medals they should include school attendance, Jubilee and Coronation, retirement or commercial mementoes. The crucial item is a named set of World War I medals (as in Card 00044) to be placed late in the series. Tell a story about the soldier named and about conditions on the Western Front in 1914-18. Then offer group work in sorting and setting, as follows:-

THE MEDALS IN THE STORY   CAN YOU FIND THEM?

You have an object in a numbered tin. Use the number to identify the object. Open each tin, study the object and number one or more of the 'boxes' which fit the object. Fill the boxes from the left and follow the arrows. For example, No:70 is a French coin and No:82 is a British medal from the Zulu war. These are filled in for you:-

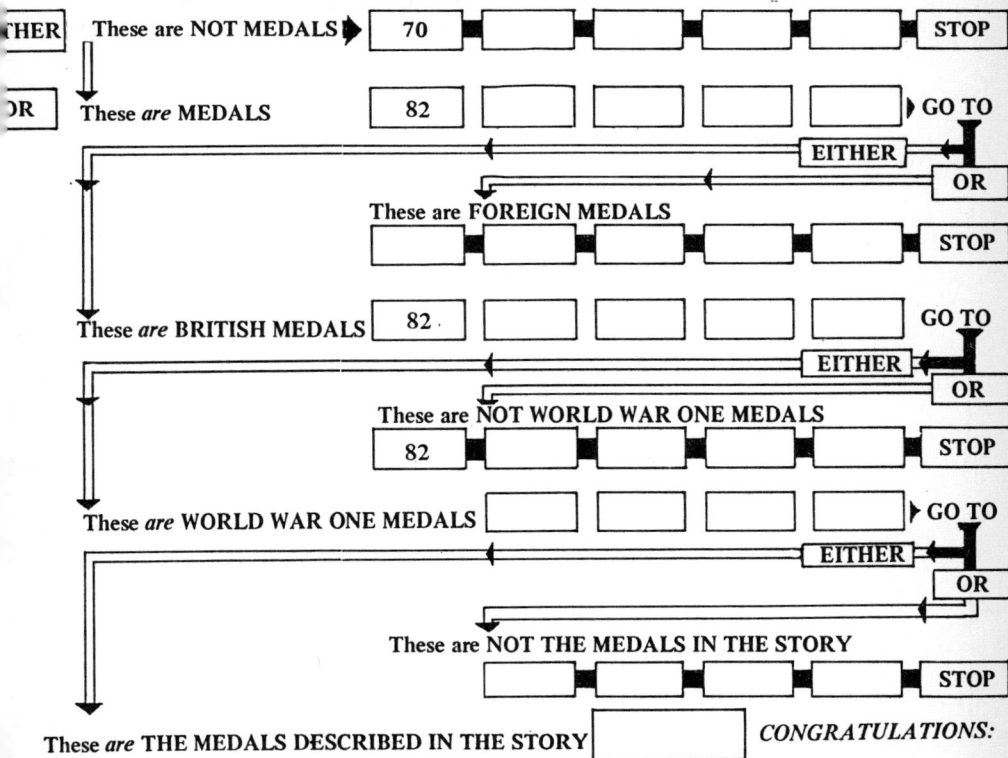

The medals are inscribed, as the story said:. . . . .

. . . .

These inscriptions are NOT as the story said: . . . .

. . . .

Fig 4: Group-work card for sorting and setting a collection of medals

CHILDREN AT WORK

Our own classroom museum is only part of a vast set of historical resources, both within the school and outside, in the children's own environment. With these, we can build a databank which combines, as well as artefacts, narrative pictures, authentic stories, the oral evidence of people who were really there, poetry and place-names, the sites and memorials of our town and village streets with all the wealth of the stories which they tell. Each story might well begin with the teacher picking up a strange and mysterious object from our own classroom collection and starting children off along its trail in Time.

CHAPTER SIX : PUZZLES AND PROBLEMS

Part of the fascination of bygones is that each artefact poses at least one peculiar problem of its own. Most artefacts too, communicate a particular ambience of their time or type. For example, the portrait of an old Queen (00080) defines Regality, just as a Palaeolithic hand-axe (00004) speaks of massive Antiquity and the baby's respirator (00009) shrieks Horror. Sometimes the problem posed is less abstract - merely "Whatever is it?" (00001), or "Is there a modern equivalent?" (00079). Children should be encouraged, when handling any ancient relic, continually to ask themselves: "What *more* does this strange object tell me?"

Here then, is a list of very brief suggestions, one per museum item, for all the objects in our catalogue (Chapter Three). These are questions of various levels of mature thought or immature response. In every case it is intended that the teacher will interpret the problem to children of various ages and to different levels of ability in the class. Or, for that matter, offer a more suitable problem of his/her own.

1: Victorian smoothing iron: Simply, "What is it?" This, until we found 086 (qv), was the ultimate Mystery Object of all! Encourage children to work out a strategy of clues, using prompt cards (page 248) which will at least move them towards a solution. Discourage wild guessing.

2: Medieval penny: Imagine a few of the thousands of business and personal transactions which wore this coin so thin. Envisage the person who lost it. What could he buy with it?

3: Roman lamp (1): Compare this lamp with 00073. How could you tell which is the replica?

4: Flint hand-axe: There is a chalky sediment embedded in one facet of this tool. Could this be subjected to carbon-dating? If so, would it help us decide the age of *the axe*? Be careful!

5: Phonograph cylinder: List the differences between this record and a CD disc. Which will last longer?

6: 78 rpm Gramophone record: Play this. What do we mean by nostalgia? Can *you* feel it, even though you weren't there?

7: Daily Mirror (1): What changes did this headline bring to you?

8: Civilian gas-mask: What does this tell us about scientific progress?

9: Baby's gas-mask: Was the baby frightened?

10: Identity card: Do we need these now? Why were they kept on after the War?

11: British war-medals: Father's? Grandmother's? or Great-grand-parents?

12: German war-medal: Why two dates?

13: British shrapnel: If your grandmother had been killed by a similar British fragment, or in a blackout traffic-accident, would she have died for freedom?

14: ARP Warden's helmet: Is it better for civilians as well as soldiers to be in the front line if war is inevitable?

15: Utility mark: Decode this label.

16: ARP Identity card: Do women get a fair deal in History's records?

17: Egyptian mirror: Draw the Egyptian girl's reflection.

18: Egyptian cat: Why are black cats supposed to be lucky? Could a cat be a goddess?

19: Egyptian papyrus: Write your own version of the story in this ancient picture.

20: The Jorvik coin: Why Thor's hammer and Christ's cross together on the same coin?

21: Egyptian amethyst beads: A present - for whom? Write the story.

22: Roman thimble: List five other everyday objects which have changed as little as this in 2000 years.

23: Egyptian Mummy's skull: This was once a living person. Imagine his/her life story.

24: War Weapons Week Badge: Collect any 6 other *small* objects from World War Two.

25: Victorian shaving-mug: Why bother with a special mug for shaving?

26: Needlework sampler: Could you do this, at 9 years-old? Would you want to? What do you do instead?

27: Jubilee plate: What does this tell us about a different Britain?

28: Cut-throat razor: Make a sequence of *five* razor-types, from earliest times until now. In your family, who once used this type?

29: Cigarette card: What sort of pop stars' materials do you collect. Are they much different?

30: Greek vase: How would you decide whether this is a replica?

31: School-room slate: Were there any advantages in using slates for school work, instead of paper? To the teacher? To the pupil?

32: Trade token: Take a rubbing of this token. What does it tell you? What *doesn't* it tell you?

33: School attendance medal: Do you wish they still gave you medals at school? What would yours be for?

34: Infant Certificate: Find a photograph, c.1896 which might have been William Williams. Which generation of your family does he represent?

35: Glove stretchers: Another mystery object. In which direction does the action work. (That's the secret.)

36: Child's button boots: 16 buttons to do up before you had breakfast! Find a tool to help you. Are these better than trainers? - Richer than trainers?

37: Button hook: The black end may be familiar to you, for its use with - - - - - - ? So, what is the metal end for?

38: Queen Elizabeth II Jubilee mug: So, what was the date of her coronation? Find another mug to fit that event.

39: Edward VII coronation cup: How do they print a photographic transparency in the bottom of a china cup?

40: George VI shaving mug: Find a pre-decimal coin to match this King. What relation is he to our Queen?

41: French steel helmet: Not a British helmet. Then whose ....? What does RF stand for?

42: Oil lamp: Compare this with 00073. In what way is this lamp similar, and in what ways is it different?

43: Columbia phonograph: If a modern, flat turntable plays discs, what was the shape of the records for this machine? Find an example to match it.

44: 1914-45 British medals: How do we know that these three medals belonged to the same person? Why are there two different kings' heads shown? Work out the owner's *possible* date of birth; his age when he joined the Army; when he died. What may he have done in 1939-45?

45: George V picture postcard: What are these pictures *for*?

46: George VI picture postcard: What relation is this king to the kings in 00039 and 00045 and the Queen in 00038? Find coins to match each reign.

47: Willcox & Gibbs' sewing machine: This machine works. Make a list of other Victorian machines which haven't worn out yet. Are modern types similar?

48: Glass photograph: Did people in those days ever look happy? Did they enjoy having their photograph taken? Do you?

49: Book of Manners: Do manners change from lifetime to lifetime? Talk to your grandmother about this.

50: Bronze spear-head: Was this for a warrior or a hunter? Tell his story.

51: Bronze palstave: Archaeologist love using difficult words for quite familiar things. They call this tool a palstave. What would you call it?

52: Socketed celt: They call this a celt. What would *you* call it? Use a dictionary to find another meaning of Celt.

53: Stone hammer: How long would it take you to make this by hand with only stone tools? Would you call its maker an expert?

54: Flint arrow head: What advantages has flint over iron? (As late as the 19th century, surgeons used flint blades for incisions. Why?)

55: Bronze arrow-head: What advantages has bronze over flint?

56: Trilobite: How long ago did this creature live, compared with dinosaurs? Before or after?

57: Ammonite: Is any fossil always older than any mammal? Find an older fossil than this one.

58: Rhinoceros tooth: What was a rhinoceros doing in Kent 2,000,000 years ago? Find out what food, climate etc. modern rhinos need.

59: Elephant's tooth: How could you prove that this tooth didn't merely come from a 19th century Zoo? How would you set about proving that it did?

60: Cretaceous lobster: How far underground would you expect to find lobsters?

61: Sea urchin: Make two lists of fossils: those of extinct creatures and those which still survive.

62: Bear's tooth: You are a hunter, cold and starving. You find shelter in a deep cave. Night comes and at the back of the cave a huge bear wakes up and moves towards you. What do you do? (Me too!)

63: Sugar Nippers: List any *six* antique kitchen tools or gadgets that we don't use any more.

64: Amphora: Why hasn't this bottle a normal flat bottom?

65: Roman wine-glass: Does this glass look modern to you? What do you mean by modern?

66: Roman statuette: List any 3 similar objects in your own home.

67: Bronze fibula: The archaeologists are showing off their vocabulary again! What would *you* call this? What sort of garment might it fasten?

68: Buckle: Would this buckle still work? What could it fasten? Why do some objects like this change so little over centuries?

69: Roman phial: How long does an ancient scent bottle keep its fragrance? Make a collection of old bottles of every sort. Can you find a reference book for your collection?

70: Celtic god: Could you say your prayers to this figure? What sort of prayers would ancient people have said to him? How could he help them?

71: The Law of Tythes: This book is about a tax which we don't pay nowadays. Make a list of taxes which we *do* pay that were not paid when the book was published.

72: Samian pot: Mass production again. Samian pottery was designed in many different patterns or forms. Archaeologists have given these forms identifying numbers, which help to identify and date particular finds. Find the form book to identify this pot's shape.

73: Roman lamp: In what ways is this genuine lamp different from the replica (0003)? In which ways is it similar?

74: Bronze brooch: How new or undamaged does this look? Why do some ancient objects keep their form, shape and newness better than others? Make two lists from our collection - (1) Looks old (2) Looks new.

75: Bronze spoon: Draw the whole spoon, filling in missing parts.

76: Ration-book: Who would need most food in wartime? Make a list of priorities - soldiers?; expectant mothers?; old folk?; children?; factory workers?; ARP workers?

77: Fossilised seed-fern: Some children today, living in centrally heated houses or flats, never see a lump of coal. Can we do something about this, and possibly find patterns in the seam?

78: Daily Mirror (2): This newspaper describes the deaths of many young pilots, British and Germans. Does it take a humane or sympathetic attitude to one day's killing? Was it wrong to keep the score like a cricket match. Was the Battle of Britain the same sort of disputed victory as the defeat of the Spanish Armada?

79: Medieval arrowhead: Compare this arrow-head with 00054 and 00055. How much technological progress took place in making this weapon over 3,000 years?

80: Queen Victoria: How does a Queen look different nowadays?

81: Civil War Musket balls: Make a map of battlefields from which these might have come. Which Civil War battlefield is nearest to you? What do you think about metal detectors? - right or wrong? Write a story about each of the five shots.

82: Mace: Is this thing any more historical or warlike than modern muggers' equipment (knuckledusters, bicycle-chains etc.)? Medieval bishops used these maces to prevent sinfully wielding the sword. Discuss this historical hypocrisy.

83: Shoe fragment: How did this child differ from the one who wore the buttoned boots? (00036).

84: Lady's stirrup: Compare this stirrup with modern examples. How much, if at all, has horses' harness changed over the centuries.

85: Greek coin: Compare the other coins in our collection (00002; 000020; 000032; 000093; 000095).   Which looks the most civilized? or attractive?   What is the only recognizable feature here?

86: Stone figure: Witchcraft? Magic? Religion? Play? Make up a story, or a song about the old woman who owned this strange little creature.

87: Medieval broadsword: Knight or robber? Crusader or outlaw? Who owned this sword? Write a story about him - or her.

88: Medieval cannon-ball: Compare this article of killing with 00004 and 00013. What do you feel about progress in warfare?

89: Leather wine-bottle: Have a conversation between the gildsman who made this and the customer who bought it.

90: Elizabethan purse: Why do some ancient objects look so much more up-to-date and real than other bits and pieces? Gather together a collection of present-day throw-outs from home. Imagine that you are a history student 400 years from now (say 2390 AD). Describe how you feel about the people who left your collection of museum objects behind.

91: Tudor knife and fork: Here are two more things that haven't changed much over 400 years. Find a menu for the last meal these were served with.

92: Horn Spoon: What were the advantages of horn for utensils, compared with metal? What were the disadvantages? Why might animal material be unpopular nowadays?

93: Georgian coin: This is a king of England. Was he an English king? Why did he choose to have the picture of a Roman Emperor? (Use a coin catalogue to check this coin).

94: Box Brownie camera: Buy a 120 film and take photographs with this camera. Are they any different from pictures taken with a modern camera?

95: Row of pennies: What reliable statements can you make about the dates of each monarch's reign *using only these pennies*?

96: Crystal Palace Souvenir: Check the recent programmes of the National Exhibition Centre near Birmingham. How would these differ from the Great Exhibition of 1851? Are there any similarities?

97: The Art of Cookery: Chose any recipes from an ancient cookery book, of dishes which you could make without any difficulty today. Which others would be difficult or impossible now? Is there anything attractive about old-fashioned food?

98: Maundy Money: Find out about charities, ancient and modern, in your locality over the past 500 years. Who need most help nowadays? Should the Queen really wash people's feet instead of giving out these unusual coins?

99: Georgian shoe buckle: Find pictures, from old paintings in your Art Gallery, of all those old-fashioned items, down to the 1970s, when men wore fancier clothes than women?

100: Elvis Presley disc: Which member of your family was last an Elvis fan? Who were your father and mother's favourite pop singers? Who did your grandparents listen to? And you great-grandparents? Try to find reproduction recordings of *early* Crosby, Jolson, Sinatra, Beatles, Florrie Ford, Marie Lloyd etc. Are any of these singers as good as Bros? - or better? Ask Mum, or Ask Mum, or Grandad!

APPENDIX A : SOURCES AND RESOURCES

Essential Guides are those which identify Museums clearly and tell us what facilities each collection offers to schoolchildren and teachers, and at what costs. These guidebooks are essential for the planning and organization of school visits, or for ordering specialised collections of picture postcards, information packs, slides and replicas.

The most technical guide is the annual *MUSEUMS YEARBOOK*, published by The Museums Association, 34, Bloomsbury Way, London WC1A 2SF @ £15.95. At first sight, this is a reference book for museum curators and administrators, rather than a teacher's guide. It is, nevertheless, a source of useful administrative data such as entrance charges, opening times, availability of parking, museum shops, cafeterias and catalogues. Area Museum Councils are listed and mapped, with a full list of administering Authorities in the British Isles and Ireland. We should not expect to find more colourful information about the Museums' collections here. The Year Book will be useful to any teacher planning a career move into museum teaching, giving details of training courses and employment opportunities.

See also: *NATIONAL MUSEUMS AND GALLERIES OF THE UK* Museums and Galleries Commission (HMSO, 1988).

For pictures and public relations, we turn instead to another annual publication: *MUSEUMS & GALLERIES IN GREAT BRITAIN AND IRELAND* (Editor: Sheila Alcock, published by British Leisure Publications @ £3.50). Well illustrated by informative advertisements, the guide is arranged by counties and indexed alphabetically, both by Museums' names and again by localities. An additional Subject Index arranges collections alphabetically, from Advertising, Aeronautics and Agriculture to

Uniforms, Watches and Witchcraft. This index is useful for indicating available resources for Topic work. Each Museum's entry is fully descriptive, with full address, telephone number and administrative authority.

A chattier, more informal handbook is *THE GOOD MUSEUMS GUIDE* by Kenneth Hudson (Macmillan 1980). Based upon personal visits by the editor himself - who has been a member of the Museum of the Year Award Jury for a long time - and a team of reporters, this book claims that "... every museum (1,600 but the Museums Association says 2,500) in Britain has been visited and reported on by at least two people." 400 museums are selected as well above average and presented as Good Museums. Reporters commented on particularly good or exciting features, refreshment facilities, car-parking, museum shop, facilities for the handicapped and, most useful to school visitors - Can the museum be seen comfortably in an hour? Museums are entered alphabetically by place-name with additional sections on Ireland, Scotland and Wales, and a set of 9 location maps. Entries are occasionally critical - "the period rooms could do with a bit of livening up ..." - but also note essential features like friendly atmosphere and good, clean toilet facilities. A startling section on "Why they didn't make it" condemns (un-named) collections which are educational, but uninspiring, "dreadful enough to put one off Museums for life." or "suffers from a clapped-out curator." Museums with outstanding special interest collections are listed, from Agriculture to Transport. Three indexes list Museums, People (collections on Adam, Brunel, Churchill, Wesley etc.) and Places. A do-it-yourself Report Form is included. This book is essential to the planning and organization of any school's Museums visit.

THE OTHER MUSEUMS GUIDE by Debra Shipley and Mary Peplow (Grafton 1988 @ £4.95) is very similar to the last-named and even chattier! Divided into regional Tourist Board areas, it describes even more small and unusual collections - for example,

Buckley's Shop Museum at Battle (E. Sussex) and the Romany Folk Lore Museum at Alton (Hants). Selected on the premise that Museums can be both fun and interesting, it includes "only those museums which we enjoyed visiting - hence the enthusiastic style!" This book too, has a Subjects Index and a Special! feature which draws attention to unusual features such as the explanation, at St. Bride's Crypt, why so many wedding cakes are decorated by that church's spire and attention to the stuffed mouse at the Museum of Grocery Shop Bygones at Wickham Market (Suffolk). Full attention is paid to the standards of toilets, picnic facilities, disabled access, cafes, shops etc. This is indeed a lively source of extra information.

Especially for 1989, *THE TIMES* published a *MUSEUMS YEAR GUIDE*, edited by Simon Tait, @ £6.95, in a handy car-convenient paperback, divided regionally, with 2-4 lines of description for each museum, including information on access for wheelchairs etc. This Guide too, has a thematic subject Index and a useful set of regional maps.

Another feature to mark Museums Year 1989 was the publication for the Museums and Galleries Commission, by HMSO and sponsored by The Times, of a new series of *EXPLORING MUSEUMS GUIDES*. These are a series of regional books, (about 160 pp. @ £7.95) providing well-illustrated, discriminating and enthusiastic introductions to the best and most interesting museums in the British Isles. The books are a source of reference rather than a step-by-step tour guide. Special educational events or facilities are also mentioned.

THE MUSEUMS JOURNAL is published quarterly by the Museums Association @ £10.00 per annum. As well as descriptive reviews of new displays in galleries and museums and technical advice on museums design and conservation, the Journal publishes regular articles on Museums and Education. Some recent features include:

Worksheets as Museum learning devices, by Heather Fry
(MJ No.87: June 1987).
Animal, vegetable, mineral : Holiday work-shops, by
Jane McMaster *(MJ No.85: September 1985)*.
Starters - Using objects from museums, by John Fines
(MJ No.83: September-December 1983).

Other useful publications of the Museums Association include:

Museums Schools Services by F. W. Cheetham 50p and:
Museums Shops (1978: £1.00)

Occasional reference to *THE BRITISH HUMANITIES INDEX*
(Library Association, annually) and *THE BRITISH EDUCATION
INDEX* (British Library Bibliographical Series, annually) will
reveal many more periodical sources to the determined searcher.
These might include, for example:

Geological education through the museums service, by
Mike Bartlett (*Geology Teaching No.10/i March 1985*)
Bring out your dead apparatus: the Science teaching
collection at South Kensington, by V.K.Chew (*School
Science Review, No.68/242, September 1986*)
Investigating learning from informal sources; listening to
conversations and observing play in Science Museums,
(*European Journal of Science Education, No.8/iv Oct-
Dec 1986*)
Jorvik - some schoolchildren's reactions, by Jeffrey
Watkin (*Teaching History No.50: January 1988*)
The First World War and its implications for education
in British museums, by Gaynor Kavanagh (*History of
Education No.17/ii, June 1988*)
Working museums and historic mills, by Dorothy
Shrimpton (*Textile History No.17, 1986*)
A better understanding of costume in education, by
Lindsay Robertson (*Costume No.22, 1988*)

Women and Archaeology, (seven articles) (*Archaeological Review Vol.7:i, Spring 1988*)

THE DEPARTMENT OF EDUCATION AND SCIENCE: has an active HMI Committee which holds a watching brief on schools' and colleges' various uses of Museums. Their list of publications about best practice includes:

A Survey of the use some Hertfordshire schools make of museum services. (40: 1986)
A Survey of the use some schools in six LEAs make of museum services. (53: 1987)
A Survey of the use of museums by some schools in the North West. (20: 1987)
A Survey of the use some Oxfordshire schools and colleges make of museum services. (312: 1987)
A Survey of how some schools in five LEAs make of museum loan services. (290: 1987)
A Survey of the use of museums and galleries in GCSE courses. (369: 1988)
A Survey of the use some pupils and students with special educational needs make of museums and historic buildings. (4: 1988)

(Copies from Publication Despatch Centre, DES Honeypot Lane, Stanmore, Middlesex HA7 1AZ)

There are several Associations which offer advice and help to museums-users and sometimes publish their findings. Some of these Societies are at hand to assist teachers in situations where no Education Officer or Schools Service is provided. In such cases, a teacher's best helpers will be:

THE GROUP FOR EDUCATION IN MUSEUMS (GEM): (Chairman: Peter Divall, Kent County Museum Service) which exists to promote and co-ordinate interest in and information about educational work in museums and art galleries. The Group publishes a lively annual *Journal of Education in Museums (JEM)*, which includes articles and talking points such as:

Mike Pond: The usefulness of schools visits - A study. (Vol.6: 1985)
John Bainbridge: Science education and museums, (Vol.1: 1980)
David Sorrell: Loan services, (Vol.1: 1980)
Gill Tanner: Role play or role work in the classroom, (Vol.9: 1988)

Back copies of the Journal are available from the Museum Education Service, Liverpool Museum, William Brown Street, Liverpool L3 8EN at £2.50 (Members) or £4.50 (Non-members).

THE BRITISH ASSOCIATION OF FRIENDS OF MUSEUMS: (Hon.Sec: Eddie Cass, 548 Wilbraham Road, Manchester M21 1LB) also aims to encourage support for museums of all kinds and to co-operate with museums professionals in all matters concerning the role of Friends, especially of those Volunteers who assist curators in contacts with schools and the public. Explicit advice is offered to those setting up new groups of Friends, who receive free copies of three Broadsheets of uptodate news a year and a beautifully produced, informative Year Book. Membership is open to groups (up to 250 at £10.00) and to individual Supporting Members at £5.00

WOMEN, HERITAGE AND MUSEUMS (WHAM!) fulfils a too-long neglected role in promoting positive images of women through museum collecting. WHAM! encourages informed museum practice through training seminars and resources lists (£4.00), publicises places where women's heritage can be studied and enjoyed, has held 3 national conferences, produces a rather disappointing national Newsletter and has regional groups running their own activities. Membership (£1.00 to £6.00 - conditional) and an excellent Resources List not always available from: Ms.

SOURCES AND RESOURCES

Margaret Brooks, Keeper of Sound Recordings, Imperial War Museum, London SE1 6HZ.

Of particular interest to children as collectors is:

THE EPHEMERA SOCIETY (12 Fitzroy Square, London W1P 5HQ): concerned with the preservation, study and educational uses of printed and handwritten ephemera - the minor documents of everyday life. The Society forms a link between collectors, serves as a formal clearing-house and repository for items of ephemera which might otherwise be destroyed. Long-term plans include the setting up of a permanent archive and the initiating of research and educational projects. *The Ephemerist,* with news, bibliography, enquiries and articles on all aspects of ephemera, is published as a quarterly journal for members only (£12.50 per annum).

Other, more specialised subject Societies, useful for reference and publication include:

THE COSTUME SOCIETY: (Hon. Sec: Nigel Arch, Court Dress Collection, Kensington Palace, London W8 4PX. Membership £10.00). This exists to promote the study and preservation of historical and contemporary costume within the context of costume history and development. This embraces documentation of surviving examples and the study of the decorative arts allied to the history of dress, as well as literary and pictorial sources. Membership offers: an illustrated annual Journal; occasional publications and newsletters; visits to public and private collections; lectures and collectors' meetings; concentrated short courses and weekend schools of costume history. For information, send to: Miss Anne Brogden, 63, Salisbury Road, Garston, Liverpoool. Costume Society publications are available from: Mrs. Helen Wood, Birtle Edge House, Birtle, Lancashire BL9 6UW.

THE FURNITURE HISTORY SOCIETY: (Membership Secretary:

Dr. Brian Austin, 1 Mercedes Cottages, St. John's Road, Haywards Heath, West Sussex RH16 4EH) whose membership consists of museum staff, antique dealers, furniture restorers, academics and others interested in the history of furniture. The Society publishes a scholarly journal, *Furniture History* annually, also a quarterly newsletter. Lectures, visits, tours and an annual symposium and Conference are arranged. Some books are published for general sale through booksellers and direct to the general public. Amongst recent publications are:

> *The Dictionary of English Furniture Makers 1660–1840.*
> *The London Furniture Trade 1700–1870.*

THE TOOL AND TRADES HISTORY SOCIETY: (Hon. Sec: Mr. John Little, 10A Beacon Close, Boundstone, Farnham, Hants. Annual subscription: £15.00; Family membership: £2.50 per head) was founded in 1983 to further the knowledge and understanding of hand-tools and the trades and people who used them. An annual weekend conference includes visits to museums, collections and places of interest, as well as talks and demonstrations. Meetings of a less formal nature take place throughout the year on a regional basis. Members receive four 48-page illustrated Newsletters and the Society's annual journal, *Tools and Trades* consisting of articles of lasting importance.

THE BRITISH ASSOCIATION OF NUMISMATIC SOCIETIES (BANS) (Secretary: K.F. Sugden, Department of Numismatics, Manchester Museum, The University, Oxford Road, Manchester) is the national Society which represents 61 numismatic societies throughout the United Kingdom. It exists to promote the study of numismatics by bringing societies and their members together to share and increase their expertise in coins, tokens and currency. The Hon. Secretary would always be very happy to advise any teacher with pupils interested in coins where to contact the nearest affiliated club. He would also be glad to suggest a local club member who would be most willing to go along to a school to give a talk on coins as they reflect some historical topic or local social history. He or she would almost certainly bring along some actual coins to show the children. The Society does not publish an annual Journal, but has produced a series of inexpensive booklets for adult collectors (e.g: *Norman mints and moneyers, Co-operative tokens* etc.) and hires out sets of slides on popular coins series to affiliated societies. BANS runs an annual Congress, organized by a local numismatic society, in a different attractive place each year, also an annual weekend lecture course with a more specifically educational programme.

THE ORDERS AND MEDALS RESEARCH SOCIETY (Membership Secretary: N.I. Brooks, 21 Colonels Lane, Chertsey, Surrey KT16 8RH; Annual subscription £6.00) is a hobby society with 2,500 world-wide members who collect medals or ribbons, and research individual regiments or themes. The bulk of the Society members would be classed as laymen and amateurs who join the society to meet others who share their interest. An excellent quarterly Journal, *Orders and Medals*. This contains Society news, items of interest and papers by members (e.g. on Crimea Medals - a Warning to collectors; Omdurman etc.)

During Autumn 1988 and Spring 1989 *BBC SCHOOLS RADIO* have produced a first-rate sound-vision programme, *History Lost and Found* which combines a slide pack and notes with the broadcast. Museum evidence presented covers the childhood of four generations, from 1900 to 1987. This slide pack has been prepared to help teachers use both the objects brought into school and the objects in any local museum more effectively. Artefacts used strip off layers of time from a Kentucky Fried Chicken take-away, Rubik's Cube and Action Man, back, via Muffin the Mule and a Pye Wireless of 1932, to penny-farthing bicycles and a photograph of a classroom Nature Study lesson of 1908. Each section incorporates discussion to investigate the evidence of these artefacts. The programme will be repeated during 1990 and 1991 and may be preserved for use (up to three years) by tape-recording.

AREA MUSEUMS SERVICE FOR SE ENGLAND: (Ferroners House, Barbican, London EC2Y 8AA) has published a fascinating set of 42 schools' case studies, entitled *MUSEUMS AND THE CURRICULUM* (1988). These show how teachers in Infant, Junior and Secondary schools (including GCSE projects) have integrated museums visits with their studies of Drama, Religious Education, Science, History and Environmental Studies. Projects included work based upon visits (e.g.) to an American dolls exhibition at Stevenage, animated film-making at the National Museum of Photography, a mock excavation at Bedford Museum, dressing in armour at the Tower of London and many more exciting ideas. There is a useful *Teachers' Check List* and a *Planning Sheet* for Museum Visits.

SPECIALIZED REFERENCE BOOKS: These are thoroughly listed for each type of artefact on individual Museums Cards in Chapter Three. A basic collection could well begin with a full set of *SHIRE ALBUMS* @ £1.25, (Shire Publications Ltd. Cromwell House, Church Street, Princes Risborough, Aylesbury, Bucks HP17 9AJ), available from most bookshops and museums. Titles, listed alphabetically on back covers, range from *Agricultural Implements* and *Anchors to Woodworking Tools* and the *Woollen Industry.* The full set of Albums numbers about 250, including unfamiliar items like *Wig, Hair-dressing and Shaving Bygones* and *Old Poultry Breeds.*

Other useful source sets can be found in many local Museums. Derbyshire's high standard of booklets on *Harvesting, Travellers and Horses, Christmas Past,* and *Sheep to Shawl* cannot pass unmentioned here, nor Cirencester Museum's score of teaching-note leaflets, ranging from *Roman Mosaics, Kitchens and Army, to Coins and Samian Pottery*, a best buy at 10p each or £1.45 the set. See also: P. H. Gosden and W. B. Stephens: *Museums of the History of Education Catalogue* (Leeds Museum, 1980 @ £1.00). In a more commercial context, no topic on *Vikings* will be complete without the wide range of colourful Information Packs, story-books, painting books and picture books published by the Jorvik Viking Centre at York. Other, similar sources of specialized Museum reference books are too numerous to list here.

General reference books on museums and museum visits include:

David Finn: *How to visit a museum* (1985 @ £6.95)
UNESCO's: *Museums and Children* (HMSO, 1980 @ £4.20)
Frank Howie: *Safety in Museums and Galleries* (1987 @ £20.00)
A Seminar Report: *Museums and the Handicapped* (Leicester Museum, 1976)
The Scottish Museums Council: *Museums are for People* (HMSO, 1985)
The Scottish Museums Council: *Working with Museums* (HMSO, 1988)
John Lucas: *The Magic of London's Museums* (1979)
Morry van Ments: *The effective use of Role-play* (1989)

Finally, though the book is, sadly, out of print, find a copy of an early seminal work by the curator of the Geffrye Museum which inspired so many of us, teachers of the '50s and '60s, and still has a great deal to offer now:

Molly Harrison : *Museum Adventure* (1950) See also the same author's later: *Changing Museums* (1967)

EXPLORING MUSEUMS: To celebrate Museums Year a new series of eleven regional guides from the Museums Association has been published by HMSO. These review the best Museums in the British Isles and are beautifully illustrated, with maps, locations and access details and descriptions of what is on view. A gazetteer lists other museums which are not described in detail. The regional guides, (*Museums and Galleries Commission* @ £7.95) are:

London: by Simon Olding

Southwest England: by Arnold Wilson

North West England and the Isle of Man: by David Phillips

North East England: by David Fleming

The Home Counties: Geoff Marsh, Nell Hoare & Karen Hull

The Midlands: Tim Schalda-Hall

East Anglia: Alf Hatton

Southern England and the Channel Islands: Keneth James Barton

Scotland: Colin Thompson

Ireland: Sean Popplewell

Wales: Geraint Jenkins

A last-minute addition to our reference books is the recently revised paperback edition of *The Cambridge Guide to the Museums of Britain and Ireland* by Kenneth Hudson and Ann Nichols (CUP 1989 @ £7.95). Now so uptodate that "two out of every three Museums in the *Guide* did not exist 40 years ago", there are more than 2,000 descriptions, including historic houses as well as museums. A useful Introduction discusses the relative merits of sites which keep objects in their original surroundings, compared with traditional museums as "receiving centres". Excellent location maps and Indexes of Subjects and Famous People's collections; also information about admission charges, car-parks, nearest BR or Underground station, bookstalls, shops, refreshment and picnic areas. Especially useful to schools is the *contact for educational visits,* also details of organizations like English Heritage which may offer free entry or preferential rates for school-children and students.

APPENDIX B : MUSEUMS AND SCHOOLS

In spite of swingeing educational cuts and continually repeated local government reorganization, many local authorities maintain a high standard of Museums provision, which they share with schools. Unlike Libraries, local museums are not a mandatory provision, so that not all counties provide a museums service. Nor do all Museums organize an Education Department. The situation is complicated by the fact that museums provision is empowered at both County and District levels and is sometimes duplicated within a county, especially by historic cities. The demise of Metropolitan counties has caused considerable reorganization of museums provision by their boroughs, acting in consortia; the abolition of GLC and ILEA will have similar effects upon London museums. The future of ILEA's *Historic Costume Collection*, for example, well-used in schools, is a matter for concern. At the time of writing it is to be hoped that this, and other valuable collections will find good homes in various London boroughs. The present incentive to privatise too, may soon have a far-reaching effect on the more familiar picture.

This Gazetteer lists the provision of county museums services, indicating Chief Officers and other administrative appointments. This indicates the probable status accorded to Museums by each authority, rather than as a more general responsibility for Arts and Leisure Services. It may be misleading to generalize about the relative standard of provision made by those county or town Museums services which appoint an independent Director but, in the author's opinion, the specific care for Museums must surely indicate an Authority's extra consciousness of their difference from squash courts.

Within each county, all museums which specifically offer an educational service are listed separately. Each local entry begins with the governing body of the museum, whether National, County, City, Borough, District or private Trustees. Many more museums, both large and small, may well offer lively services to teachers and children without the designation of specialist educational appointments but these cannot easily be identified.

It is a rare occurrence to find, as in Derbyshire, the appointment of an LEA Adviser with specific responsibility for Museum education. This brief is no doubt faithfully and actively observed by many a History or Humanities Adviser, Audio-visual aids Officer or Teachers' Centre Warden. More significant is the provision in some LEAs, like Derbyshire and Warwickshire, of a specialized Museums Resources Centre for schools, whose staff act in an advisory capacity and organize extensive loans services. Some authorities, like the Yorkshire boroughs, operate on a consortium basis, providing services to several local museums or to other boroughs' schools.

The appointment of an Education Officer to any Museum, responsible for liaison with local teachers, is another important advantage to schools. The most practical appointments are undoubtedly the provision of qualified advisory teachers, experienced in both schools and museums. These teachers preferably move from school to school, demonstrating the many different uses of artefacts as well as organizing their own busy classrooms at the Museum. Museums or LEAs which employ Education Officers, Keepers of Education, Schools Services Officers or advisory teachers are listed for each county or borough. A database review of museums statistics (*Museums UK*) identified more than 250 practising advisory teachers employed by national, LEA and private museums in 1987. Regrettably, ongoing economic and fiscal policies keep these posts continually at risk.

Many different Museum appointments, by job-specification, require teaching qualifications and experience. The designation

Officer can often be equated with Teacher, as in *Interpretative, Extension* and *Outreach* services. Many Museums Directors and their Deputies also have teaching qualifications, though no specific Educational designation. On balance, Museums' Officers have more educational expertise than teachers have museums experience. By the same token a few LEA Museum and Resources Centres have lacked adequate museums' qualification for their staff. Combined in-service training is an essential feature of this field of education.

Loans services - *almost invariably restricted to schools within a Centre or Museums's LEA,* - are indicated by *L. Other services, such as the organization of intra-mural or extra-mural teaching, in-service courses (similarly restricted to teachers within the LEA), information packs and teachers' notes, (sometimes available to visitors and often of a high standard of publication at low cost), are also listed. The intention of this Appendix is to offer information to aspiring or mobile teachers about those authorities in which schools' uses of museums are likely to be best served. The author will be grateful for any additional information which would update these lists and apologizes for unintentional omissions, and for any losses by reorganization of posts since going to print.

COUNTY COUNCILS

AVON: No County Museums service.

Bath Museums Services, 4 the Circus, Bath (City Council)
City of Bristol Museum and Art Gallery: (City Council; Schools Service Department; Organizer, with two Assistants.)
The American Museum in Britain, Bath (Trustees: Director of Education)
Bath Industrial Heritage Centre offers social history packs and demonstrations.
Bath Postal Museum. (Postal Museums Trust; Education Officer)

BEDFORDSHIRE: No County Museums service.

County has: Head of Teaching Media Resource Service.
Bedford Museum: (Borough Council; Education Officer (post frozen); intra-mural and some extra-mural teaching; holiday activities; *L Services available to North and Mid-Bedfordshire)
Luton Museum and Art Gallery: (Borough Council; Keeper of Extension and Education Services; Worksheets; *L)
Stockwood Craft Museum, Luton: (Crafts for Schools programme.)

BERKSHIRE: No County Museums service.

Reading Museum and Art Gallery: (Borough Council: Schools Service Section; Keeper of Education and Museum Schools Officer; *L to all schools and colleges in Reading and Berkshire)

BUCKINGHAMSHIRE: County Museums Service : Museums Officer (3rd tier).

Buckinghamshire County Museum, Aylesbury: (County Council: Schools Museum Service; Keeper of Extension and Education Services; *L)
Chiltern Open Air Museum, Chalfont St. Giles. (Ltd. company; Education Officer)

CAMBRIDGESHIRE: County Museums (Libraries & Information) Service: Museums Officer (3rd tier).

Duxford Airfield: (National museum; Schools Officer: Worksheets)
Fitzwilliam Museum, Cambridge: (University; Education Officer) County post)
Sedgwick Museum of Geology: (University; Education Officer)

CHESHIRE: County Libraries, Museums & Arts Service : Principal Officer (Director of Libraries & Museums, 3rd tier)

The Boat Museum, Ellesmere Port: (Boat Museum Trust; Education Officer; worksheets)
Grosvenor Museum, Chester: (City Council; Education Services Officer; teachers' packs)
Norton Priory Museum, Runcorn: (Priory Trust and County Council; Education Officer)
Quarry Bank Mill, Styal: (National Trust; Education Officer; information packs; Worksheets)
Warrington Museum and Art Gallery: (Borough Council; Education Officers)

CLEVELAND: County Museums Service: Museums Officer (4th tier).

Cleveland Gallery, Middlesbrough: (County Council; Museums Schools Service Officer)
HMS *Warrior*, Hartlepool: (Trust; Educational Liaison Officer)

CLWYD: This county's Museums administration was drastically reorganized in April, 1989, as follows:

Tourism and Leisure Department at Bodelwydden Castle, Mold, will appoint a County Museums' Development Officer, responsible for the following Museums:
Bodelwyddan Castle: (fine reconstruction of the Victorian era.)
Bersham Industrial Heritage Centre
Libraries/ Information Service: to administer all collections housed in Libraries. The Education Authority to fund the appointment of a Museums' Education/Interpretation Officer for schools, with particular attention to the following Museums:
    Rhyll Library, Museum & Arts Centre
    Denbigh Museum (opening September 1989)
    David Owen Museum, Mold

National Museum of Wales, Cardiff: (National; organizes loans in schools of Clwyd and other Welsh counties.

CORNWALL: County Museums Service: Director (2nd tier)

Pencarrow House, Bodmin: (Education Officer; Victorian teaching pack)
Poldark House, Helston: (Schools Liaison Officer)

CUMBRIA: No County Museums service.

Kendal Museum: (Lakeland district; Education Officer)

DERBYSHIRE: County Museums Service: Museums Officer (2nd tier).

Derbyshire Museums Service, Matlock: (County Council; Museum Education Adviser)
Derbyshire Museum Loans Service: at Schools Resources Centre, Derby. *L
Derby Museums and Art Gallery: (City Council; Museums Education Officer and Assistant.
Museum of Childhood, Sudbury Hall: (County Council; Assistant Curator, Education)

DEVON: No County Museums service.

Torquay Resources Centre: (Education Officer; Heritage sites etc. *L)
Plymouth City Museum and Art Gallery Service for Schools: (City Council; Education Officer (County appointment)
Royal Albert Memorial Museum, Exeter: (City Council; Education Officers)
Alscott Farm Agricultural Museum, Shebbear: (Trust; Education Officer)
British Photographic Museum, Totnes: (Private Trust; Schools Administrative Officer)

Devonshire Collection of Period Costume, Totnes: (Education Officer)
Exeter Maritime Museum: (International Sailing Craft Assn.; Education Officer; activity sheets)

DORSET: No County Museums service.

Dorset County Museum, Dorchester: (DH & Arch. Soc; Schools Organizer)
Bridport Museum and Art Gallery: (West Dorset District; Education Officer)
East Dorset Heritage Trust Wimborne: (Education Officer)
Guildhall Museum, Poole: (Borough Council; Museums Officer: Education)
Maritime Museum, Poole: (Borough Council; Museums Officer: Education)
Sea Life Centre, Weymouth: (Education Officer; teachers' packs)
The Tank Museum, Wareham: (Education Officer)

DURHAM Co: County Museums Service : Curator (3rd tier)

Bowes Museum, Barnard Castle, Co.Durham (County Council; Museum Education Officer)
Museum Education Service, Darlington: (Education Officer; *L)

DYFED: County Museums Officer (4th tier).

National Museum of Wales, Cardiff: organizes loans in Dyfed schools.
Scolton Manor Museum, Haverfordwest: (Education Officer, frozen)

EAST SUSSEX: No County Museums service.

East Sussex Museum Loans Service, Seaford: (Loan and Exhibition service to schools)

Bexhill Manor Costume Museum: (Private and Rother District; Education Officer)
Brighton Art Gallery and Museum: (Borough Council; Education Officer)
Ditchling Museum: (Trust; Education Officer)
Royal Pavilion, Art Gallery and Museums, Brighton: (Borough Council; Education Officer; worksheets and teachers' packs)
Hove Museum and Art Gallery: (Borough Council; Education Officer; workshops)

ESSEX: No County Museums service.

Colchester and Essex Museum Resource Centre: (Borough Council; Schools Service Officer; *L)
Chelmsford and Essex Museum: (Borough Council; *L)
Harlow Museum: (Harlow District; *L; Museum Assistant, Local History and Education)

GLOUCESTERSHIRE: No County Museums service.

Gloucester City Museum and Art Gallery: (City Council; Service to schools)
Cotswold Country Museum, Northleach: (Cotswold District; Education Officer)
Corinium Museum, Cirencester: (Cotswold District; *L; teachers' notes)
Cheltenham Museum and Art Gallery Service: (Borough Council; Education Officers)

GWENT: No County Museums service.

National Museum of Wales, Cardiff: organizes loans in schools of Gwent.
Newport Museum and Art Gallery: (Borough Council: museum-teacher; *L; Schools Museum Officer)
Segontium Roman Fort Museum, Caernarfon: (National museum; Education Officer)

GWYNEDD: No County Museums service.

National Museum of Wales, Cardiff: organizes loans in schools of Gwynedd.
Museum of Childhood, Beaumaris: (Private: Education Officer)

HAMPSHIRE: County Museums Service : Director (Chief Officer)

Hampshire County Museums Service, Winchester: Extension Services Officer
Southampton City Museums Education Service: (City Council; Education Officer; teaching and resources service)
Southampton Museums and Art Gallery: (City Council; Education Officer; worksheets; teachers' courses)
Maritime Museum, Bucklers Hard: (Ltd. Co; Head of Education and Interpretation; education packs and worksheets.)
National Motor Museum, Beaulieu: (National Motor Museum Trust; Head of Education)
Portsmouth City Museum and Art Gallery, Southsea: (City Council; Education Services: Education & Visitor Services Officer; Education Services Organizer; Education Services Technician; *L)

HEREFORD & WORCESTER: County Museums Service : Museums Officer (3rd tier — vacant)

County Museum, Hartlebury Castle, Kidderminster: (County Council; Education Assistant; classroom; *L)
Worcester City Museum and Art Gallery: (City Museum Service; Education Officer and technicians)
Avoncroft Museum of Buildings, Bromsgrove: (Trust; Full education service available)

HERTFORDSHIRE: No County Museums service.

Stevenage Museum Education Service: (Borough Council; Education Officer; *L)

Museum School Service, Hitchin: (District Council; Keeper of Museum Schools Service)
Verulamium Museum, St.Albans: (City & District Council; Keeper of Education)

HUMBERSIDE: County Museums Service: County Heritage Officer (3rd tier).

Schools Services Department, Hull: (City Council; Keeper of Schools Service; worksheets, classrooms; *L)
Scunthorpe Museum Services: (Borough Council: Education Officer)
Hornsea Museum: (Trust; Education Officer; comprehensive educational material)
Welholme Galleries, Great Grimsby: (Borough Council; *L)

ISLE OF WIGHT: No County Museums service.

Carisbrooke Castle Museum, Newport: (Trust; Museum Education Service; Museum Schools Officer; *L)
Osborne House, East Cowes (English Heritage): (DoE; Education room, education pack)

KENT: County Museums Service : Museums Officer (3rd tier).

County Museum Service, West Malling: (Education Officer; classroom; *L)
Hever Castle, Edenbridge: (Education Officer; information packs)

LANCASHIRE: County Museums Service, Preston : Museums Officer (3rd tier).

Lancaster City Museum: (City Council; Education Officer (County post); intra- and extra-mural teaching; *L)
Museum of Lancashire Textile Industry, Rossendale: (County Council; Museum teacher)

Judges' Lodgings, Lancaster: (County Council; Education Officer)
Lancaster City Museum: (City Council; Education Officer; County post)
Ribchester Roman Museum: (Trust; Education Officer)

LEICESTERSHIRE: County Museums Service: Director (Chief Officer)

Leicestershire Museums, Art Galleries and Records Service, Leicester: (County Council; Keeper of Education and 4 Teacher-leaders)
Rutland County Museum, Oakham Castle: (County Council; Education Officer)
Leicester University Department of Museum Studies: (University)

LINCOLNSHIRE: County Museums Service: Assistant Director (Leisure and recreational Services) Museums (2nd tier)

Lincoln City and County Museum: (County Council; loan packs *L)
Museum of Lincolnshire Life, Lincoln: (County Council; Teachers' and pupils' notes and activity sheets; school loan kits *L)

LONDON BOROUGHS and ILEA (*):

Barnet:	**Royal Air Force Museum, Hendon:** (National museum; Education and PRO)
Brent:	**Grange Museum of Local History, Neasden:** (Borough provision; Education Officer)
Camden:	**Freud Museum, Hampstead:** (Private; Education Officer) **The British Museum, WC1** (National; Head of Education and 4 Education Officers)

Greenwich*:	**The National Maritime Museum:** (National museum: (Education Officer and Deputy)
Hackney*.	**The Geffrye Museum, Shoreditch:** (ILEA provision; Head of Education Services and Deputy
Kensington & Chelsea*:	**National Army Museum, SW3:** (National museum; Department of Education) **Science Museum:** (National museum; (Education Assistant) **Victoria and Albert Museum:** (National museum; Keeper of Education and two Assistants)
City of London:	**London Transport Museum, Covent Garden:** (London Regional Transport; Museum-teacher) **Museum of London, London Wall** (Board of Governors; Education Officer, 2 Assistant Education Officers and Education Assistant) **Royal Armouries, Tower of London Education Centre:** (National museum; (Education Officer and Assistant)
Southwark*:	**Imperial War Museum** (National Museum; Education Officer)
Tower Hamlets*:	**Bethnal Green Museum of Childhood:** (Branch of V&A; Education Officer; excellent answer-phone description of Museum's services)
City of Westminster*:	**London Transport Museum** (London Regional Transport; museum-teacher)

MANCHESTER METROPOLITAN BOROUGHS:

Bolton:
Museum and Art Gallery: (Borough Council; holiday activities; *L)

Manchester:
Museum of Science and Industry: (Trustees; teachers' courses; museum teacher)
The Manchester Museum: (University; Head of Education Department and 4 museum teachers; teaching and lecturing service for Manchester and Cheshire: *L to Manchester)
Gallery of English Costume: (City Council; Education Officer)
Manchester Jewish Museum: (Trustees: Education Assistant)
Manchester University Postgraduate Diploma in Art Gallery and Museum Studies: (University)

Stockport:
Stockport Museum and Art Gallery: (Borough Council; Education Officer and Assistant)

Tameside:
Tameside Museum Service, Stalybridge: (Borough Council; Education Officer)

Wigan:
Wigan Pier Heritage Centre: (Borough Council; *L); Metropolitan Wigan Schools Centre; Teacher-in-charge; extensive education service.

MERSEYSIDE METROPOLITAN BOROUGHS:

Liverpool: National Museums and Galleries on Merseyside, Liverpool: (Trustees: Intra-mural teaching, publications and teachers' courses; mobile exhibition service for schools; Keeper of Education Service; 2 Museum Education Officers, (Humanities & Science) and Assistant Museum Education Officer) and 4 Assistant museum teachers). This team organizes educational activities in the following Liverpool Museums:-

Merseyside Museum of Labour History,
Merseyside Maritime Museum
The Walker Art Gallery
Sudley Art Gallery
Collections at St.Georges Hall

and at:

Lady Lever Art Gallery, Port Sunlight, Wirral

Croxteth Hall and Country Park, Liverpool: (Trustees: educational provision)

Wirral: **Williamson Museum and Art Gallery, Birkenhead:** (Wirral District; educational activities)

MID GLAMORGAN: No County Museums service.

National Museum of Wales, Cardiff: organizes loans in schools of Mid Glamorgan.

MUSEUMS AND SCHOOLS

NORFOLK: County Museums Service : Director (Chief Officer)

Museum Education Department, Castle Museum, Norwich: County Council: The museums Education Officer and 3 Assistant Education Officers organize educational provision, including intra-mural teaching, handling sessions, holiday activities and work-sheets in this and other Norwich Museums, which include:-

Strangers' Hall Museum; Bridewell Museum and St.Peters, Hungate.
Additional educational provision is made by Norfolk's Museums teachers and Education Officers, with occasional *ad hoc* second-ment at:
Norfolk Rural Life Museum, Gressenhall:
Norfolk Archaeological Unit, Gressenhall
Elizabethan House Museum, Great Yarmouth: (Museum teacher)
Lynn Museum, Kings Lynn: (Deputy curator (Education); hand-ling sessions; *L)
Museum of Social History, Kings Lynn
Maritime Museum for East Anglia, Great Yarmouth: (Museum teacher)
Nelson's Monument, Great Yarmouth
Tolhouse Museum, Great Yarmouth
The Exhibition Galleries, Great Yarmouth
Cromer Museum
Ancient House Museum, Thetford
Shirehall Museum, Little Walsingham

NORTH YORKSHIRE: County Museums Service: Curator (3rd tier)

Yorkshire Museum: (County Council; *L)
National Railway Museum, York: (National museum: Head of Education and Education Officer)
York Castle Museum: (City Council; Education Officer; teaching notes)

Jorvik Viking Centre (York Arch. Trust; Education Officer; information packs)

NORTHAMPTONSHIRE: No County Museums service.

Northamptonshire Museums Education Service: (Keeper of Education; *L)
Northampton Museum and Art Gallery: (Borough Council; Keeper of Education and Extension Services)

NORTHUMBERLAND: County Museums Service : Museums Officer (3rd tier).

Northumberland County Museums Service, Morpeth: (County Council; Education Officer)
Chesterholme Museum, Hexham: (Education Officer; information packs; Worksheets)

NOTTINGHAMSHIRE: No County Museums service.

Nottinghamshire Education Resources Service: (County Council; General Adviser for Teaching and Learning Resources)
Castle Museum, Nottingham: (City Council; Education Officer; teachers' courses; consultative programme for schools' visits)
Brewhouse Yard Museum; (City Council; Education Officer)
Museum of Costume and Textiles: (City Council; Education Officer

OXFORDSHIRE: County Museums Service: Director (Chief Officer) (subject to amalgamation with Libraries & Archives as Assistant Director)

Oxfordshire County Council Department of Museum Services, County Museum Woodstock: (Head of Education, 3 Education Officers and Admin. Asst. (Education); teaching services; *L)
Ashmolean Museum, Oxford: (University; Education Officer)

Banbury Museum: (County Council and District Council; classes or workshops; Worksheets)
Cogges Farm Museum, Witney: (County Council and Ltd. Co.; Education Officer)

SHROPSHIRE: County Museum Service, Church Stretton: Cultural Services Officer (2nd tier)

Acton Scott Working Farm Museum: (County Council; Assistant Keeper of Interpretation/Education; teachers' notes)
Ironbridge Gorge Museum, Telford: (Trustees: Educational Development Officer) includes:
Toll House and Information Centre; Jackfields Works and Tile Museum; Long Warehouse, Coalbrookdale; Blists Hill, Madeley; Coalbrookdale Museum of Iron and Furnace; Coalport China Works and the recently opened Museum of the River.
Ironbridge Gorge Youth Hostel and Walker Field Study Centre: (YHA and Ironbridge Trust)

SOMERSET: County Museums Service : Museums Officer (2nd tier).

Somerset Museum Education Service and County Museum, Taunton: (County Council; County Museums Officer; Organizer, Museum Education Service; intra-mural teaching; advisory service; *L)
Somerset Rural Life Museum, Glastonbury: Education Officer
Fleet Air Arm Museum, Yeovilton: (Trustees: Education Officer; Worksheets)

SOUTH GLAMORGAN: No County Museums service.

National Museum of Wales, Cardiff: (National museum: Museums Schools Service; Acting Senior Officer) organizes loans in schools of South Glamorgan.

Welsh Folk Museum, St Fagan's Cardiff: (National museum: Education Officer)

SOUTH YORKSHIRE METROPOLITAN BOROUGHS:

Doncaster: **Museum and Art Gallery:** (Borough Council; Education (Loans) Officer; *L)

Rotherham: **Rotherham Libraries, Museum and Arts Department:** (Borough Council; Director of Libraries, Museums and Arts)
Rotherham Museum and Art Gallery: (Borough Council; Keeper of Education and Extension Services; teachers' courses; intra-mural teaching; classroom; *L)

Sheffield: **Sheffield City Museum:** (District Council; Keeper of Extension Services and 3 Assistants)
Graves Art Gallery, Sheffield: (Education Officer)

STAFFORDSHIRE: County Museums Service : Curator (3rd tier)

Staffordshire County Museum, Shugborough: (County Council; Education Officer; reconstructed Victorian classroom)
City of Stoke-on-Trent Museum and Art Gallery: (District Council; Education Officer)
Chatterley Winfield Mining Museum, Stoke-on-Trent: (Trustees: Education Officer; free education services)
Bass Museum of Brewing History and Shirehorse Stables: (Bass Plc; Education Officer)

SUFFOLK: No County Museums service.

Ipswich Museum: (Borough Council; Museum Education Service: Museum Educational Liaison Officer)

SURREY: No County Museums service.

Chertsey Museum: (Borough Council; Education Officer; activities tailored to teachers' requirements)
Farnham Museum: (Borough Council Leisure and Culture Department; Education Officer; holiday activities; *L)
Old Kiln Agricultural Museum, Farnham (Private; demonstrations of e.g: horse-shoeing etc)
Guildford Museum: (Borough Council; *L)
Surrey Heath Museum, Camberley: (Borough Council; Education Officer)

TYNE AND WEAR METROPOLITAN BOROUGHS:

Tyne and Wear Museums Services (Headquarters), Newcastle upon Tyne: Director of Museums and Art Galleries; Consortium of Districts with Educational provision in 3 Groups, (East, West and Science), each with a Group Education Officer. Educational packs, *L)

Gateshead:	**Shipley Art Gallery, Gateshead**: (District Group Consortium; West Group Education Officer)
Newcastle:	**Laing Art Gallery, Newcastle**: (District Consortium; West Group Education Officer) **Museum of Science and Industry**: (District Consortium; Science Group Education Officer)

	John George Joicey Museum: (District Consortium; West Group Education Officer)
	Hancock Museum, Newcastle: (University and Society Trustees: Loans Officer, teachers' guides; *L)
North Tyneside:	**Museum Store and Transport Workshop, North Shields:** (District Consortium; Science Group Education Officer)
	Wallsend Heritage Centre: (District Consortium; Educational provision)
South Tyneside:	**South Shields Museum and Art Gallery:** (District Consortium; East Group Education Officer)
	Arbeia Roman Fort, South Shields: (District Consortium; East Group Education Officer)
	Bede Monastery Museum, Jarrow: (Development Trust; Education Officer)
Sunderland:	**Grindon Close Museum, Sunderland:** (District Consortium; East Group Education Officer)
	Sunderland Museum and Art Gallery: (District Consortium; East Group Education Officer; *L)
	Monkwearmouth Station Museum, Sunderland: (District Consortium; East Group Education Officer)

WARWICKSHIRE: County Museums Service : Curator (3rd tier)

Museum Education and Resources Centre, St.John's House, Warwick: County Council Museum Service; Keeper of Museum

Education Service; Schools Resources Officer. Educational services
to:-

> **Warwick Museum**
> **St.John's House, Warwick**
> **Warwickshire Museum of Rural Life**
> **The Doll Museum, Warwick**

The Shakespeare Properties, Stratford-upon-Avon: (Shakespeare
Birthplace Trust: Education Officer)
Nuneaton Museum and Art Gallery: (Borough Council; Education
Liaison Officer)

WEST GLAMORGAN: No County Museums service.

Glynn Vivian Museum and Art Gallery, Swansea: (City Council;
Education Officer; films and lectures)
Swansea Maritime and Industrial Museum: (City Council; Educa-
tion Officer; Worksheets)
Swansea Museum: (University; Education Officer; teachers'
courses, workshops and residencies; Worksheets)

WEST MIDLANDS METROPOLITAN BOROUGHS:

Birmingham: City Museums and Art Gallery: City Council;
Schools Liaison Department with 5 Liaison Officers and Extension
Services Officer, offering educational provision in the seven
Museums and to all Birmingham and Midlands schools. (Excellent
workbooks):

> **Aston Hall:** (Museum teacher)
> **Birmingham Museum of Science and
> Industry**
> **Blakesley Hall:** (Museum teacher)
> **Sarehole Mill**
> **Weoley Castle**

Birmingham Railway Museum: (Private; Education Officer)

Coventry: **Herbert Museum and Art Gallery**: (City Council; Education Officer: teachers workshops and courses; information packs; *L)

Dudley: **The Black Country Museum**: (Trustees: Visits Organizer; the Museum has no Education Officer but uses 15-20 expert local teachers as guides and instructors: teachers' seminars and other services to schools nationwide; demonstrations; handling objects; information packs)

WEST SUSSEX: No County Museums service.

Amberley Chalk Pits Museum, Arundel: (Trustees: Assistant Director, Education)
Chichester District Museum: (District Council; Workshops; *L)
Fishbourne Roman Palace and Museum: (Sussex Arch. Soc; Education Officer; special emphasis on schoolchildren; work book)

WEST YORKSHIRE METROPOLITAN BOROUGHS:

Yorkshire Consortium for Education. Joint services, Educational Resource Service, Wakefield: (District Council; Loan service to schools in Wakefield, Bradford, Kirklees and North Yorkshire)

Bradford: One of the most outstanding City schools-museums provisions, now under threat of reorganization under Libraries and Leisure. 93% of Bradford Museums' services had gone into schools, including:

                       Museums Loans Service: (City District Council: Loans Officer *L)
                       City of Bradford Art Galleries and Museums: (City Council; Keeper of

Education; teaching rooms; handling sessions; workshops; museum teacher; Worksheets; *L)
Bradford Industrial Museum: (City Council; Keeper of Museums Education service)
Bolling Hall, Bradford: (City Council: museum teacher)
Cartwright Hall, Bradford: (City Council; Assistant Keeper Education Service; museum teacher)

National Museum of Photography, Film and Television, Bradford: (National museum: Education and Interpretation Service by City Council)

Leeds:

Temple Newsam House: (City Council; Keeper of Education Services, with educational provision also to:

Leeds City Art Gallery and Lotherton Hall (City Council; Senior Assistant Keeper (Education)

Wakefield:

Wakefield Museum and Art Gallery: (District; Education Outreach Service with 2 Education Officers)
Clarke Hall, Wakefield: (District Council; role-play for children; museum teacher)

WILTSHIRE: County Museums Service: Museums Officer (3rd tier).

Wiltshire Library and Museum Service, Trowbridge: (County Council; Director of Libraries and Museums; Local Studies Officer; *L)
Devizes Museum: (Topic boxes)

APPENDIX C : SAMPLE CARD AS MODEL

The following blank card is offered as a master-card, to photocopy for future accessions to the school's own collection. This may be completed by children as a classification exercise. The illustration (5"x 4") can be a drawing or a photograph. Drawings may be attempted by able pupils. Insert children's unaided conjectures on first sight of each object, under **Possible identity**, **Description** and similar entries are useful exercises in testing children's powers of observation and concise note-making.

Overleaf (**Main Features**) can also be offered to children as part of the **Twenty Questions** approach to identifying accessions. (See Chapter Three (passim). The appropriate boxes can be blacked out, or punched for use on a light-deck (see Chapter Four on retrieval).

Main features

[ ]	Natural	[ ]	Man-made
[ ]	Immobile	[ ]	Portable
[ ]	Inexpensive	[ ]	Precious
[ ]	Simple	[ ]	Ornate
[ ]	Functional	[ ]	Ornamental
[ ]	Industrial	[ ]	Domestic
[ ]	Outdoor	[ ]	Indoor
[ ]	Mechanical	[ ]	Non-mechanical
[ ]	Factory-made	[ ]	Hand-made
[ ]	Authentic	[ ]	Fake
[ ]	Facsimile	[ ]	Replica
[ ]	Dated	[ ]	Undated

SAMPLE CARD AS MODEL

No:

Date:

Period:

From:

Exit Date:

Measurements:

Weight:

Materials:

Location:

SIHC No:

SAMPLE CARD AS MODEL

Description:

Condition:

Distinguishing Marks:

Possible identity:

Reference Books:

Museums:

Data: